Mahabharata

The Classic Hindu Epic of War and Philosophy

Swami Divyananda

GRAPEVINE INDIA

Published by

GRAPEVINE INDIA PUBLISHERS PVT LTD

www.grapevineindia.com
Delhi | Mumbai
email: grapevineindiapublishers@gmail.com

Ordering Information:
Quantity sales: Special discounts are available on quantity purchases by corporations, associations, and others.
For details, reach out to the publisher.

First published by Grapevine India 2024

Printed at Nutech Print Services - India

Ganapati, The Scribe

BHAGAVAN Vyasa, the Vedas' compiler, was Parasara's son. He created the Mahabharata and wondered how to share it with the world. He meditated on Brahma who appeared to him. Vyasa saluted him and said, "Lord, I've thought an amazing work, but I can't think of someone to transcribe it."

Brahma praised Vyasa and told him to request Ganapati as his scribe. Ganapati agreed to help and wrote the Mahabharata as Vyasa dictated. Before printing, books were learned and passed on orally. Suka, Vyasa's son, taught it to others. If not, future generations may have lost the book.

In the forest of Naimisa, Suka addressed an assembly of sages led by Rishi Saunaka. "I had the excellent pleasure to hear Vyasa's Mahabharata to teach dharma and other goals of life. I'll explain." He then told the gathering the whole Mahabharata.

Here is the Mahabharata's plot.

After King Santanu's death, Chitrangada ruled Hastinapura and was followed by Vichitravirya. Dhritarashtra and Pandu were his sons. Pandu, the blind eldest brother, ascended the throne.

He spent many years in the wilderness with his two wives in penance for an offence. His wives, Kunti and Madri, gave birth to the five Pandavas in the jungle. Pandu died in the jungle and sages raised the young Pandavas.

When his eldest son Yudhishthira became 16, the rishis escorted them back to Hastinapura and gave them to Bhishma. The Pandavas quickly mastered the Vedas, Vedanta, and the kshatriya skills. The Kauravas, sons of the blind Dhritarashtra, were jealous of the Pandavas and hurt them. The Pandavas and Kauravas began ruling separately from Indraprastha and Hastinapura after Bhishma's intervention.

The Kauravas and Pandavas played dice according to the kshatriya code of honour. Yudhishthira was vanquished by Kauravas' Sakuni. As a result, the Pandavas were exiled for thirteen years. With Draupadi, they fled the kingdom for the wilderness.

According to the game, the Pandavas spent twelve years in the wilderness, and one incognito. When they returned and requested their paternal inheritance from Duryodhana, he refused. War ensued. The Pandavas overcame Duryodhana and recaptured their land.

In this old and great epic of our nation, there are many colourful tales and profound teachings. Mahabharata is an ocean of pearls and diamonds. With the Ramayana, it is a live source of our principles and culture.

Section I

Adi Parva

Devavrata

"REGARDLESS of who you are, you must become my wife," said the mighty King Santanu to the goddess Ganga, enthralled with her superhuman beauty. The monarch sincerely gave his entire kingdom, all of his riches, and even his life in exchange for her love.

"O king, I shall become your wife," Ganga replied. "But only under one condition: you must never ask me who I am or where I come from. You must never hinder my actions—good or bad—and you must never have any animosity toward me. Do you agree?"

The enamoured king promised his approval and she married him and lived with him. Her modesty, grace, and the constant affection she gave the king captured his heart. King Santanu and Ganga lived a life of perfect contentment.

She had numerous children, each of whom she brought to the Ganges and threw into the river before joyfully returning to the monarch. Despite being overwhelmed with agony at such evil behaviour, Santanu endured it in silence because of the commitment he had made.

She killed seven kids in this manner. When the eighth child was born, Santanu could no longer take it. "Stop, stop," he yelled, "Why are you determined to commit this dreadful murder?"

"You have forgotten your pledge, O mighty king, and I shall go. But before you judge me, consider my story. I, the goddess Ganga, am revered by men and gods. The Vasishtha curse forces me to portray this evil character. I was to be the mother of the eighth Vasus, who were cursed to be born in the world of mankind. You will prosper in return for the service you provided to the Vasus. I'll raise your final child and give it back to you as a gift."

The deity then vanished with the infant after saying these remarks. This youngster went on to become known as Bhishma.

[This is how the Vasus came to be subject to Vasishtha's curse. The Vasus visited Vasishtha's hermitage on vacation with their wives. One of them noticed Nandini, Vasishtha's cow, grazing nearby and asked her husband to get the graceful animal for her.

"What requirement do we, the devas, have for cow's milk?" he said. "Drinking its milk will make man immortal, but as we are already immortal, this will be of little benefit to us. Should we provoke Vasishtha's wrath just to appease a whim?"

She was not, however, deterred by this. "In the mortal world, I have a great friend. I ask you to do this for her." Her spouse finally gave in. Together, all of the Vasus brought the cow and its calf with them.

By using his yogic awareness, Vasishtha understood what had happened. He became furious and cursed the Vasus. They were intended to be born into the world of men, according to the sage, whose only riches was his asceticism.

When the Vasus learned of the curse, they pleaded for pardon.

"The curse must unavoidably run its course," Vasishtha replied. The Vasu who took the cow, Prabhasa, will enjoy a long and glorious life in this world, but the other Vasus will be released from the curse as soon as they are born. I won't be able to stop the curse entirely with my words, but I can at least ease it some."

The Vasus approached the goddess Ganga, saying, "We wish that you become our mother. We implore you to come to earth and wed a respectable man for our sake. As soon as we are born, throw us into the ocean to free us from the curse." The goddess answered their petition, travelled to the planet, and wed Santanu.

The monarch ruled as an ascetic after the goddess Ganga vanished with the eighth child. He came upon the youngster while he was strolling along the Ganges riverbanks one day. The boy had the appearance and physical attributes of Devendra, the ruler of the gods. He was building an arrow dam across the Ganges, just as he had done as a child.

The goddess Ganga revealed herself to the king, who was awed by the sight. "This is Devavrata, the eighth child I gave birth to," the queen said. "Take him back with you; he's a great archer, a hero, and a master of diplomacy." She gave the boy a blessing, gave him to his father, and left.

Bhishma's Vow

DEVAVRATA, a radiant and young prince, was welcomed into the monarch's realm, and was crowned as the *yuvaraja*, the heir apparent.

Four years later, the monarch was strolling along the Yamuna River's banks. The air was suddenly filled with a wonderful aroma one day. He traced the fragrance to a young woman, as beautiful as a goodness. The fragrance she had received as a sage's blessing. The sight of this lovely girl overwhelmed him with yearning and he proposed to her.

The young woman proclaimed, "I am a fisherwoman and the daughter of the fishermen's chief. You must obtain his permission."

The father was a cunning man. "This maiden, like all others, must definitely be married to someone, and you are undoubtedly deserving of her. But you must first promise me that her child will succeed you as king."

This would have meant discarding Devavrata, the son of Ganga's heir. So the king was unable to keep his promise. Sick with longing, he made his way back to Hastinapura, his home city.

Devavrata remarked to his father, "My father, you have all that one could desire. Why are you still unhappy?"

The father was too embarrassed to reveal the truth. "Dear son," the monarch said. "You are my only child. If anything bad happens to you, our family will be lost forever. This is why I am worried."

The discerning Devavrata realised there must be another reason for his father's mental state. After questioning the king's charioteer, he learned of his encounter with the fishermaiden. He went to the fishermen's chief and pleaded for his daughter's hand.

The fisherman was respectful but firm. "If my daughter can marry the monarch, shouldn't her son succeed her as king? But you have been named the heir-apparent, and that is the problem."

Devavrata then vowed, "The son born of this woman shall be king, and I resign my right as heir-apparent."

"O greatest of the Bharata race, you have done what no one else born of royal blood has ever done," the chief exclaimed. "I am now willing to give my daughter to the king. However, will your offspring give up their birthright? They are destined to be heroic warriors like you and may attempt to take the country by force."

Devavrata was determined to grant the king's wish. He made the ultimate renunciation: "I pledge myself to a life of uninterrupted virginity."

The gods rained flowers and screams of "Bhishma" on him as he spoke these words of renunciation. "Bhishma" refers to a person who makes a dreadful vow and keeps it. From that point forward, that name was Devavrata's epithet.

The young Satyavati was then brought to the king by his son. Santanu received two sons from Satyavati: Chitrangada and Vichitravirya.

[Dhritarashtra and Pandu, the two sons of Vichitravirya, were the offspring of his two queens, Ambalika and Ambika. The Kauravas were the name given to Dhritarashtra's 100 sons. Five of Pandu's sons rose to fame as the Pandavas. Until the conclusion of the renowned battle of Kurukshetra, Bhishma lived a long life and was revered by all as the pater-familias.]

Amba And Bhishma

CHITRANGADA died in a fight with a Gandharva. As he had no children, his brother Vichitravirya was formally anointed king. Until he reached adulthood, Bhishma presided over the realm in his name.

In accordance with the kshatriya custom, he travelled to Kasi to obtain princesses for his brother. The three princesses were renowned for their accomplishments and beauty. The princes gathered competed in trials to win them. After routing the gathering princes, Bhishma left with the three princesses for Hastinapura. The princess Amba had already made up her mind to marry Salva. The prince stopped and confronted Bhishma, who defeated him easily.

At the wedding in Hasinapura, Amba said to Bhishma, "I have mentally selected Salva, the king of Saubala, as my spouse. Do as you were taught to do by the scriptures."

So Bhishma sent her to Salva. The two younger sisters, Ambika and Ambalika, were married to Vichitravirya.

When Amba went to Salva and told him all that had happened, Salva responded, "Bhishma defeated me openly, and I have been shamed. I cannot accept you as my wife."

She then returned to Bhishma and Vichitravirya. However, Vichitravirya resisted the idea of wedding a woman whose heart had been given to someone else. Out of options, Amba pleaded with Bhishma to marry her, but he advised her to convince Salva instead.

However, she was too proud to do this, and lived in Hastinapura for a long time. Out of pure desperation, she finally went to Salva. He denied her again.

Amba bitterly hated Bhishma for six years as the cause of her miserable existence. She looked for a champion to battle him, but even the greatest warriors feared Bhishma. Finally, Lord Subrahmanya handed her a garland of perpetually fresh lotuses. Whoever wore it would turn against Bhishma. However, no one had the courage to do so. She left for the jungle after hanging the garland at Drupada's palace entrance.

Many ascetics advised her to visit Parasurama, another renowned fighter. Parasurarna took pity on her and engaged Bhishma in combat. After a long battle, Parasurama was forced to concede defeat.

Overcome with wrath, Amba travelled to the Himalayas and engaged in strict penance to win Siva's favour. Siva gave Amba the wish that she would kill Bhishma in her following incarnation.

Amba leapt into a raging fire because she couldn't wait for her rebirth. She was born as King Drupada's daughter. A few years after her birth, she noticed the never-fading flower garland that was still immaculately displayed at the royal gate. She wrapped it around her neck.

King Drupada feared that Bhishma would be enraged by her boldness. He exiled his daughter to the wilderness. She engaged in penance, and eventually changed into a man. She took on the name Sikhandin, a warrior.

On the Kurukshetra battlefield, Sikhandin served as Arjuna's charioteer. Bhishma was aware that Sikhandin was born a woman. He couldn't attack Sikhandin out of chivalry. Bhishma realised that his arduous trial on earth was up and agreed to be defeated. This is how Arjuna could defeat him while being guarded by Sikhandin.

In his last moments, Bhishma was hit by arrows. He pointed to the ones that had struck him most severely and declared, "This is Arjuna's arrow, not Sikhandin's." So this mighty warrior was defeated.

Devayani And Kacha

IN the distant past, the devas (gods) and asuras (demons) fought fiercely for control of the three planets. Brihaspati led the devas, while the asuras were guided by Sukracharya. Sukracharya was the only person who knew Sanjivini's secret to bring the dead back to life. This gave the asuras a significant edge.

The devas pleaded with Kacha, Brihaspati's son, to study under Sukracharya and discover the secret. Kacha worked closely with Sukracharya for a long time and perfected his studies. Sukracharya had a beautiful daughter Devayani, who was dear to him. Kacha succeeded in winning her favour without violating his brahmacharya vows.

The asuras believed Kacha's goal was to get Sanjivini's secret from Sukracharya. To prevent this, some asuras attacked and killed him one day when Kacha was tending to his master's livestock.

Devayani was alarmed when the cattle came back without Kacha. She hurried to her father, crying out, "I think something terrible has happened to Kacha!"

The loving father conjured the deceased child's appearance using Sanjivini art. Kacha came back to life and admitted that the asuras killed him.

This happened a second time, with the asuras killing Kacha and Sukracharya restoring him to life. The third time it happened, he was powdered into wine, which the asuras then offered to Sukracharya.

Devayani again pleaded with her father for Kacha. Sukracharya said, "The asuras seem determined to murder him. Death is a frequent occurrence, and it is wrong for a thoughtful soul like you to lament it."

Devayani had a strong affection for Kacha. Wise words have never eased the pain of loss. She began a fast to death.

Sukracharya used the Sanjivini technique to summon Kacha's presence. Kacha was scattered as he was in the wine within Sukracharya's body. He could not leave and could only respond to his name.

"How did you get into me?" Sukracharya cried out. "Is this also the asuras' work?"

Kacha somehow managed to tell him the story.

"Dear daughter, there is a dilemma for you," Sukracharya said, turning to face his daughter Devayani. "My stomach must be torn open for Kacha to survive, which would mean my death."

"Alas!" Devayani cried. "In any case, I will die since I cannot survive if one of you dies."

Sukracharya realised that the only way to resurrect Kacha was to teach him Sanjivini. Sukracharya fell to the ground lifeless as Kacha emerged from his corpse. Kacha immediately revived Sukracharya using his Sanjivini.

Kacha bowed before Sukracharya and stated, "You are also my mother since I sprang from your flesh."

Kacha soon left to go back to the realm of the gods. Devayani requested him, "I have loved you long and sincerely. I want you to love me in return and make me happy by marrying me."

However, Kacha replied, "I emerged from your father's corpse. I am thus your brother. My sister, asking me to marry you is not right." He then moved to Indra's home.

The Marriage Of Devayani

ONE day Devayani and the asuras' daughters bathed in a pool. Princess Sarmishtha, the king's daughter, accidentally wore Devayani's garments when they returned. Devayani teased the disciple's daughter for wearing the master's daughter's attire.

Princess Sarmishtha angrily said, "I'm of a royal line that proudly provides, while you beg and take, and you dare to talk so to me." She slapped Devayani and pushed her down a well.

Devayani couldn't climb out of the well. The Bharata emperor Yayati came to that spot to find water while hunting. He was shocked to see a damsel in the well, and pulled her out.

Devayani was frightened to return to the asuras' palace because of Sarmishtha. She told Yayati, "You've grasped a maiden's right hand; marry her. You are a worthy spouse."

Yayati said, "I'm a kshatriya and you're a brahmana virgin. How can we marry?" (A kshatriya girl could marry a brahmana, but a brahmana maiden couldn't.) And Yayati returned to his capital.

Devayani refused to return to the asuran kingdom as she had been insulted. "It is not right to live with people without respect or decorum. Virtuous people should avoid them."

Sukracharya went to Vrishaparva and said, "O king, faults will damage prosperity sooner or later. Kacha was my loyal servant and your servants killed him. Your daughter hurt my honourable daughter. She will not stay in your kingdom any more. Without her, I can't stay. I shall leave now."

The king was startled and answered, "I am unaware of these claims. If you abandon me, I will die."

Sukracharya answered, "I care more about my daughter's happiness than yours. If you can pacify her, I will be content. I leave otherwise."

Devayani insisted that Sarmishtha become her handmaiden. Sarmishtha apologised and submitted to the condition.

Devayani repeated her request to the reluctant Yayati. Finally, they went to Sukracharya for permission to marry, and it was granted to them.

Yayati was one of the Pandavas' forebears. He obeyed the rules of the sastras, worshipped the gods, and paid tremendous homage to his forefathers. He rose to fame as a leader who was committed to the welfare of his people.

Sarmishtha secretly approached Yayati and begged to be his wife, and he agreed. In his anger, Sukracharya cursed Yayati with early ageing. Yayati begged Sukracharya for pardon so meekly that he yielded. He said, "The curse cannot be retracted, but if you can convince someone to give his youth for yours, the transaction will take effect."

Yayati "attained that old age which ruins beauty and brings on sufferings," as the Mahabharata's poet put it. He was suddenly an elderly man, yet his need for physical pleasure persisted. He beseeched his five sons, "One of you should exchange his youth for mine. He will control my empire if he consents to this and gives me his youth. I want to experience life while I'm still young and vibrant."

His four oldest sons, though, turned down his requests.

Yayati was devastated by the four boys' rejection. He begged his final son, who had never before refused to go against his desires, saying, "You must rescue me. I will enjoy life for a little while longer if you accept these ailments, after which I will return your youth to you and begin my old age with all of its woes."

The youngest son, Puru, said, "Father, I joyfully offer you my youth."

Yayati embraced him after hearing these remarks. The moment he touched his son, Yayati transformed into a boy. Puru, who realised that his father was becoming older, controlled the kingdom and became well-known.

Yayati enjoyed life for a while but was unsatisfied. He later returned to Kubera's garden and spent a lengthy time with an apsara girl. The truth finally hit him after many years of fruitless attempts to gratify desires.

He went back to Puru and said, "Dear son, sensual need is never sated by indulgence, just like fire is now stoked by adding ghee to it. I had read and heard about this, but I hadn't realised it until today. Nothing, not bread, not riches, not livestock, not women, can ever satisfy a man's hunger. Only by mental stability that goes beyond likes and dislikes can we achieve tranquillity. Reclaim your youth, and govern the kingdom judiciously."

Yayati betrayed his advanced age with these statements. Yayati, who withdrew to the wilderness, appointed Puru as king once he recovered his youth. He lived a life of frugality there for a while before eventually reaching paradise.

Vidura

THE sage Mandavya dedicated his days to seeking truth and repentance. Some bandits were being pursued by the king's officers. They went inside the ashrama to hide. The king's men followed their tracks and arrived at the ashrama.

"Did you see the robbers pass by? Where have they been?" The army commander said sternly of Mandavya, who was absorbed in intense meditation.

The sage didn't say anything. Insolently, the commander asked the same question again. However, the sage was silent. Some of the attendants found the stolen items in the ashrama and informed their commander.

"Now I see why the brahmana claimed to be a guru," the commander thought. "He is the leader of these bandits."

He ordered his men to watch the area and returned to the king. At hearing that a thief had pretended to be a sage, the monarch was infuriated. He ordered the commander to impale him without verifying the information. The commander returned to the hermitage, impaled Mandavya with a spear, and delivered the stolen goods to the king.

The sage was doing yoga when he was impaled, therefore yoga's power kept him alive. Other forest elders asked Mandavya how he ended up in that dreadful situation.

Mandavya replied, "The king's employees who guard the world are responsible for this punishment."

When the king was told that the sage was still alive and that the other forest sages were surrounding him, he was shocked and terrified. He hurried to the woods and gave the order to remove the sage from the spear. He then knelt at his knees and earnestly asked for forgiveness.

Instead of confronting the king in his rage, Mandavya went straight to Dharma, the supreme judge, and questioned him, "What crime have I committed to deserve this?"

Lord Dharma responded modestly, "O sage, you have tormented bees and birds. Do you not realise that every action, no matter how minor, has a reaction, whether positive or bad?"

Lord Dharma's response caught Mandavya off-guard. He enquired, "When did I commit this offence?"

"When you were a youngster," Lord Dharma responded.

Mandavya cursed Dharma, saying, "This penalty you have imposed is far too severe for a mistake made by an uneducated youngster. I curse you to take human birth and enter the world as a mortal."

As a result of the sage Mandavya's curse, Lord Dharma took the form of Vidura. He was conceived by Ambalika's servant-maid. Thus, Vidura was a manifestation of Dharma.

The wise men of the world recognised Vidura as a mahatma whose wisdom in dharma, sastras, and statesmanship was unmatched. While he was still in his teens, Bhishma appointed him as the principal advisor to king Dhritarashtra.

Kunti Devi

SURA, Sri Krishna's paternal grandfather, was a deserving member of the Yadava race. Sura gave his daughter Pritha to his cousin Kuntibhoja who was without children. Since then, people have called her Kunti after her adopted father.

Kunti served the sage Durvasa for a year when he stayed at her father's home. He was pleased with her service and gave her a holy mantra. "If you invoke any deity by repeating this mantra, he will appear to you and provide you the blessing of a son who is equal to him in grandeur." He knew of the sorrow her future husband would suffer. He gave this blessing to her as compensation for his knowledge.

Kunti was curious and wanted to test the mantra's effectiveness right away. She invoked the Sun, which she could see beaming in the skies. The Sun god stood admiringly in front of her.

"O God, who are thou?" Kunti questioned, overwhelmed by the wonderful glimpse of her celestial guest.

"I am the Sun," the Sun said in response. "The magic cast by the incantation you sang has called me to you."

In shock, Kunti said, "I am an unmarried girl and depend on my father. I do not want to be a mother because I'm not ready for it right now. I just wanted to see how strong the boon was. Please accept my apology for this foolish behaviour."

The strength of the chant, however, prevented the Sun god from doing so. She, on the other hand, dreaded the idea of being blamed by the public. However, the Sun god comforted her, saying, "You shall restore virginity after giving birth to my son."

Kunti was blessed by the Sun, who gives the entire world its light and life. Divine births occur instantly without the nine-month human gestation. Karna was born from her, with celestial armour and earrings, brilliant and lovely like the Sun.

She wondered what she should do with the child. She finally put the infant in a sealed box and cast it adrift in a river. When a childless charioteer saw the floating casket, he was pleased to see a lovely child within. He gave it to his wife, who showered it with motherly affection. Thus Karna, the Sun God's son, was raised as a charioteer's child.

When it was time to give Kunti in marriage, Kuntibhoja organised a swayamvara so she could pick her spouse. The swayamvara attracted a large number of suitors because of the princess's widespread reputation for beauty and morality.

King Pandu, the representative of the Bharata race, had the garland put on his neck by Kunti. King Pandu's charisma outshone the brilliance of all the other princes there. The marriage was solemnised, and she travelled to Hastinapur with her spouse.

On Bhishma's recommendation, Pandu chose Madri, the sister of the king of Madra, as his second wife. The monarchs of ancient times married two or three times to ensure progeny, not for sensuous whims. But Pandu was cursed by a guru so that he would never have offspring. The following chapter will tell this story.

Death Of Pandu

KING Pandu went hunting one day. A sage and his wife were also hunting in the guise of deer. Unaware that the deer was a sage in disguise, Pandu shot him with an arrow.

"You will die the instant you experience the joys of the bed," the rishi cursed Pandu.

Out of heartbreak over this curse, Pandu withdrew to the forest with his wives. He lived a life of perfect celibacy after leaving his empire in the hands of Bhishma and Vidura. Kunti realised his Pandu's desire for progeny. She told him the tale of the mantra she had learned from Durvasa. He asked Kunti and Madri to recite the mantra. As a result, the five Pandavas were born to Kunti and Madri from the gods. They were born and raised among ascetics.

One day in the spring, the effect of the season caused Pandu's resolve to crumble despite Madri's vehement protest. The sage's curse immediately went into effect, killing Pandu.

Madri begged Kunti to take care of her two children. She burned herself on her husband's funeral pyre, blaming herself for the king's demise.

The grieving Kunti and the Pandavas were brought to Hastinapura by the forest elders, who gave them to Bhishma. At the time, Yudhishthira was just sixteen years old.

The entire kingdom was overcome with grief when the sages announced Pandu's passing in the forest. The burial ceremonies were carried out by Vidura, Bhishma, Vyasa, Dhritarashtra, and others. Everyone in the kingdom wept as though they had experienced a personal loss.

Vyasa addressed the grandmother Satyavati, saying, "The past has been happy, but the future holds many hardships. Time moves irrevocably. You don't have to wait to witness the suffering and calamities that will befall this race. You should live out the remainder of your days in a hermitage in the woods."

Satyavati consented and joined Ambika and Ambalika in the wilderness. These three elderly queens avoided sharing in their children's suffering by ascending to higher realms of happiness via holy asceticism.

Bhima

AT Hastinapura, the five sons of Pandu and the one hundred sons of Dhritarashtra grew up in joy and good times.

Bhima was the strongest of them all physically. He used to drag Duryodhana and the other Kauravas by their hair and beat and bully them. Because of Bhima's practical jokes, the sons of Dhritarashtra would always have bruises on their bodies. Naturally, the sons of Dhritarashtra had a strong animosity for Bhima from an early age.

As the princes got older, Kripacharya instructed them in archery, the use of weapons, and other topics appropriate for princes. Due to his envy of Bhima, Duryodhana engaged in various wrongdoings that clouded his judgement.

Pandu was in charge of the realm as his father was blind. Yudhishthira, the heir apparent, would eventually succeed him and rule after his death. Duryodhana was extremely concerned at this. He believed that the murder of Bhima would weaken the Pandavas' influence. So he devised a plan to kill Bhima in order to stop Yudhishthira from assuming the throne.

Duryodhana and his brothers planned to throw Bhima into the Ganges, imprison Arjuna and Yudhishthira, and then seize control of the country. To accomplish this, Duryodhana went swimming in the Ganges with his brothers and the Pandavas. They slept in their tents after the sports since they were exhausted.

Bhishma had worked harder than the others and his meal had been poisoned. He felt terribly sleepy and laid down beside the river. He was tied with untamed creepers by Duryodhana before being dropped into the river, who had already set razor-sharp spikes so that Bhima would be impaled and die.

Fortunately, Bhima did not strike a single spike as he dropped. His body was bit by poisonous water snakes. Bhima was unharmed since the snake venom neutralised the toxic meal he had consumed. He was eventually swept to a bank beside the river.

Duryodhana was positive that Bhima had passed away. Together with the rest of the group, he joyfully made his way back to the city.

As soon as he returned, Yudhishthira questioned his mother about Bhima's whereabouts. When he learned that Bhima hadn't returned, he suspected that someone had harmed his brother. He went back to the jungle with his brothers and looked everywhere. But Bhima was nowhere to be seen. They returned in deep grief.

Bhima eventually woke up and went drowsily back home. He was welcomed and hugged by Kunti and Yudhishthira with tremendous enthusiasm. Bhima was made more powerful than before by the poison that had entered his body.

"Duryodhana is evil and ruthless," Kunti informed Vidura in private. "He wants to dominate the country, and so he intends to assassinate Bhima. I'm very concerned about this."

"This is true, but keep your opinions to yourselves," Vidura responded. "If Duryodhana is charged or held accountable, his rage and hostility will only grow.

You should not worry, since your sons are blessed with lengthy lives."

Additionally, Yudhishthira advised Bhima to keep quiet about the situation. "In the future, we must exercise caution, take care of one another, and safeguard ourselves."

When Bhima resurfaced, Duryodhana was taken aback. His resentment and anger grew.

Karna

KRIPACHARYA was the first person to teach the Pandavas and the Kauravas how to use weapons. Drona was the next. A day was set aside for a demonstration of their competence with weapons and a test.

There was a big and happy throng, since the people had been invited to see their favourite princes. The large crowd was in awe of Arjuna's superhuman ability with his swords. Envy and hatred darkened Duryodhana's brow.

The sound of massive arms being raised in challenge suddenly emanated from the arena's entrance at the end of the day. It was loud and compelling, like thunder in a storm. Everyone looked in that direction.

A godlike youngster with the appearance of light and might entered. The gathering moved aside in quiet reverence.

He looked triumphantly at the crowd and approached Arjuna. Unaware of their same ancestry, the brothers faced one another; for it was Karna.

Karna said, "Arjuna, I shall demonstrate greater ability than you have exhibited," in a voice as loud as rumbling thunder. Drona permitted him to perform. He, the battle-lover, immediately imitated all of Arjuna's achievements with carefree ease.

Duryodhana was delighted. "Welcome, great warrior! You are a source of good fortune for us," he said as he wrapped his arms around Karna. "You have control over both this empire and me."

"I, Karna, am grateful, O king," he said. "I just want two things: your love and a one-on-one fight with Partha (Karna)."

Again encircling Karna in his arms, Duryodhana said, "My wealth is all yours to enjoy."

As love overwhelmed Duryodhana's heart, rage filled Arjuna's. "O Karna, you will soon go to the pit assigned for those who come uninvited and babble without permission." And he glared at Karna.

"This arena is accessible to everyone, O Arjuna," scoffed Karna. "Law is established on the idea that might is the sanction of sovereignty. But what good is simple language, the weapon of the weak? Shoot arrows instead of words."

This was a clear challenge. Drona approved the battle. Arjuna quickly hugged his brothers and prepared for combat. Karna, who had left the Kuru brothers, met him with a weapon.

Indra of the thunderclouds and Bhaskara of the limitless rays together appeared in the skies. It was as though the heroes' celestial parents were trying to encourage their children.

On seeing Karna, Kunti instantly recognized him as her firstborn, and fainted. She was soon restored by the maidservant's care and stood helpless.

"This prince who engages with you is the son of Pritha and Pandu, and a descendant of the Kuru race," said Kripa as they were preparing to engage in a fight. Kripa was knowledgeable about the customs of single combat. "High-born princes are forbidden from fighting alone with strangers. Partha can only battle with you after learning about your ancestry."

Karna bowed his head as if a lotus was being drenched by rain as he heard these remarks.

"If the fight can't happen just because Karna isn't a prince, that can be fixed," Duryodhana stated as he rose up. "Karna is now crowned the ruler of Anga."

Then, after receiving the approval of Bhishma and Dhritarashtra, he carried out the requisite ceremonies. He gave Karna the crown, jewels, and other symbols of the Anga kingdom, and invested Karna with its rule.

Adhiratha, the charioteer who was Karna's foster father, approached the gathering right then, trembling in terror. Karna, the recently crowned king of Anga, lowered his head in homage as soon as he saw him. The elderly man sobbed with happiness as he embraced the man with his frail, shaking arms.

Bhima yelled with amusement at this sight. "O, he is merely the son of a charioteer! Then, as befits your ancestry, take up the driving whip. You are not deserving of Arjuna's execution. You shouldn't have a monarchical position in Anga."

Karna's lips quivered in agony at these obscene words, and he sighed deeply as he stared up at the setting sun. But Duryodhana intervened angrily, saying, "You, O Vrikodara, are not fit to speak so. The hallmark of a Kshatriya is courage; it is nonsense to trace the origins of great heroes or powerful rivers. I could tell of several brilliant people who came from low beginnings. But I shall now, as it could raise embarrassing questions about your own background. Look at this warrior, his godlike stature, armour, jewellery, and mastery of the sword. He must have some mystery surrounding him. How could a tiger come from an antelope? Did you claim that the monarch of Anga is unworthy? I really believe he deserves to govern the entire planet."

And Duryodhana loaded Karna onto his chariot and fled in a fit of rage. The throng departed in a commotion as the sun sank.

Indra anticipated that his son Arjuna and Karna would engage in a last combat. He then dressed as a brahmana and went to Karna, who was known for his generosity, asking for his armour and earrings.

The Sun god had previously forewarned Karna that Indra would try to trick him. Karna, however, could not bring himself to turn down any request for a present. He thereupon took off his birth jewellery and armour and offered them to the brahmana.

The ruler of the gods, Indra, was surprised and delighted. He thanked Karna for doing what no one else would and advised him to seek for any boon he desired after taking the gift.

"I want to obtain your weapon, the Sakti, which has the ability to slay opponents," Karna responded.

The blessing was bestowed by Indra, but with a fatal condition. "You can only use this weapon against one adversary. Once the killing is done, this weapon will no longer be yours but will be given back to me."

Karna went to Parasurama and pretended to be a brahmana in order to gain his discipleship. He acquired the mantra for wielding the legendary Brahmastra sword.

A stinging worm once burrowed into Karna's leg as Parasurama lay back with his head on Karna's lap. Karna endured the excruciating agony without flinching, out of concern for his master's sound sleep.

When Parasurama awakened, he saw the bloody wound. "A kshatriya alone may stay unmoved under bodily suffering," he said. "Tell me the truth, please."

Karna admitted that he had lied when he claimed to be a brahmana and that, in reality, he was the son of a charioteer. In his rage, Parasurama cursed him, saying, "Since you betrayed your teacher, the Brahmastra you have learned will fail you at the predetermined time. When your time comes, you won't be able to remember the invocatory incantation."

Karna had full knowledge of the Brahmastra spell. Yet, due to this curse, he was unable to recall it during the critical moments of his final battle with Arjuna.

Drona

THE brahmin Drona excelled at archery after finishing his studies. Drupada, the son of the king of Panchala, studied alongside Drona in the hermitage. Their warm camaraderie of youth blossomed. Drupada frequently promised Drona in his childlike exuberance that when he rose to the throne, he would give him half of the country.

Drona married Kripa's sister after finishing his studies, and the couple had a son named Aswatthama. He wanted to become rich for their sake. He went to Parasurama first after learning that he was sharing his wealth with the brahmanas. However, he was too late as Parasurama had already distributed all of his riches.

Out of his desire to help Drona, Parasurama volunteered to teach him how to wield weapons. He was a supreme expert at this skill. Drona enthusiastically concurred, and while already being a skilled archer, he became the undisputed master of the military art.

After his father passed away, Drupada succeeded to the Panchala kingdom. Drona approached him in the sure knowledge that she would receive kind treatment. But he saw that the monarch was very different from the pupil. Drupada displayed no interest in meeting him when he introduced himself as an old friend. Rather, he thought it was an insufferable insult.

"O brahmana, how dare you greet me familiarly as your friend," raged Drupada. "There can only be friendship between equals. A ruler cannot befriend a wandering beggar." With such insults, Drona was escorted from the palace. He mentally vowed to avenge the haughty monarch for this affront.

He stayed in Hastinapura for a few days at the home of his brother-in-law Kripacharya. The princes were playing with a ball one day beyond the city's boundaries. The ball and Yudhishthira's ring fell into a well. The princes could not think of a way to remove it. However, they were unaware that a brahmana was standing close and watching them.

He startled them by declaring, "Princes, you are the offspring of the valiant Bharata race. Why are you unable to shoot at the ball, as any competent archer should be able to do? Should I handle it for you?"

"O brahmana, if you take out the ball, we shall ensure that you have a wonderful lunch in the house of Kripacharya," Yudhishthira said laughingly.

Drona uttered a few magical words to a blade of grass that would make it fly like an arrow. The grass immediately accelerated and ploughed into the ball. He launched many successively identical blades that stuck together to form a chain, with which Drona removed the ball.

He was urged to get the ring as well. Borrowing a bow, Drona attached an arrow to the string, and fired it directly into the ring. The ring was raised by the arrow's rebound, and the brahmana smiled as he gave it to the prince.

The princes were astounded by these deeds and saluted the brahmana, asking, "Who are you? Are there any other ways we can help you?"

"Go to Bhishma and learn from him who I am," he commanded the princes.

Bhishma recognised the brahmana as the renowned master Drona based on the princes' descriptions. He concluded that Drona was the best candidate to provide the Pandavas and Kauravas with more training. Bhishma treated him with great honour and hired him to teach the princes how to use weapons.

As soon as the Kauravas and the Pandavas had mastered the art of war, Drona ordered Karna and Duryodhana to capture Drupada and bring him back alive at their master's command. They followed his instructions but were unable to carry out this mission.

Arjuna was then dispatched by the master on the same mission. He took Drupada and his minister prisoner after defeating him in battle and brought them to Drona.

Then Drona turned to Drupada with a smile and said, "We were friends when we were young, but you were willing to forget that and dishonour me. After capturing your realm, I am now a king. Since you believe that friendship can only exist between equals, I grant you half of your kingdom. We are now on equal footing."

Drona decided that this was adequate retaliation for the insult he had received. He released Drupada and treated him with respect.

Drupada's pride was wounded, and revenge never puts an end to hatred. Drupada's hatred of Drona grew to dominate his existence. The monarch persuaded the gods to provide him a son who would kill Drona and a daughter who would marry Arjuna. His efforts were rewarded with the birth of Draupadi, the Pandavas' consort, and Dhrishtadyumna, who led the Pandava army in Kurukshetra and defeated the near-invincible Drona.

The Wax Palace

BHIMA'S physical prowess and Arjuna's agility increased Duryodhana's envy. Karna and Sakuni took on the role of Duryodhana's malevolent advisors and they devised cunning plans. Duryodhana tried several times to slay the Pandavas. Each time, the Pandavas escaped with their lives thanks to Vidura's covert assistance. The minister wished to spare the family from a serious transgression.

Poor Dhritarashtra was undoubtedly a knowledgeable man who also loved his brother's children, but he lacked willpower and was overly devoted to his own children. His concern caused him to think of terrible options as good, and he occasionally even deliberately took the wrong path.

The offence that Duryodhana thought was unforgivable was the open praise of the people for the Pandavas. The people proclaimed that only Yudhishthira was qualified to rule the city. They would congregate and quarrel, saying, "Dhritarashtra could never be king since he was born blind. Because he is committed to his promise, Bhishma is also ineligible to be king. So, only Yudhishthira should be given the throne. The Kuru race and the country can only be justly ruled by him." To hear these words was poison to Duryodhana, who writhed and burned with resentment.

He went to Dhritarashtra and criticised the talk in the streets, saying, "Father, the people talk useless nonsense. They contend that Yudhishthira ought to be anointed king right now. A catastrophe would result from this. Where do we go if Yudhishthira is to succeed his father? What chance do our offspring have? We shall become utterly dependent on them and impoverished. Better than that would be to spend eternity in hell!"

Thoughtfully, Dhritarashtra said, "Son, what you say is true. Yudhishthira won't deviate from the righteous path, though. And all the ministers and generals that Pandu had won over with his noble demeanour will support his cause. The populace reveres the Pandavas as gods. We are powerless to confront them. If we commit a wrong, they will revolt and murder us or drive us out. We shall simply bring shame upon ourselves."

"Your fears are unfounded," Duryodhana responded. "Aswatthama is loyal to me. His father Drona and uncle Kripa will also support us. Bhishma would, at worst, be neutral. Vidura lacks the fortitude to publicly disagree with us. I've had enough sorrow; I can't take it anymore. Send the Pandavas to Varanavata right away; we'll fortify our allies."

Efforts were made to persuade several legislators to join Duryodhana's party. Their leader was Kanika, a Sakuni minister. He warned the monarch, "O king, defend yourself from the sons of Pandu. Their kindness and power pose a threat to you. The Pandavas are your brother's sons, but danger always gets closer with closer relatives."

As proof of his success in gaining supporters, Duryodhana told Dhritarashtra, "I have persuaded the ministers to support our cause. The entire kingdom will support us if you can convince the Pandavas to travel to Varanavata. Then, they won't have the capacity to hurt anyone, and it could even be feasible to allow them to return." Dhritarashtra gave in as a result of mental anguish.

The plot now only needed to be put into effect. The ministers started praising Varanavata's beauty in the Pandavas' presence and mentioning that a significant celebration would be held in Siva's honour. The Pandavas were easily convinced, especially when Dhritarashtra urged them to attend the festivities and that the locals were anxious to greet them. After saying goodbye to Bhishma and other wise men, the Pandavas travelled to Varanavata.

At Varanavata, Duryodhana hatched a scheme with Karna and Sakuni to murder Kunti and her sons. They sent for the minister Purochana and handed him secret directives, which he swore to diligently follow out.

Purochana had a magnificent palace constructed for their welcome. Jute, lac, ghee, oil, and fat were all utilised in the building as combustible elements. He expertly placed flammable, dry objects around the structure while strategically placing attractive seating and bedsteads near other, more combustible areas. It was intended to be lit on fire at night, when the Pandavas were fast sleeping.

The extravagant affection and concern shown to the Pandavas would dispel any doubt. The fire would be seen as a tragic example of an unavoidable accident. Nobody would ever think to blame the Kauravas.

The Escape Of The Pandavas

BEFORE leaving for Varanavata, Vidura subtly warned Yudhishthira, "He who thwarts the designs of a cunning opponent will escape peril. A rat hiding in a hole or a porcupine burrowing in the ground cannot be harmed by the fire that destroys a forest."

Yudhishthira responded that he understood Vidura's warning and shared it with Kuntidevi. They continued their voyage in grief and dread.

Varanavata residents greeted the Pandavas when they arrived in their city. Purochana directed them to enter the palace. Ironically, the deathtrap was given the name "Sivam," which means wealth.

Yudhishthira meticulously investigated the entire area, remembering Vidura's warning, and realised that the structure was made of flammable materials. Bhima advised Yudhishthira not to make Purochana suspect that his plan was known to them, as that would make their escape more challenging. As a result, they continued to live carefree in that mansion.

Vidura privately dispatched a skilled miner to aid them. The miner laboured for several days to dig a tunnel leading from the wax house and around the moat and the fortifications.

Purochana's apartments were located near the palace's entrance. The Pandavas stood guard with weapons at night. During the day they would go hunting in the forest, seemingly enjoying themselves but actually learning the trails.

Purochana waited a full year before carrying out the plan. He wanted to allay any suspicions and make the horrific fire appear accidental. Finally, he decided that he had endured enough. The vigilant Yudhishthira knew the fated hour had come. He gathered his brothers and warned them that it was now or never for them to go.

On that particular day, Kuntidevi planned a lavish feast for the guests. She intended to lull them to sound slumber at night after a good meal.

Bhima started several fires throughout the palace at midnight. The Pandava brothers and Kuntidevi hurried out through the underground passage, stumbling in the pitch-blackness.

The palace was currently engulfed in flames, and a growing number of terrified bystanders were lamenting all around them. Some hurried aimlessly in vain attempts to put out the fire. Everyone joined in the cries. "Alas! Alas! This is unquestionably Duryodhana's doing, and he is murdering the upright Pandavas!"

The palace was burned to the ground. Before he could flee, Purochana's house caught fire, and he was an unlucky victim of his own nefarious scheme.

The telegram from Varanavata to Hastinapura read: "The palace that was the Pandavas' residence has burned down and no one in it escaped alive."

The heart of Dhritarashtra was both warm with joy and frigid with sadness, much as the water of a deep pool is cool at the bottom and warm on the surface. The Kauravas carried out the propitiatory funeral ceremonies in simple clothing to resemble grieving relations. No visible sign of heartbroken grief was withheld.

Some people observed that Vidura wasn't as distraught as the others. This was attributed to his intellectual tendencies. But the underlying cause was that he was aware that the Pandavas had managed to flee and find refuge. He was actually picturing the tired Pandavas' wanderings when he appeared dejected. When Vidura noticed that Bhishma was very depressed, he quietly consoled him by telling him how they had managed to flee.

Bhima noticed that his mother and brothers were worn out from keeping watch every night as well as from worry and terror. He supported Yudhishthira and Arjuna with his two hands while carrying his mother on his shoulders and Nakula, Sahadeva, and Nakula on his hips. He pushed through the woodland like a lordly elephant.

When they arrived at the Ganges, a boatman was waiting for them. They entered a large forest after crossing the river in the dark. They spent the entire night in a quiet that was horribly disturbed by the horrible sounds of wild creatures. They finally sat down after succumbing to sleepiness and thirst.

"Even if the sons of Dhritarashtra are present to take me away," Kuntidevi said, "I must stretch my legs." She immediately fell asleep.

Bhima waded through the dense jungle, searching for water, and came upon a pool. He then soaked his top garment, constructed cups out of lotus leaves, and delivered water to his mother and brothers. Bhima was the only person awake and meditated as the others slept.

"Do not the forest's flora and creepers support one another and coexist peacefully? Why would the evil Dhritarashtra and Duryodhana strive to harm us in such ways?" he wondered. Bhima, who was sinless himself, was overcome with anguish and unable to comprehend the causes of others' immorality.

The Pandavas continued their march despite facing several challenges and peril. They would occasionally sprint against one another, bursting with vitality and the magnificent vigour of youth. Sometimes, when they were too exhausted to continue with their amazing endurance, they would stop and rest instead of carrying their mother to increase their speed.

On the way, they ran across Bhagavan Vyasa. They bowed before him and listened to his excellent advice and words of encouragement. When Kunti informed him about their woes, Vyasa comforted her by saying, "No sinner is evil enough to exist in one welter of vice, nor is any virtuous man strong enough to live in virtue at all times. Everyone has engaged in both good and bad deeds, and life is a complicated web. Every person is responsible for the effects of their actions. Do not give in to sadness."

They then dressed in brahmana clothing and travelled to Ekachakra. They waited for better times there in a brahmana's home.

The Slaying Of Bakasura

THE Pandavas remained disguised as brahmanas and begged for food in the brahmana streets. They carried what they were given to their mother, who anxiously awaited their return. The meal they brought would be split into two equal halves by Kunti. Bhima would receive half, and the other half would be split between the mother, the other brothers, and Bhima.

Bhima was extremely strong and had a voracious appetite because he was a Wind god's child. One of Bhima's names, Vrikodara, means wolf-bellied, and wolves have insatiable appetites. Bhima's constant hunger and the poor quality of the food he used to eat at Ekachakra were inextricably linked. As a result, he constantly lost weight, much to the dismay of his mother and siblings.

Bhimasena and his mother were left behind one day when the other brothers left to ask for alms. They overheard raucous lamentations coming from their brahmana landlord's home. Kunti entered to find out what the problem was.

To his wife, the brahmana said:

"You cannot be executed while I am still alive. It is wrong to sacrifice this young daughter, a gift from God, and equally difficult to allow the death of our son. How can we continue to live after losing both our only source of comfort in this life and our hope for eternal life? Alas! It's best if we all die at the same time!" And the brahmana broke into tears.

"It is difficult for me to look after two fatherless orphans," the wife responded. "I should be given to the rakshasa, that would be ideal. The woman who moves on to the afterlife while her husband is still living is blessed. The scriptures say this, as you are aware. Take another wife once I'm gone. Give me your blessing, cheer me with a courageous smile, and send me to the rakshasa."

When his wife spoke these things, the brahmana gently hugged her and sobbed like a child, completely moved by her love and bravery. "O dear and honourable one, what words are these?" he said once he could speak. "Could I handle living without you? Protecting his wife is a married man's primary responsibility. If I continued to live after sacrificing both love and duty by delivering you to the rakshasa, I would undoubtedly be a miserable sinner."

The daughter, who was overhearing this pitiful dialogue, intervened with tears, saying, "You can spare no one else except me for the rakshasa. You may save the other souls by sacrificing one of your own."

When he noticed that everyone was crying, the youngster, who was a little older than a newborn, lisped and said, "Father, do not grieve. Mother, try not to cry. Sister, don't cry," he said, going to each one and taking turns sitting on their laps.

Then he stood up and declared in his lovely, childlike voice, "I shall kill the rakshasa with this stick." He then grabbed a piece of firewood. They smiled through their tears at the child's behaviour and remarks, but it made them feel more deeply sad.

Kuntidevi entered, sensing that now was the right time to step in. She inquired about the source of their grief and whether there was anything she could do to assist them.

"Mother, this is a sadness much beyond your assistance," the brahmana remarked. "Near the city, there is a rakshasa by the name of Bakasura who is vicious and extremely powerful. Thirteen years ago, he took our city and kingdom by force, and randomly slays and hacks men, women, and children in this city whenever he pleases.

"The residents pleaded with the rakshasa to make a binding agreement. They pleaded, 'We will bring you enough meat, rice, curds, intoxicating liquors, and many more delights once a week. These will be brought to you in a carriage carried by two bullocks and driven by a person selected randomly from each residence. Make a meal out of the rice, together with the bullocks and the guy, but avoid this insane ritualistic massacre.' This agreement has been in place for a very long time.

"There hasn't been a hero to save this nation from this scourge since every valiant man who has attempted has been slain and vanquished by the rakshasa. Now it is our time to send a person to the rakshasa as prey. I don't have the money to buy a replacement. I'll go to him with my entire family since none of us can stand to live after sending one of us to a torturous death. Only God can aid us, but even in that, we have given up hope."

After discussing the situation with Bhimasena, Kunti went back to the brahmana. "Good man, don't give up," she said. "God is great. I have got five sons. The meal will be delivered to the rakshasa by one of them."

The brahmana gasped in awe and amazement, but he refused to hear about the substitution sacrifice. "Brahmana, do not be terrified," Kunti commanded. "My son has superhuman abilities that come from mantras. But do not tell anyone about this since doing so will negate his influence."

Kunti feared that if the tale spread around, Duryodhana's warriors would see the Pandavas' hand and learn where they were.

Bhima was ecstatic and enthusiastic beyond measure. When his brothers returned, Dharmaputra observed Bhimasena's face, which had been long unfamiliar to him, as being bright with delight. He realised that he was prepared for a dangerous adventure and questioned Kunti about what she had told him.

"What is this?" said Yudhishthira. "Bhima is our current defence and our best hope for the future. Now you put his life at danger. I worry that your numerous tribulations have tainted your judgement."

"Dear sons, we have lived peacefully in this brahmana's residence for many years," Kuntidevi responded. "Repaying the favour one has received is a man's duty, no, his ultimate virtue. I have no concerns since I am aware of Bhima's bravery."

Then, with a chariot driven by two bullocks and filled with a variety of meat, delicacies, jugs of curd, and alcoholic beverages, the townspeople arrived at the brahmana's home. Bhima boarded the vehicle and began his journey to the rakshasa cave.

When they arrived at the familiar location, the residents turned around to head back to safety, leaving Bhima to continue in the carriage by himself. The area in front of the rakshasa's lair was filled with rodents and ants, as well as with bones, hair, and gore.

The food that had been intended for the rakshasa was devoured voraciously by Bhima as he halted the chariot. He told himself, "I must consume the food before it gets thrown in the pandemonium of my struggle with the rakshasa. Additionally, once I kill him, I will get contaminated through touch with the corpse and won't be able to consume anything."

The rakshasa was furious when he denounced what Bhima was doing. His patience had already been frayed by the prolonged waiting. The rakshasa, who had a gigantic physique, red hair, beard, and moustache, as well as a mouth that stretched from ear to ear, charged at Bhima.

Bhima simply grinned carefreely avoided the gripping hands by turning to face the rakshasa while eating. Bhima didn't pay attention to the rakshasa or stop eating as he rained strikes from his arrogantly turned back. He didn't get up and face the rakshasa until he had finished, right down to the last pot of curds, and washed his mouth with a sigh of relief.

The rakshasa was used as a plaything by Bhima, who would hurl him to the ground and then command him to get back up and continue fighting. Bhima frequently threw the rakshasa up as if he were a ragged toy. After throwing him to the ground, Bhima put his knee on his back, breaking his bones. The terrifying wail of anguish and despair from the rakshasa was followed by its death.

The corpse was dragged by Bhima to the city's gates. To his mother's great satisfaction, he returned to the brahmana's home, had a bath, and then recounted the events of the day.

Draupadi's Swayamvara

NEWS of the swayamvara of Draupadi, daughter of Drupada, reached the Pandavas when they were hiding. Many brahmanas from Ekachakrapura made travel plans to Panchala in the hopes of attending a royal wedding and collecting the usual gifts.

With her maternal intuition, Kunti understood her sons' ambition to visit Panchala and win Draupadi. "Since we have lived in this city for so long, it is time to consider moving somewhere else," she said to Yudhishthira. "The amount of charity given to us is decreasing. Let us travel to Drupada's kingdom, which has a reputation for being kind and rich."

The Pandavas mingled with the brahmanas who had come to see the swayamvara. The group arrived in the lovely city of Drupada after an arduous march, and they took up residence in a potter's home.

Despite the fact that Drupada and Drona appeared to be at peace, the former was never able to forget or forgive Drona for the humiliation he had caused. His only desire was to marry Arjuna with his daughter.

Drona plainly adored Arjuna and could scarcely see his pupil's father-in-law as his deadly adversary. If there were a battle, Drupada would be stronger due to being Arjuna's father-in-law. He was devastated to learn that the Pandavas had been killed at Varanavata, but he afterwards heard a rumour that they had managed to flee.

The marriage hall was elegantly furnished and constructed. A tastefully organised set of brand-new guest homes was created to host the swayamvara suitors and visitors. The audience was entertained for fourteen days straight with beautiful events, attractive sights, and exciting sports.

The wedding hall was furnished with a powerful steel bow. The potential princess's hand-winner had to rig the bow, and use it to fire a steel arrow through the centre of a rotating disc at a high target. It needed almost superhuman strength and ability. Drupada decreed that this feat should be accomplished by the hero who would win his daughter.

There were several brave princes assembled from all around Bharatavarsha. There were the sons of Dhritarashtra, Karna, Krishna, Sisupala, Jarasandha, and Salya.

The cacophony that ensued sounded like the ocean crashing, and over it all came the joyous sound of festive music played on countless instruments. Draupadi was sitting on an elephant while her brother Dhrishtadyumna rode in front of them on horseback. Draupadi dismounted and entered the swayamvara hall, filling it with the sweetness of her presence and exquisite beauty. She had just had her auspicious bridal bath and was dressed in flowing silk.

She approached the dais holding a garland while coyly staring at the brave princes, who on their part were silent in awe of her. The brahmanas offered oblations in the fire while reciting the customary mantras. Dhrishtadyumna escorted Draupadi to the centre of the auditorium after the peace prayer was chanted and the music had ceased flourishing.

Then he declared in a strong, distinct voice, "Listen, princes assembled in this assembly; the bow is here. Here are the arrows, and there is the target. If he has a decent family and presence, the person who shoots five arrows in a row through the wheel's hole and consistently strikes the target will win my sister."

Numerous illustrious kings rose and attempted in vain to string the bow, but they were too intimidated and embarrassed by its weight and stillness to succeed. These included Sisupala, Jarasandha, Salya, and Duryodhana.

Everyone present anticipated that Karna would succeed when he stood up, but he narrowly fell short. The massive bow sprang out of his hands like a creature of life as the string slid back blazing. There was a lot of commotion and irate conversation. Some said that the exam was an impossibility set up to humiliate the monarchs. Then everyone became silent when a young man emerged from the brahmanas and made his way over to the bow.

It was Arjuna who had arrived in brahman attire. When he stood up, the audience erupted in a frenzied clamour once again.

The brahmanas themselves were divided in their opinions; some were overjoyed that there should be a young man among them with the fortitude to compete, while others, who were more envious or wiser in the ways of the world, said it was impudent for this brahmacharin to appear on the lists when heroes like Karna, Salya, and others had failed.

However, there were still those who spoke in a different way. "We sense from his appearance that he is going to win," they said. "He exudes self-assurance and appears to be well aware of his objectives. Although the brahmana may be physically inferior, is it really only a matter of strength? How effective are austerity measures? Why not give it a shot?" They also wished him well.

"Can a brahman attempt to bend the bow?" Arjuna inquired of Dhrishtadyumna as he neared the location where the bow was lying.

"O finest of brahmanas, my sister will become the life partner of anybody from a decent family and presence who bends the bow and hits the target," Dhrishtadyumna said.

Then Arjuna grabbed the bow in his hands and skillfully strung it after meditating on Narayana, the Supreme God. As the crowd went silent in amazement, he put an arrow on the string and smiled as he gazed around. The target dropped to the ground as he fired five arrows in rapid succession through the rotating mechanism without pausing or thinking. There was a clamour of musical instruments, and the audience was in uproar.

The brahmanas shouted for glee and exulted while holding up their deerskins as though they had all just won Draupadi. The commotion that ensued was indescribable.

Draupadi radiated a youthful beauty. She turned to face Arjuna with a smile on her face. She walked over to him and put the wreath around his neck. Sahadeva, Nakula, and Yudhishthira hastily made their way back to the potter's home to tell their mother the happy news. Only Bhima stayed in the gathering because he thought Arjuna would be in danger from the kshatriyas.

Bhima had expected the princes' fierce fury. "The practice of swayamvara, the selection of a bridegroom, is not common among the brahmanas," they declared. "If this young lady doesn't want to wed a prince, she should stay a virgin and commit herself by setting herself ablaze. How could a brahmana propose to her? To defend virtue and preserve the swayamvara practice from the danger it faces, we should oppose and prohibit this marriage."

Anticipating a fight, Bhima grabbed a tree by the roots, stripped it of its leaves, and then stood ready for anything with this powerful bludgeon by Arjuna's side. Draupadi remained still, hanging onto the deerskin skirts that Arjuna was wearing.

Balarama, Krishna, and others made an effort to placate the princes who had caused the commotion. Arjuna and Draupadi made their way to the potter's home.

Dhrishtadyumna accompanied Bhima and Arjuna as they carried Draupadi to their temporary home and silently observed all that happened there. He was astounded and thrilled by what he saw, and returning, he whispered in King Drupada's ear, "Father, I think these are the Pandavas. I saw all five of them, and a wise and regal woman who I am sure is Kunti herself."

Kunti and the Pandavas went to the palace at Drupada's invitation. The monarch was informed by Dharmaputra that they were the Pandavas. This knowledge made Drupada ecstatic and all his worries about Drona's animosity were put to rest.

He was also told by Dharmaputra of their shared desire to wed Draupadi. This was rejected by Drupada, who remarked: "How unjust! How did this morally repugnant notion that contradicts conventional use enter your mind?"

In response, Yudhishthira said, "O king, pardon us. We promised to share everything in common during a time of grave danger, and we cannot go back on that promise. Our mother has told us to do this."

Drupada eventually gave in, and the wedding was celebrated.

Indraprastha

VIDURA was thrilled when the swayamvara news reached Hastinapura. He told Dhritarashtra, "O King, our family is stronger now that Drupada's daughter is our daughter-in-law. Our stars have aligned."

Dhritarashtra thought Duryodhana won Draupadi out of blind love for him. He said, "Bring Draupadi. Let's greet Panchali."

Vidura quickly corrected. "The Pandavas are alive, and Arjuna won Drupada's daughter," he said. "The five Pandavas married her according to the sastras."

Vidura's statements frustrated Dhritarashtra, but he hid it. "O Vidura, I'm thrilled by your words," he said. "The Pandavas? We buried them. Our son-in-law is Drupada's daughter. Excellent!"

Duryodhana's resentment and wrath redoubled when he learned the Pandavas had escaped the wax palace. Not only that, he had become more powerful through an alliance with the king of Panchala.

He and his brother Dushasana told their uncle Sakuni, "Uncle, we're destroyed. Purochana failed us. Our enemies are smarter and more fortunate than us. They've allied with Dhrishtadyumna and Sikhandin. What are we to do?"

Karna and Duryodhana visited Dhritarashtra. Duryodhana said, "You promised Vidura better days. Is it a 'good time' that our natural foes, the Pandavas, have become so strong they will destroy us? Either we kill them now or we perish. Please advise us."

Dhritarashtra said, "Yes, son. We should not speak to Vidura about this, though. Let me hear your ideas."

Duryodhana remarked, "We may use the fact that the Pandavas have different mothers to create hostility between Madri and Kunti's kids. We can also bribe Drupada. Wealth can do anything."

Karna smiled and replied, "Utter nonsense."

Duryodhana added, "We must prevent the Pandavas from claiming our kingdom. We can commission some brahmanas to propagate rumours in Drupada's city and warn the Pandavas that Hastinapura is dangerous. The Pandavas would fear coming here, and we'd be protected."

Karna answered, "This is mere chatter. This won't scare them."

"Can we create division among the Pandavas who have jointly married Draupadi? Experts will sow mistrust and jealousy among them. We will win. We can seduce some of Kunti's sons and turn Draupadi against them. If Draupadi suspects one of them, we can invite him to Hastinapura and use him to succeed."

Karna laughed outright. "None of your ideas are good," he said. "The Pandavas can't be outwitted or divided. Drupada cannot be bribed. He'll never abandon the Pandavas. Draupadi is also unconquerable. As kshatriyas, we should assault before they get stronger. Trickery is useless."

Dhritarashtra was caught between emotions. He consulted Bhishma and Drona.

Bhishma was glad to hear that the Pandavas had married the daughter of King Drupada of Panchala. He advised welcoming them back and giving them half the kingdom. "Citizens want this too. Our family's dignity requires this. The wax house fire is much-discussed. Invite the Pandavas and give them half the kingdom to clear your name."

Drona gave similar counsel, and recommended sending a messenger to reach a peaceful settlement.

Karna, who was dedicated to Duryodhana, became enraged. "I'm amazed that Drona, who has gained wealth and honours from you, would recommend this," he said to Dhritarashtra. "A king should carefully consider his ministers' advice before accepting it."

Drona exclaimed, "O wicked man, you're counselling the king improperly. If Dhritarashtra doesn't follow our advice, the Kauravas would be destroyed soon."

Vidura advised Dhritarashtra to heed Bhishma, the leader of his race, and Drona, the master. "The Pandavas are also your children, just like Duryodhana and his brothers. Those who suggest harming them want to destroy the race. They and their allies are impossible to vanquish. Karna and Sakuni are immature, unskilled advisers. Do not listen to Duryodhana, but follow Bhishma's advice."

Dhritarashtra gave half the kingdom to Pandu's sons to establish peace. He despatched Vidura to get the Pandavas and Draupadi.

Vidura hurried quickly to King Drupada's city to ask him to send the Pandavas to Hastinapura for Dhritarashtra. Drupada mistrusted Dhritarashtra, but he responded, "The Pandavas may do as they like."

Vidura prostrated himself before Kuntidevi, who said, "Vichitravirya, you saved my sons. They are your children also. I'll follow your advice."

She questioned Dhritarashtra's motives. Vidura told her, "Your children won't perish. They'll inherit the throne and gain fame."

Vidura, the Pandavas, Kunti, and Draupadi, and Drupada finally returned to Hastinapura.

Hastinapura's streets were decked with water and flowers to welcome the Pandavas. As planned, the Pandavas got half the kingdom and Yudhishthira was anointed king.

Dhritarashtra blessed Yudhishthira and said goodbye. "My brother Pandu enriched the kingdom. May you inherit his fame! King Pandu followed my advice. You too, do the same. My sons are proud and wicked. I formed this settlement to avoid contention and animosity. Khandavaprastha was our ancient capital. Re-establish that and be famous."

Thus Dhritarashtra spoke cordially to Yudhishthira. The Pandavas restored the wrecked city, constructed palaces and forts, and called it Indraprastha, which blossomed in richness and beauty. The Pandavas and Draupadi ruled there for 36 years, always following dharma.

Section II

Sabha Parva

Jarasandha

INDRAPRASTHA was ruled gloriously by the Pandavas. Yudhishthira was pressured by those around him to carry out the Rajasuya sacrifice and accede to the title of "Emperor." Even then, imperialism exuded an alluring glamour.

Yudhishthira asked Sri Krishna for guidance on this. "My people beg me to conduct Rajasuya. But as you are aware, only those who acquire the respect and loyalty of all kings can carry out that sacrifice and achieve the rank of emperor. Counsel me. You are not blinded by your affection, and you do not advocate simply doing what you are told. Furthermore, you are not among those who give advice merely to appease others and whose advice favours pleasure above sound judgement."

"You cannot rule as emperor as long as the great Jarasandha of Magadha is still alive and unconquered," Krishna responded. "He has subdued numerous rulers by conquest. Every Kshatriya, including the legendary Sisupala, is terrified of his might and submits to him.

"I and my people assaulted Jarasandha after Ugrasena's son, the evil Kamsa, joined Jarasandha as an ally and son-in-law. We had to admit defeat after three years of combat, so we abandoned Mathura and migrated to Dwaraka in the west, where we established a new city and today live in peace and plenty.

"Jarasandha would undoubtedly oppose you taking the title of emperor, even if Duryodhana, Karna, and others do not object to it. The only way to get rid of him is to vanquish and kill him. The monarchs who are imprisoned by him can then be rescued, and you can win their allegiance in addition to performing the Rajasuya."

"I concur," Yudhishthira said. "I am only one of many kings who live contented, unambitious lives while presiding over their kingdoms with fairness and justice. The urge to rule as an emperor is nothing more than ego and vainglory. Why can't a king be content with his own realm and rest? In reality, I am not attracted to the term of emperor; it is my brothers who desire it. What chance do we have when even you fear Jarasandha?"

This attitude of timid happiness did not sit well with Bhima. "Ambition is the highest quality in a ruler," he declared. "If one does not understand their own strength, what use is it to be strong? Strength enhanced by cunning will undoubtedly accomplish a great deal. What task cannot be performed by my physical might, Krishna's knowledge, and Arjuna's deftness? If we work together and attack it fearlessly, we can defeat Jarasandha's might."

"Jarasandha should definitely be killed and he deserves it," Krishna chimed in. "Injustice was committed when he imprisoned eighty-six princes. He is waiting to seize fourteen more of the hundred kings he has planned to immolate. If Bhima and Arjuna agree, I will go with them, and together we will kill that ruler and release the princes."

This counsel did not sit well with Yudhishthira. "This might actually end with the death of Bhima and Arjuna, who serve as my eyes. And this is all to fulfil a hollow desire to rule as an emperor. It would be better for me to abandon the concept entirely than to send them on this risky mission."

Arjuna said, "What use is it to us, born as we are of a famous line, to live without performing great deeds? Even though a kshatriya possesses all other positive traits, he will not become famous if he does not put in effort. Even a strong person can fail if they neglect to use their resources due to laziness. Most often, failure results from being unaware of one's own strength.

"We are confident in our strength and do not hesitate to exert all of it. Why would Yudhishthira think that we can't do this? Once we reach old age, it will be time to don the ochre robe, retreat to the forest, and spend the remainder of our days in fasting and penance. We should now lead demanding lives and perform brave deeds befitting the traditions of our race."

When Krishna heard these words, he was ecstatic and said: "What other advice can Arjuna, a Bharata race member born of Kunti, offer? Death comes to everyone, both the hero and the sluggard. Yet, the highest responsibility of a kshatriya is to uphold the principles of his race and religion while defeating his enemies in just war in order to obtain glory."

Finally, Yudhishthira agreed with the group's consensus that killing Jarasandha was their duty.

THE SLAYING OF JARASANDHA

BRIHADRTHA, who oversaw three regiments, ruled the Magadha kingdom and gained fame as a great hero. He wed the identical twin daughters of the raja of Kasi and made a promise to them that he would not favour one over the other.

For a long time, Brihadratha was denied the gift of procreation. When he grew old, he gave his ministers control of the kingdom, took his two wives to the forest, and began to live a life of austerity. He went to the Gautama family's Sage Kausika with a heartbroken desire for children.

The sage was touched by compassion and asked him what he wanted. He replied, "I am childless and have come to the forest giving up my kingdom. Please give me children."

The sage was brimming with sympathy. A mango fruit landed in his lap while he was considering how to assist the king. He blessed it, and handed it to the monarch. "Your wish will come true."

The fruit was divided in half by the monarch and given to each of his wives. He did this in order to uphold his promise to neither side to be partial.

The wives became pregnant shortly after eating the fruit. The delivery happened as scheduled, but instead of bringing them the joy they had anticipated, it left them much more heartbroken than before, because each woman only gave birth to a half-child. With one eye, one limb, half a face, one ear, and so on, they were in fact two equal and complimentary parts of one baby.

They were so distraught that they gave the order to their servants to cut the halves into hideous bits and throw them away. The attendants followed orders and placed the cloth bundle on a pile of trash on the street.

That location was discovered by a cannibal rakshasi. The two bits of flesh filled her with joy. And as she was gathering them both up, they accidentally fit together correctly and instantly fused to form a complete, living child that was faultless in every aspect.

The shocked rakshasi had no desire to murder the kid. She pretended to be a lovely woman and went to the monarch to present the infant, saying, "This is your child."

This youngster was given the name Jarasandha. He developed into a man of tremendous physical power, but his body had one flaw. Because it was created by the joining of two distinct parts, it could be split in half again with enough force.

When it was decided to conquer and kill Jarasandha, Sri Krishna declared: "Jarasandha's allies, Hamsa, Hidimbaka, Kamsa, are no longer with him. Now that he is alone, it is appropriate to kill him. Armies are of no service in battle. He needs to be engaged in one-on-one battle and killed."

(In accordance with the rule of honour of the time, a kshatriya was required to accept a challenge to a duel, whether it involved weapons or not. The latter was either wrestling or a combat to the death using weighted gauntlets. For the sake of killing Jarasandha, Krishna and the Pandavas followed this kshatriya tradition.)

With bark-fiber garments on and sacred darbha grass in their hands, they pretended to be men who had taken religious oaths. As a result, they crossed into the Magadha kingdom and arrived in Jarasandha, the capital.

Jarasandha was troubled by ominous portents. He had priests perform propitiatory rites, and he personally engaged in fasting and penance to fend off the looming peril.

Arjuna, Bhima, and Krishna entered the castle without weapons. They were greeted with reverence by Jarasandha because of their dignified bearing, which seemed to reflect an honourable origin. To avoid having to utter lies, Bhima and Arjuna did not respond to his words of welcome.

They were represented by Krishna, who said: "These two are performing austerities by keeping a vow of silence for the time being. Only after midnight can they communicate. After entertaining them in the sacrifice hall, Jarasandha went back to the palace."

As it was Jarasandha's custom to meet and converse with aristocratic visitors who had made vows at their leisure and convenience, he called them at midnight. Jarasandha was sceptical of their behaviour, and he also noticed that they possessed the proud demeanour of kshatriyas in addition to the scars left by the bowstring on their hands.

They came clean when Jarasandha pressed them for the truth, declaring, "We are your enemies and seek immediate conflict. You are free to pick anybody you want to battle with."

Jarasandha introduced himself and stated, "Krishna, you are a cowherd, and Arjuna is a simple child. Bhima is well known for his might. I therefore want to fight him." Jarasandha bravely consented to battle Bhima without a weapon because he was unarmed.

As Krishna and Arjuna watched in alternating hope and worry, Bhima and Jarasandha engaged in a continuous thirteen-day battle without stopping for rest or food due to their equal strength.

When Jarasandha began to exhibit indications of tiredness on the fourteenth day, Krishna told Bhima that it was time to put an end to him. Bhima spun him a hundred times in a circle before throwing him to the ground. and by grabbing his legs, he split his body in half. And Bhima screamed with joy.

The two halves instantly fused, and Jarasandha, now whole, once more assaulted Bhima.

Bhima was horrified by the sight and unsure of what to do. He saw Krishna take up a straw, break it in half, and hurl the pieces in opposing directions. Heeding the advice, when he tore Jarasandha in two, he tossed the two pieces in opposing directions to prevent them from coming together and joining. Jarasandha died in this manner.

The captured princes were then freed. Krishna, Bhima, and Arjuna went back to Indraprastha and Jarasandha's son was anointed King of Magadha.

With Jarasandha gone, the Pandavas could finally perform the Rajasuya with all due pomp and circumstance. Yudhishthira assumed the title of Emperor.

Only one event ruined the celebrations. When the first honour was being paid toward the end of the festivities, Sisupala disrespectfully acted in front of the princes and incited a fight with Krishna in which he was killed. The following chapter tells the rest of this tale.

The First Honour

AT the time, India was made up of twenty-one separate states. Even though there was only one dharma and one culture in the entire country, each state's independence was meticulously upheld. Occasionally, a powerful and ambitious monarch would ask his peers for their consent to rule, which was occasionally accorded without hesitation. Following this approval, he would offer a massive Rajasuya sacrifice, to which all the consenting monarchs would be invited as a sign of respect for his sovereignty.

After killing Jarasandha, the Pandavas performed the Rajasuya and invited the other monarchs in accordance with this tradition. The moment had come to perform the appropriate formalities. It was customary to give first honour to the visitor who was deemed most deserving of precedence over all other guests. The question was about whom to honour first.

The grandsire, who shared Yudhishthira's viewpoint, was adamant that Sri Krishna, the monarch of Dwaraka, should be honoured first. Yudhishthira heeded the counsel, and Sahadeva presented to Sri Krishna the customary honours required by custom as per Yudhishthira's instructions.

Sisupala, the king of Chedi, could not stand it because he despised Krishna in the same way that only evil can despise good.

"This is absurd and unfair, but I am not shocked," he added, laughing out loud. "The man who asked for counsel was an illegitimate child. (This was a derogatory reference to Kunti's sons.) The man who offered advice was descended from a constant descendant of high to low. (This is a reference to the fact that Ganga, the river that naturally flows from upper to lower levels, gave birth to Bhishma.)

"Additionally, the honoree was an illegitimate child. And what can I say about the man who was honoured? By birth an idiot and by breeding a cowherd. If none of the people in this assembly have anything to say about this, they must be really unwise. The place is not for honourable men."

Sisupala was praised by a few of the assembled princes. He turned to Yudhishthira after hearing their cheers. "It is unfortunate that you gave Krishna the top honour when there are so many rulers present. Failing to show respect where it is due and showing respect where it is not deserved are both serious offences. It is unfortunate that you are unaware of this despite your imperial pretensions."

As his anger increased, he said, "You have paid royal honours to a cowherd boor, a mere nobody. Is this the right time and place to display your obscene favouritism for Krishna, Devaki's son? Is this deserving of the Pandu children?

"O sons of Pandu, you are immature, uneducated adolescents who have no idea how to handle a royal assembly. You were led astray by this idiot Bhishma, who also made a fool of you. Krishna—why, he's not even a ruler! He is not even related to royalty. You picked Krishna for the first honour instead of him out of infantile prejudice, despite the fact that he is nothing more than a humble cowherd and is neither royal, heroic, learned, holy, nor even old. By doing this, you have degraded everyone you invited here.

"Why, O Yudhishthira, did you have the temerity to accord this wretch first honour among this distinguished company of kings? He doesn't even have the benefit of age, and isn't his father still living if you want grey hair? You could not have honoured him as your preceptor, since Drona, who is present in this assembly, is your preceptor. Do you regard him as a master at making sacrifices because you have honoured him?

"Vyasa, the great master, is present, hence it is impossible. Even if Bhishma is a dotard, it would have been preferable if you had given him the first honour. He has the advantage of being the oldest man in your household. Kripacharya, your family's instructor, is also present at this gathering. Then, how could you give this cowherd the first honour? The hero who is knowledgeable in all sastras, Aswatthama, is present. How did you decide on Krishna, oblivious to him?

"O kings, we did not consent to Yudhishthira acquiring the title of 'emperor' out of fear. Whether he is a friend or foe is not particularly important to us. However, after hearing so much about his righteousness, we were eager to witness him defend the dharma. After all that rhetoric of morality and dharma, he has now willfully denigrated us. What virtue or dharma did he uphold by giving Jarasandha's unjustly murdered killer Krishna first place in his honour? From now on, you must refer to Yudhishthira as being unjust.

"Oh Krishna, what arrogance on your part to accept this honour that these foolish Pandavas bestowed upon you! Have you lost yourself? Or did you disregard respectable customs? Or was it only a case of a dog stealing a piece of food that nobody bothered to claim or protect? Do you not realise that this farce is an abomination and an embarrassment to yourself?

"As absurd as presenting a girl in marriage to a eunuch or showing attractive things to a blind person. Likewise, you are being insulted by these regal honours. It is now clear that Krishna, the elderly Bhishma, and the would-be emperor Yudhishthira are all formed of the same substance."

After saying these severe comments, Sisupala got up from his chair and left, urging the other kings to follow him in rejecting the insult. They all flocked to follow him.

They were too enraged to be placated, so Yudhishthira hurried after them and sought to comfort them with kind words of peace. When Sisupala's aggressive conceit reached a violent fever pitch, a horrific brawl broke out between the two men, ending with Sisupala's death.

The Rajasuya was appropriately observed, and Yudhishthira acknowledged the emperor.

Sakuni Comes In

THE princes, priests, and elders who had assembled for the Rajasuya returned when the Rajasuya ended. Vyasa arrived to bid adieu as well. With all due respect, Dharmaputra welcomed him and sat by his side.

"O son of Kunti, you have the title of 'emperor,' which you admirably merit," the sage remarked. "Give me permission to go back to my hermitage."

Yudhishthira bowed before his guru and ancestor and said, "O master, you alone can allay my fears. From portents, wise men have anticipated the occurrence of tragic disasters. Has Sisupala's passing resulted in the fulfilment of this prophecy?"

"Far from it," Bhagavan Vyasa replied. "Good child, the next thirteen years hold a lot of sadness and anguish. Despite Sisupala's passing, there are still portents that point to the kshatriya race's doom. Not at all. This calamity will result from the animosity between your relatives the Dhritarashtras, and you and your brothers. It will come to a head in a battle that would effectively wipe off the kshatriya race. Nobody has the power to defy fate. Stand solid and unwavering in your justice." And Yudhishthira was blessed by Vyasa.

Yudhishthira was grieved and greatly repulsed by worldly ambition and life itself as a result of Vyasa's comments. He warned his brothers about the impending race catastrophe. He perceived life as a sour and exhausting endeavour, and his fate as particularly cruel and intolerable.

"You are a monarch, and it is improper for you to be agitated," Arjuna remarked. "Let's face destiny and fulfil our obligations."

"Brothers, may God protect us and grant us wisdom," Yudhishthira responded. For my part, I make a thirteen-year commitment to never be critical of my brothers or other family members. I will stay clear of any excuse for a fight. The main source of enmity is anger, which I will never give in to. I will never give someone a reason to be angry or hostile. We will benefit from Bhagavan Vyasa's caution in this way." His brothers agreed with him amicably.

The gambling game in which Yudhishthira was duped by Duryodhana's wicked genius Sakuni, who was Duryodhana, was the first event of the series that resulted in the horrific massacre on the blood-stained field of Kurukshetra. Why did the enlightened and righteous Yudhishthira allow himself to be persuaded to take this action?

His unwavering commitment to maintaining good relations with his relatives was the key factor. Since the etiquette of the day made it a point of honour to accept a game of equal risk, a cordial request to dice could not be declined. In trying to spread goodwill, he created a fertile ground for the deadly germ of hatred and violence.

While Dharmaputra was careworn with solicitude to avoid a dispute at all costs, Duryodhana was burning with resentment at the prosperity of the Pandavas which he had witnessed at the Rajasuya sacrifice. In Yudhishthira's court-hall, he had observed incredible wealth, beautiful and sight-eluding crystal doors, and numerous works of exquisite art that all suggested immense fortune. He also observed the joy with which the monarchs of many nations welcomed their alliance with the Pandavas. His agony over this was intolerable.

He was first oblivious to Sakuni speaking to him since he was so preoccupied with sorrow at the success of the Pandavas. Sakuni was standing by his side.

"Why are you sighing," Sakuni questioned. "Why are you suffering from sorrow?"

"Yudhishthira, who is encircled by his brothers, is like Indra, the ruler of gods," Duryodhana responded. "Sisupala was killed in front of the assembled kings, but not one of them had the bravery to step forward to exact revenge. How can I not grieve? What is the purpose of life?"

"O Duryodhana, the Pandavas are your brothers," Sakuni remarked. "You shouldn't be envious of their wealth. They are only now taking advantage of their legal inheritance. They have prospered and thrived thanks to their good fortune without harming anyone else.

"What makes you jealous, exactly? Your brothers and family support you and submit to you. Aswatthama, Karna, and Drona are on your side. When Bhishma, Kripa, Jayadratha, Somadatta, and I are on your side, why do you weep? You have the power to rule the entire globe. Do not give in to sadness."

Duryodhana responded, "O Sakuni, it is true that I have a great deal of support. Why not start a battle and expel the Pandavas from Indraprastha?"

Sakuni countered, "I am aware of a way to expel Yudhishthira from Indraprastha without a struggle or any bloodshed."

Duryodhana's eyes brightened, but it felt too good to be true. "Uncle, is it possible to defeat the Pandavas without losing any lives? How?"

"Yudhishthira enjoys the game of dice," Sakuni responded. "He is completely unaware of its tricks and the chance it presents to those who are more intelligent since he lacks skill. He would accept if we invited him to a game, as is customary among kshatriyas. I will represent you because I am familiar with the game's strategies. Against me, Yudhishthira will be as helpless as a child. Without spilling a drop of blood, I will take his country and riches for you."

The Invitation

SAKUNI and Duryodhana travelled to Dhritarashtra. Sakuni started the discussion. "O king, Duryodhana is wan with sorrow and worry," he remarked. "His excruciating pain is going unnoticed by you. Why is that?"

The adoring father Dhritarashtra embraced Duryodhana and said, "I do not understand why you should be dejected. What do you dislike about this place? The entire world is at your disposal. You have studied under the top instructors, learning the Vedas, archery, and other sciences. You have inherited the throne as my firstborn. What more do you have to desire? Tell me."

"Father, like anyone else, rich or poor, I eat and hide my nakedness, yet I find life intolerable," Duryodhana responded. "What purpose does such a life serve?" Then he spoke of the abundance he had observed in the Pandava palace, which, in his opinion, was more bitter than losing everything.

"Contentment with one's situation is not characteristic of a kshatriya," he exploded. "Fear and sympathy diminish a king's stature. Since I have seen the greater riches of Yudhishthira, my money and pleasures no longer satisfy me. The Pandavas have expanded, whilst we have contracted, O King."

"Beloved child, do not harbour any animosity toward the Pandavas. The only outcome of hatred for family members, especially when they are innocent, will be sorrow and death. Why are you supposed to be envious of your brother? Isn't his success also ours? He doesn't harbour the slightest resentment or jealousy for us. In terms of bravery and ancestry, you are comparable to him. Why are you supposed to be envious of your brother? No. Do not harbour jealousy."

The old king was overly fond of his son, yet occasionally did not hesitate to state what he believed to be right.

The father's suggestion did not sit well with Duryodhana, and he responded in an impolite manner. "The individual who lacks common sense yet is steeped in learning," he said, "is like a wooden ladle immersed in savoury food which it neither tastes nor benefits from. You are quite knowledgeable about statecraft but are completely lacking in state wisdom. The way the world operates is one thing, but running a state is quite another.

"According to Brihaspati, 'Forbearance and contentment are not virtues in monarchs, even though they are the obligations of ordinary men.' The kshatriya's duty is to pursue victory constantly."

When Sakuni interfered, he explained in great detail how he would invite Yudhishthira to a dice game, completely defeat him, and strip him of everything he owned without using force.

"It is enough if you just send for the son of Kunti to play the dice game," he concluded. "Let me handle the rest."

"If you would just agree to invite Yudhishthira, Sakuni will win for me the wealth of the Pandavas without a battle," continued Duryodhana.

"Your suggestion does not seem appropriate," Dhritarashtra responded. "Ask Vidura about it, please. He will give us sound advice."

But Vidura's advice was not welcomed by Duryodhana. "Vidura will simply provide us with the clichés of everyday morality, which will not help us achieve our target," he stated to his father. "Kingly policy must be much stricter than the maxims found in textbooks. And success serves as the yardstick. In addition, Vidura prefers the Pandavas and does not like me. You are as aware of this as I am."

"The Pandavas are strong," declared Dhritarashtra. "The dice game will only breed animosity. I do not believe it is wise to provoke them."

However, Duryodhana was insistent: "Wise statesmanship rests in putting off all fear and guarding oneself by one's own means. Should we not try to force the matter now that we are stronger than they are? That demonstrates true forethought. Kshatriyas have always enjoyed the game of dice, and if it can help us win this battle without resorting to violence, what damage can it do?"

In the end, Dhritarashtra conceded after being defeated in argument, and giving up hope of convincing his son. He then gave the servants instructions to set up a hall for games. However, he could not resist talking to Vidura about it in private.

"O king, this will without a certain bring about the demise of our species by arousing unquenchable hatred," replied Vidura.

In response to his son's desire, Dhritarashtra, who was unable to object, said: "If luck is on our side, I have no worry about this game. On the other hand, how could we stop it if bad luck struck us? Because fate has unlimited power. On my behalf, send an invitation to Yudhishthira to come play some dice." Vidura went to Yudhishthira with an invitation after receiving this order.

THE WAGER

WHEN Yudhishthira first saw Vidura, he asked in worry, "Why are you so dejected? Are all of our relationships in Hastinapura going well? "How are the princes and the king doing?"

He was made aware of his purpose by Vidura.

Yudhishthira appeared to consult Vidura and say, "Wagering games cause disputes among kshatriyas. If possible, a sensible man will stay away from them. What do you want us to do?"

"I tried my best to fight against this notion," Vidura replied. "Still, the king ordered me to extend the invitation, so I did. The choice is yours."

Yudhishthira travelled to Hastinapura with his siblings and entourage despite the warning.

One could wonder why the sage Yudhishthira accepted the offer. Three explanations are possible. Yudhishthira enjoyed playing the slots. And it was considered polite and honourable in the kshatriya tradition to accept an invitation to a dice game.

There is also a third explanation. By declining Dhritarashtta's invitation, Yudhishthira wouldn't offer anyone cause for complaint or anger. These motivations combined with his inherent propensity led Yudhishthira to accept the invitation and travel to Hastinapura.

Following the exchange of formal greetings, Sakuni informed Yudhishthira that the game's cloth had been spread and extended an invitation.

At first, Yudhishthira uttered the following: "O monarch, Asita, Devala, and other rishis have declared that gambling should be avoided since it provides room for deception. Additionally, they have stated that the kshatriyas should follow a path of conquering in battle."

Yudhishthira wanted to play, though, in his heart of hearts. This internal tension was obvious in his conversation with Sakuni. This weakness was immediately recognised by the quick-witted Sakuni, who asked: "What is wrong with the game? What is a battle? Every time, the stronger man prevails. There is nothing wrong with it because it is simply a strength or talent test. If you are scared, do not play, but do not use the tired justification of good and wrong."

"Well, who is to play with me?" Yudhishthira responded.

"It is my task to find the stakes," declared Duryodhana. "I will let my uncle Sakuni roll the dice in my place."

Yudhishthira had assumed that he would be able to overcome Duryodhana through play, but Sakuni was a renowned specialist. As a result, he paused before declaring: "I think it is not normal for one man to play on behalf of another."

"I see that you are fabricating another justification," Sakuni shot back in jest.

Yudhishthira reddened and said, "Well, I shall play," disregarding prudence.

The room was completely packed. There were Dhritarashtra, Vidura, Kripa,

Bhishma, Drona, and Kripa seated. They sat unhappy spectators watching what they could not stop even though they knew the game would finish brutally. The assembled princes were enthused and highly interested in the game.

At first, they bet on jewels, then on gold and silver, and then on chariots and horses. Yudhishthira lost continuously. He staked his servants and lost them as well. He gave up his army and elephants. The dice Sakuni threw appeared to always bend to his desire.

Yudhishthira lost everything—cows, sheep, cities, villages, people, and all other belongings. However, he would not stop, since tragedy had drugged him. In addition to the clothing they were wearing, he also lost his brothers' and his own jewels. Still, bad luck followed him, or more precisely, Sakuni's deceit was too much for him.

"Is there anything else you can wager on?" Sakuni questioned.

"Here is the lovely Nakula with the sky-complexioned complexion," said Yudhishthira. "He is among my wealth. He is a wager that I make."

"Is that the case?" Sakuni asked. "If we can win your beloved prince, we will be happy." With these remarks, Sakuni threw the dice, and the outcome was as predicted.

The audience trembled.

"My brother Sahadeva is here," Yudhishthira said. "He is well known for having a vast understanding of all the arts. Even though it is wrong, I still gamble on him."

"I have played and I have won here," Sakuni said as he threw the dice. And Sahadeva was lost by Yudhishthira.

The evil Sakuni feared that Yudhishthira may end his journey there. He scolded Yudhishthira by saying, "There is no doubt that the sons of Madri are more precious to you than Bhima and Arjuna, who are your full brothers. You won't make them an offer. I know."

The scornful accusation that he thought his step-brothers were cheap hurt Yudhishthira to the core, and made and lost Arjuna and Bhima in their turn.

"Is there anything else you can provide?" the evil Sakuni inquired.

"Yes, Dharmaputra answered. "I will be your slave if you win."

Sakuni rolled the dice and won. After that, Sakuni loudly announced that the five Pandavas had now become his legal slaves as he stepped up in front of the group.

The group watched in startled silence. "There is one jewel you still own that you can still free yourself from by staking," Sakuni stated, turning to face Yudhishthira alone. "Can't you make Draupadi your bet?"

"I pledge her," Yudhishthira muttered with despondent trembling.

In the area of the gathering where the elders were seated, there was audible anguish and agitation. 'Fie! Fie!" cries of enormous volume soon erupted from all directions. The more sensitive sobbed. Others began to perspire and thought the end of the world had arrived.

Sakuni threw the dice and exclaimed, "I have won," once more. Karna, Duryodhana, and his brothers yelled in joy.

Immediately, Duryodhana turned to Vidura and ordered, "Go get Draupadi, the

Pandavas' cherished wife. She must therefore sweep and tidy our home from today. Let her arrive right now."

"Are you so crazy that you hurry to certain destruction?" Vidura exclaimed. "You cannot see it, but you are dangling precariously over an infinite chasm! Yudhishthira had no right to stake Panchali because he had already forfeited his freedom," he continued as he faced the crowd. "The Kauravas are about to perish, and despite the counsel of their friends and well-wishers, the sons of Dhritarashtra are headed in the direction of hell, in my opinion."

Vidura's remarks incensed Duryodhana, who said to his charioteer Prathikami, "Vidura is jealous of us and he is terrified of the Pandavas. But you are unique. Go ahead and bring Draupadi right away."

Draupadi's Grief

AS directed by his master, Prathikami travelled to Draupadi.

"O cherished princess, Yudhishthira fell under the grip of the dice game, and bet and lost even you," he said. "You are now owned by Duryodhana. By Duryodhana's order, I have come to take you to work as a maid in his home."

Draupadi was perplexed by this odd message. "Prathikami, what do you say? Which prince would give his wife in marriage?"

Prathikami responded, "He played offering you as a stake because he had previously lost all other belongings and had nothing else left." The entire tale was then narrated to her.

Even though the news was enough to crush a person's heart and kill their soul, Draupadi quickly regained her composure and said, "O charioteer, return. Inquire of the player if he lost his wife or himself in the game initially. Ask him this in front of everyone; when you get his response, you can take me."

Prathikami entered the gathering and addressed Yudhishthira, asking him the query posed by Draupadi. Yudhishthira was still and silent.

Duryodhana then ordered Prathikami to bring Panchali there so she could confront her husband. Once more, Prathikami approached Draupadi and respectfully informed her that cruel Duryodhana wanted her to go before the assembly and address her own query.

"No," Draupadi responded. "Bring up the issue again in front of the group and demand an answer."

Prathikami did so. Furious, Duryodhana turned to his brother Dushasana. "This man is an idiot and terrified of Bhima. Even if you have to drag Draupadi here, go get her."

The evil Dushasana immediately hurried with joy on his mission. He walked up to where Draupadi was and yelled, "Come, why are you holding up? We now own you. Be brave, lovely lady. Now that you have been won over by us, make yourself agreeable to us. Come to the assembly," he commanded, appearing impatient to drag her there.

Heartbroken, Panchali ran to the inner apartments of Dhritarashtra's queen for safety. Following her quickly, Duhsasana grabbed her by the hair and dragged her to the gathering.

Draupadi managed her distress as she entered the gathering and pleaded with the elders gathered there, saying, "How could you approve of the king staking me when he was himself caught up in the game and deceived by wicked people? How could he risk anything at all now that he was no longer a free man?

"If you have loved and cherished the mothers who produced you, if the honour of wife, sister, or daughter has been dear to you, if you believe in God and dharma, desert me not in this horror crueller than death," she sobbed, extending out her arms and raising her pouring eyes in agonised pleading.

The elders hung their heads in despair and humiliation at this heart-breaking cry, which sounded like a poor fawn who had been struck to death.

Bhima could no longer contain himself. He turned to Yudhishthira and shouted angrily, "Even abandoned professional gamblers would not bet the harlots who live with them. And you, worse than they, have left the daughter of Drupada to the mercy of these ruffians. You are to blame for this terrible act. Bring fire, Sahadeva. The hands that threw the dice will be burned by me."

But Arjuna gently corrected Bhima, saying, "The plan hatched by our adversaries is entwining us in its webs and inspiring us to do evil. We shouldn't give in and participate in their game."

Bhima managed to restrain his rage with superhuman willpower.

The sorrow of Panchali was too much for Vikarna, the son of Dhtitarashtra, to bear. He stood up and questioned the silence of the Kshatriya heroes.

"Although I am only a young person, your silence begs me to speak. Listen. This lady did not belong to Yudhishthira alone; he had no right to promise this woman. Additionally, Yudhishthira already had his freedom taken away. There is also an additional objection. It is against the rules of the game that Sakuni proposed her as a pledge. If we take into account all of these factors, we must acknowledge that Panchali was not legitimately won by us."

There were loud cheers of approval. "Dharma has been saved, Dharma has been saved," the elders cried out.

"O Vikarna, you lay down the rule though you are just a stripling," Karna roared as he stood up. "When Yudhishthira was a free man in the beginning, he surrendered everything he had, which naturally included Draupadi. Draupadi was in Sakuni's custody already. Even the clothes they are wearing now belong to Sakuni. O Dushasana, take hold of robes of the Pandavas and Draupadi and deliver them to Sakuni."

The Pandavas threw off their upper garments to demonstrate that they were prepared to walk the road of honour and right at whatever cost.

Duhsasana went to Draupadi to forcefully take her clothing. She cried out for divine mercy. "O Lord of the World, whom I adore and trust, abandon me not in this dreadful affliction." And then she passed out.

While the evil Duhsasana began pulling at Panchali's robes and good men trembled and turned away, even then, by the grace of God, a miracle took place. Duhsasana laboured vainly to remove her clothing because as he did so, ever-new clothes could be seen covering her body.

Before the assembly, a massive mound of splendid clothing quickly built up till Duhsasana finally gave up and sank down in exhaustion. The crowd shook in awe at this miracle as honourable men worshipped God and sobbed.

Bhima uttered the awful oath, "May I never enter the blessed dwelling of my forefathers unless I rip open the breast and drink the blood of this immoral Duhsasana, this humiliation of the Bharata race," with quivering lips.

Suddenly, jackals howling could be heard. Strange dissonant sounds emanating from all directions, including those of grazing donkeys and predatory birds, foretold impending disasters.

Dhritarashtra acted wisely and bravely when he realised that this occurrence would finally lead to the extinction of his species. He beckoned Draupadi to his side and made an effort to comfort her with kind and loving words.

Then, turning to face Yudhishthira, he said, "You are so innocent that you can have no foes. The sin that Duryodhana committed should be forgiven in your magnanimity, and you should forget about it. Reclaim your empire, wealth, and everything else to enjoy freedom and prosperity. Visit Indraprastha once more."

The Pandavas then exited the hall of curses, confused and in awe of the miracle that was their quick deliverance from disaster. But it was too good to endure.

Duryodhana chastised his father for derailing their carefully set plans just as they were about to succeed. He cited Brihaspati's maxim, according to which no instrument that aimed to eliminate powerful foes could be deemed improper. Duryodhana managed to get his adoring father's reluctant consent to a scheme to tempt Yudhishthira to a game of dice once more.

As a result, a messenger was sent to follow Yudhisthira when he left for Indraprastha. Before Yudhishthira arrived at his destination, he approached him and requested him to return on behalf of king Dhritarashtra.

Yudhishthira responded to this request by saying, "Good and evil arise from fate and cannot be avoided. An honourable person cannot turn down a dice challenge." The entire assembly attempted to talk Dharmaputra out of playing with Sakuni. But he returned to Hastinapura.

The stake was that the defeated party would exile to the forest with his brothers for twelve years and spend the following year in secret. If they were discovered in the following year, they would have to go into exile once more for another twelve years.

Naturally, Yudhishthira lost this battle as well, and the Pandavas accepted the vows of those who would enter the jungle. The assembly's participants all bowed their heads in shame.

Dhritarashtra's Anxiety

WHEN the Pandavas left for the jungle, a loud outcry of mourning erupted from the crowds of people. They crowded the streets and climbed houses, towers, and trees to see them leave. The princes, who previously departed in the company of mourning throngs while riding on lordly elephants or jewel-encrusted chariots, now went away on tired feet.

Shouts of "Fie! and "Alas!" could be heard from every angle. "Does God not see this from His heavenly position?"

Blind Dhritarashtra sent for Vidura and requested that he give a description of the Pandavas' banishment.

"Yudhishthira, the son of Kunti, walked with his face covered by a garment," Vidura said. "Bhima moves behind, keeping his gaze fixed on his arms. Arjuna sprinkles sand in his route. Dust is strewn all over Nakula and Sahadeva. Tears flow from Draupadi's eyes as her messy hair covers her face."

Dhritarashtra was gripped by a growing sense of worry and terror. "What do the people say?" he enquired.

"'Our leaders have left us'," Vidura responded, using their own words. "'Fie on the Kuru race's elders who allowed such atrocities to occur! The sons of Pandu have been driven into the forest by the avaricious Dhritarashtra and his sons.' There are other bad omens, as well as cloudless lightning, disturbed earthquakes, and trouble in the heavens."

The sage Narada suddenly appeared in front of them. "Fourteen years from today, the Kauravas will become extinct as a result of the evil perpetrated by Duryodhana." And he disappeared from view.

Fearful, Duryodhana and his comrades prayed to Drona not to leave them.

"My job is to battle for the sons of Dhritarashtra who depend on me and whose salt I eat," Drona replied solemnly. "However, fate holds all power. The Pandavas will undoubtedly return angrily from exile. I recognise rage because it was my wrath against Drupada that caused me to dishonour him.

"He made a sacrifice in order to be granted a son who would murder me, and it is stated that Dhrishtadyumna is that son. He is the Pandavas' brother-in-law and close friend, and everything is going according to fate. Make peace with Yudhishthira, is my advice to Duryodhana. Of course, you are free to follow your own preferences." But Drona's remarks were not received by Duryodhana.

Dhritarashtra used to receive sincere advice from Vidura. He frequently told him, "Your son has done a terrible wrong. Was it not your responsibility to guide your kids down the right path? Even now, you should appoint for the return of the kingdom you gave the Pandavas. In the event that Duryodhana refuses to accept reason, you should even use force to detain him."

Dhritarashtra would at first be mournful and quiet as Vidura spoke, but eventually his forbearance ran out. "O Vidura, you always argue for the Pandavas and against my sons," he said. "How can I let go of Duryodhana? I no longer have faith in you. You may visit the Pandavas if you choose." Then he left Vidura behind and went into the apartments.

Vidura truly believed that the Kuru race would be destroyed. He drove to the forest where the Pandavas dwelt.

Dhritarashtra was overcome by fearful regret. “What have I done? By causing the sage Vidura to fall into the Pandavas’ clutches, I have only served to strengthen them even more.” He ordered Sanjaya to deliver a message of regret to Vidura pleading for him to come back.

Sanjaya hurried to the hermitage and discovered the Pandavas dressed in deer skin and surrounded by sages. He also found Vidura and told him what Dhritarashtra had said, adding that if he did not return, the blind monarch would die heartbroken.

Vidura, who had a tender disposition, was deeply moved and went back to Hastinapura. The division between Dhritarashtra and Vidura was erased by tears of affectionate embrace.

The sage Maitreya was greeted with great respect when he arrived at the palace of Dhritarashtra one day.

“Revered sir, you have undoubtedly met my darling children in Kurujangala,” Dhritarashtra said, pleading for his blessing. “Are they healthy?”

“I stumbled into Yudhishthira in the Kamyaka forest,” remarked Maitreya. “When I heard about the events in Hastinapura, I was astounded that such atrocities could have happened when Bhishma and you were still living.”

Later, Maitreya ran into Duryodhana in the court and counselled him to reconcile with the Pandavas for his own sake. But Duryodhana was stubborn and foolish. He simply laughed, slapped his thighs in mockery, and turned away.

When Maitreya saw Duryodhana, he became enraged and yelled at him, “Are you so conceited and do you slap your thighs in mockery of one who wishes you well! You will be killed on the battlefield after Bhima’s mace breaks your thighs.”

Dhritarashtra sprang up at this point and knelt at the sage’s feet to ask for pardon.

“My curse won’t operate if your son makes peace with the Pandavas,” stated Maitreya. Otherwise, it will be fulfilled,” he declared as he marched out of the crowd.

Section III

Aranyaka Parva

Krlshna's Vow

AS soon as his companion Salva learned that Krishna had killed Sisupala, he grew furious and surrounded Dwaraka with a powerful force. The garrison endured severe hardships. When Krishna returned, the suffering in his beloved city broke his heart. He instantly ordered Salva to raise the siege by attacking and overpowering him.

Krishna didn't learn about the events at Hastinapura, the dice game, or the exile of the Pandavas until thereafter. He immediately left for the forest where the Pandavas lived.

Many people travelled with Krishna, including members of the Bhoja and Vrishni tribes, the Chedi country's king Dhrishtaketu, and the Kekayas, who were all dedicated to the Pandavas. When they learned of Duryodhana's perfidy, they were seized with righteous fury and cried out, "Surely the earth will drink the blood of such evil people!"

Draupadi approached Sri Krishna and described her transgressions in a voice drenched in tears and torn with weeping.

"I was pulled to the gathering when I had only one garment on my body," she claimed. "The sons of Dhritarashtra made the obscenest insults toward me and revelled in my suffering. They harassed and mistreated me because they believed I had become their slave.

"Even Bhishma and Dhritarashtra ignored my origins, my ancestry, and my connection to them. I was degraded despite being the wife of five heroes. Even you, Madhusudana, had abandoned me." She stood shaking, almost unable to speak because of how sickened by grief she was.

Deeply moved, Krishna comforted the distraught Draupadi. He declared: "Those who tortured you will perish in the bloody gore of a defeated fight. I'll do whatever I can to assist the Pandavas. You are going to be an empress. I swear this," Krishna said in front of Draupadi.

Dhrishtadyumna also comforted his sister by explaining how the Kauravas would fall victim to nemesis. "I shall kill Drona," he declared. "Bhishma will stumble because of Sikhandin. The evil Duryodhana and his brothers shall perish at the hands of Bhima. The charioteer's son, Karna, will be killed by Arjuna."

After that, Krishna left and went back to Dwaraka with Subhadra, Arjuna's wife, and their son Abhimanyu. The sons of Draupadi were taken by Dhrishtadyumna when he returned to Panchala.

Pasupata

WHEN Bhima and Draupadi first moved into the forest, they occasionally quarrelled with Yudhishthira.

Bhima was bursting with rage and couldn't wait to retake the kingdom from Duryodhana. He believed that warriors should not continue to live submissively in the jungle. Draupadi would also cite passages from the Vedas. This worried Yudhishthira when he thought about the dishonour she had endured at the hands of Duryodhana, Karna, and Duhsasana.

"We should uphold the commitment we made," Yudhishthira said forcefully. He would occasionally respond with clichéd political adages and mention the relative power of the parties. In this way, he struggled to control the younger Pandavas' impatience.

Arjuna later travelled to the Himalayas to practise austerities in order to get new weapons from the devas, as directed by Vyasa. After saying goodbye to his brothers, Arjuna headed to Panchali to say his final goodbyes.

"O Dhananjaya, may you succeed in your task," she wished. "May God grant you all Kuntidevi wished and hoped for before she gave birth to you. Come back when you have new weaponry."

Arjuna arrived at the summit of Indrakila after traversing thick jungles, where he saw an elderly brahmana. "Child, you are wearing armour and carrying weapons; they are of no use here," the ascetic said with a smirk. "In this place of ascetics and saints who have subdued rage and passion, what do you seek in this kshatriya garb?"

That was the ruler of the gods, Indra, who had come to meet his son.

"I seek arms. Bless me with weapons," Arjuna murmured as he bowed before his father.

"O Dhananjaya, what is the utility of weapons?" Indra responded. "Ask for joys or try to find happiness in greater worlds."

"O monarch of gods, I do not covet the joys of higher worlds," Arjuna said. "I left Panchali and my brothers in the forest and came here. I only seek weapons."

"The three-eyed god Siva would grant you divine weapons if you are fortunate enough to see him and win his grace," the thousand-eyed declared and vanished.

Arjuna then travelled to the Himalayas to perform atonement and win Siva's favour. Along with his celestial spouse Umadevi, Siva disguised himself as a hunter and entered the forest in search of game.

A wild boar suddenly charged at Arjuna who dispatched it with an arrow from his Gandiva. At the same time, it was pierced with a shaft from the hunter Siva's bow, the Pinaka.

"Who are you?" Arjuna shouted. "You shot at the target I was aiming at. How dare you!"

The hunter responded that the boar had been slain by his shaft and that Arjuna was welcome to engage in a duel if he felt differently.

Arjuna could not have been more pleased. He leaped up and shot arrows that resembled snakes. He was astounded when they appeared to have no impact on the hunter, and retreated like rain blown by a storm from a mountain peak.

He began to arrow Siva with his bow, but the hunter didn't appear to pay attention. He quickly yanked the bow from Arjuna's grasp and started laughing.

He drew his sword and continued the fight unfazed. On the hunter's tough frame, the sword broke to pieces.

Now he had no choice but to fight by hand, but once more he was outmatched. In a tight iron clutch, Arjuna was rendered completely defenceless.

Worn out and overpowered, Arjuna meekly prayed to God and focused on Siva. His clouded thinking suddenly became clear, and he realised who the hunter actually was. He knelt at the Lord's feet and cried out in a weak voice of admiration and contrition, asking for pardon.

"I pardon you," Siva replied with a smile, returning Gandiva and the other weapons he had been denied. Arjuna received the magnificent Pasupata weapon from him as well.

A hundred times stronger and more brilliant than before, Arjuna's body, ravaged in the unfair conflict, was made whole and faultless by the heavenly touch of the three-eyed god. Siva said, "Go to heaven and give due homage to your father Indra," and then he disappeared from view like the sun setting.

"Have I actually seen the Lord face to face and been graced with his heavenly touch?" Arjuna shouted, filled with delight. "What more do I require?"

At that very moment, Matali, Indra's charioteer, arrived there in his chariot. He transported Arjuna to the realm of the gods.

Bhima And Hanuman

DRAUPADI used to bemoan how unattractive the Kamyaka forest was without Arjuna. This misery was shared by the other Pandavas.

"I have sent Arjuna to win Indra's favour and obtain weapons from him because there is no other way to destroy the Kaurava heroes," Yudhishthira said to his priest Dhaumya. "However, we are unable to live comfortably here because we miss him in all of our usual haunts. I wish to leave as I think that will help us cope with being apart. Where do you think we should go?"

Dhaumya spoke of several forests and sacred sites. The Pandavas visited each of those locations in an effort to ease the pain of separation. They invested several years in their pilgrimage, listening to the customs that gave each site its sanctity. Draupadi would frequently become weary from traversing the mountains and forests. Bhima would assist them, encourage them, and make their labours simple, sometimes with the assistance of his son Ghatotkacha.

They arrived to Kulinda, the kingdom of Subahu on the Himalayas, during their wanderings over the Himalayan regions. They graciously accepted the honours bestowed upon them by that king and took some time to relax. Later, they made their way to Narayanasrama's lovely woodland and camped there.

A lovely flower was once carried by a breeze that was blowing from the northeast toward Draupadi. When Draupadi took it in her hands, she was so enchanted by its aroma and beauty that she ardently displayed it to Bhima. "What a lovely scent! I will give this to Yudhishthira now. Bring some of these flowers. This plant ought to be grown in our Kamyaka forest."

Bhima set off in search of the plant because he wanted to delight his lover Draupadi. Without giving the wild animals that crossed his path a second thought, he walked alone towards the direction from which the scent appeared to be carried by the breeze.

He soon arrived at a garden of plantain trees at the base of a mountain when he noticed a large monkey. It was sleeping directly in his way, gleaming like a flaming fire. He shouted at the animal in an attempt to scare it away from his path.

It drawled, only partially opening its eyes, "I am ill, which is why I am resting here. How come you woke me up? Where are you headed? Men cannot go beyond this point on the mountain trail. Take what you want from the local produce, and if you're wise, return home in peace."

Bhima was used to being taken seriously. He became enraged and yelled, "Who are you, you monkey, engaging in such tall talk? I am a Kuru ancestor and a son of Kunti. I am a kshatriya hero. I am the Wind God's son. Now leave the path; attempt to stop me at your peril."

Still grinning, the monkey responded, "I am a monkey, as you claim. But if you try to force a path, you will come to ruin."

"I don't want your advice, and it doesn't matter if I end up in ruins," Bhima remarked. "If you don't get up and move, I will make you."

The primate responded, "Being only a very old monkey, I lack the strength to rise up. Jump over me if you have to leave at any costs."

"Nothing could be simpler, yet the scriptures ban it," Bhima said. "If not, I should leap over both of you and the mountain in a single motion like Hanuman did when he crossed the ocean."

"O finest of men, who is that Hanuman that crossed the ocean?" the monkey exclaimed, appearing surprised. "Tell me his tale if you are familiar with it."

"Have you not heard of Hanuman, my older brother, who travelled across an ocean one hundred yojanas wide to look for and find Sita, the wife of Rama?" Bhima screamed. "In terms of bravery and strength, I match him. That's all I have to say, so start moving and make room so I won't injure you."

The monkey replied, "O brave hero, have patience. Be as strong as you are soft, and show mercy to the elderly and helpless. I am so old and frail that I lack the strength to get myself up. Since you are hesitant to jump over me, kindly push my tail aside and clear a space for yourself."

To his surprise, after using all of his might, Bhima was unable to move it in the slightest. He bowed his head in shame and said, "Who are you?" in a contrite tone. "Please pardon me and let me know if you are a gandharva, god, or siddha."

"I am that Hanuman, the son of the Wind god whom you named. You will face peril if you continue down this path, which leads to the spiritual realm where the yakshas and rakshasas reside. For this reason, I'm stopping you. Beyond this, no one can live. However, this creek has depths where you can locate the Saugandhika plant you were looking for."

"I count myself the most fortunate of men in that I have been blessed to meet my brother," exclaimed Bhima, who was filled with joy. He bowed in front of Hanuman and said, "I want to see the shape in which you crossed the ocean."

Hanuman appeared to engulf the landscape as he grinned, grew larger physically, and stood four square to the globe. When Bhima first saw this older brother's celestial form, which had previously only been described to him, he was overjoyed. He shielded his eyes because he could not stand the brilliant light coming from that figure.

"Bhima, my body can grow much more in the presence of my foes," said Hanuman. He then shrank back to his original size by contracting his body and gave Bhimasena a gentle embrace.

When Hanuman hugged Bhima, according to Bhagavan Vyasa, he felt entirely renewed and grew more stronger than before.

"O hero, go to your dwelling," Hanuman commanded. "When you're in need, keep me in mind. When I hugged you, I experienced the same joy that I had when I had the good fortune to touch Sri Rama's heavenly body. Ask any favour you'd like."

"Bless the Pandavas, for I have had the good fortune to see you," Bhima remarked. "We will definitely defeat our adversaries with your strength."

"While you roar like a lion in the battlefield, my voice shall join yours and strike dread into the hearts of your adversaries," Hanuman said as he bid his brother farewell. "I'll be there riding the flag of your brother Arjuna's chariot. You will win the battle."

Bhima was shown by Hanuman where the Saugandhika blossoms bloomed in a stream. This made Bhima think of Draupadi, who was waiting for him to return. He quickly gathered the flowers and went back to her.

The Wicked Are Never Satisfied

MANY brahmanas paid the Pandavas visits while they were in exile. One of them went to meet Dhritarashtra, who honoured him appropriately. The brahmana explained how the Pandavas, who were born princes, were subject to the whims of the sun and wind and endured severe hardships.

Although Dhritarashtra was unhappy to hear this, the implications for his own boys were what bothered him the most. He was concerned that the Pandavas' rage would one day surpass its boundaries and cause a catastrophic flood.

He thought, "Bhima's wrath is yawning below to receive Sakuni, Karna, Duryodhana, and the blind Duhsasana to their demise. They are poised dangerously up a tree in search of a honeycomb."

The blind king pondered, "Alas, why did we fall victim to covetousness? We gave in to the craving for power and possession. We craved what was not ours instead of enjoying our limitless abundance in serenity. Arjuna has brought celestial weapons back from heaven. What other than the desire for retribution may tempt one to return to earth from heaven?" He would be tormented by these thoughts and unable to relax.

Sakuni, Karna, and Duryodhana, however, were deliriously joyful. Duryodhana was informed by Karna and Sakuni that they now held the kingdom that Yudhishthira had previously held.

"O Karna, would it not be a joy of joys to watch with my own eyes the sufferings of the Pandavas and bring their anguish to a culmination by a display of our happiness?" Duryodhana said. "However, my father will decline to grant it. He fears the Pandavas and prevents us from entering the forest out of concern for our safety. But I'll tell you, everything we've done thus far has been wasted labour. We haven't even seen Draupadi, Bhima, or Arjuna's agony in the forest. We need to find a means, Sakuni and you, to get the king's permission to go to the forest."

Karna went to Duryodhana early the following morning and cheerfully declared that he had discovered a solution to the problem. "What do you think about attending the annual stock-taking of the cows at our ranches in Dwaitavana? There is no way the king could oppose that." This was a brilliant proposal, and Sakuni and Duryodhana sent the cowherds' chief to ask the king's approval.

However, the king would not agree. "The princes do benefit from hunting," he noted. "It might be a good idea to count the cows as well. However, I find out that the Pandavas live in that jungle. While there is still cause for resentment and conflict, I cannot consent to sending you to a location close to Bhima and Arjuna's home."

Duryodhana declared, "We won't approach them. Instead, we'll take great care to stay away from them."

"However cautious you may be, there is danger in just being close by," the monarch said in response. "Additionally, interfering with the Pandavas' suffering while they live in the jungle is wrong. Any one of your men could trespass and cause trouble if they did. You can send someone else to count the animals in your place."

"O monarch, Yudhishthira is aware of and adheres to the path of dharma," said Sakuni. "The Pandavas will do what he requests because he made his vow in front of everyone. Don't fight against Duryodhana, who enjoys hunting. I'll go with him and make sure that none of us approaches the Pandavas."

As usual, the king was easily persuaded.

Duryodhana Disgraced

WITH a sizable army and following, The Kauravas arrived in Dwaitavan. Duryodhana and Karna set up camp four miles away from the Pandava home in opulent guesthouses.

They examined the cow herds and conducted an inventory of them. They enjoyed the dance, the hunt, the sylvan sports, and other entertainment provided for them. Duryodhana and his hunting party came to a picturesque pond close to the Pandavas' retreat. He gave the order to set up a camp on its bank.

The king of the gandharvas, Chitrasena, and his entourage had already set up camp next to the pool. They blocked the men of Duryodhana from setting up camp.

They returned to Duryodhana and said that a mischievous prince was causing them problems. Duryodhana ordered his guards to evict the young prince. The attendants went back to the lake but discovered there were too many gandharvas for them. They were forced to flee in the rain.

Furious, Duryodhana led a sizable army into battle to vanquish the bold adversaries who had dared to oppose his pleasure. The army of Duryodhana and the gandharvas engaged in a fierce battle.

The battle initially favoured the Kauravas. But as Chitrasena rallied his warriors and started employing his magic weapons, the situation swiftly changed. Karna and the other Kaurava heroes were forced to flee in haste and shame when their chariots and weapons were lost.

Only Duryodhana remained on the battlefield. Chitrasena quickly apprehended him, chained him from head to foot, and blew his conch as a sign of triumph. Many of the renowned Kauravas were captured by the gandharvas.

Bhima was delighted and amused to learn of Duryodhana's defeat and capture. "These gandharvas have done our duty for us," he said to Yudhishthira. "Duryodhana, who undoubtedly came here to make fun of us, has received his due. I want to thank our gandharva friend right now!"

The Buddha's disciple Yudhishthira chastised him, saying, "Dear brother, now is not the time for you to celebrate. The humiliation suffered by the Kauravas at the hands of outsiders belongs to us because they are our relatives. We cannot remain silent and accept this. We have to save them."

This didn't seem very sensible to Bhima. "Why should we save this sinner who attempted to burn us alive in the wax home? Why should you feel sorry for the person who tainted my food, tried to drown me in the river, and humiliated Draupadi in front of everyone?"

They were then vaguely aware of Duryodhana's agonising cries in the distance. Being deeply moved, Yudhishthira disregarded Bhima's protest and ordered his brothers to help the Kauravas. Bhima and Arjuna assembled the dispersed Kaurava soldiers at his command and challenged the gandharvas to combat.

Chitrasena, however, had no desire to battle the Pandavas. He set free Duryodhana and the other prisoners as they drew near. He declared that his only goal was to humiliate the haughty Kauravas. The dishonoured Kauravas hastily travelled back to Hastinapura with Karna, who had been chased from the fight and had since joined them.

In extreme shame and despair, Duryodhana declared his intention to fast until death. He felt it would have been better if Chitrasena had slain him. Duhsasana was told to take over the rule of the kingdom. Duhsasana gripped his brother's feet and sobbed as he pleaded his ineligibility to rule.

Karna was unable to endure seeing his brother's anguish. "This does not fit heroes of the Kuru race. What good does it do to give in to grief? Only your adversaries will benefit from it. Just observe the Pandavas. Despite the shame they have endured, they have avoided fasting."

"If you truly regret what you have done up to this point," Sakuni said, "You should return the Pandavas' kingdom to them."

When Duryodhana heard this, his evil side once again took control. Losing the kingdom was to him a hundred times worse than losing or being humiliated. "I shall defeat the Pandavas," he cried.

"That is how a king speaks," said Karna. "What purpose does death serve? You must be living in order to accomplish something significant.

As he made his way home, Karna declared, "I swear to you by all that is sacred that, when the specified term of thirteen years is through, I will kill Arjuna in combat." As a sign of the oath, he then touched his sword.

Duryodhana celebrated a significant sacrifice with tremendous pomp and circumstance while the Pandavas were living in the jungle. He wished to offer the Rajasuya sacrifice, but he could not while Yudhishthira and Dhritarashtra were still alive. The brahmanas persuaded him to offer the Vaishnava sacrifice instead. He took this advice into consideration and celebrated the Vaishnava in grand style.

After the ritual, however, the people started to complain among themselves that Duryodhana's sacrifice had fallen short of the splendour of Yudhishthira's Rajasuya by not even a sixteenth of that amount. On the other hand, Duryodhana's companions applauded him and the sacrifice he had commemorated. They compared it to those made by Yayati, Mandhata, Bharata, and other people. The court sycophants did not hold back.

Karna reiterated that his role would be to kill Arjuna and informed Duryodhana that his Rajasuya had only been delayed until the Pandavas were vanquished and murdered in combat. "Until I've killed Arjuna, I won't consume meat or alcohol, and I won't decline anyone's request for a prayer." Such was the solemn oath Karna took in front of everyone. The sons of Dhritarashtra were ecstatic and yelled with glee as though the Pandavas had already died.

The Pandavas in the jungle received word of Karna's vows from spies. Yudhishthira was quite worried because he thought highly of Karna's ability. Karna was unquestionably a powerful hero who was born with heavenly armour.

Sri Krishna's Hunger

THE wise man Durvasa once travelled to Duryodhana with ten thousand of his followers. Knowing the sage's temper, Duryodhana took great care to see to every detail of the guests' welcome and showed such extravagant hospitality that the sage was pleased and told him to request any boon.

Duryodhana was incredibly glad to have survived the ordeal so unscathed. The great sage asked him to beg for a boon. He saw that this was his chance to unleash the irate sage on the Pandavas. He responded, "You have blessed us, great sage, by accepting our hospitality. In the woods are our brothers. Kindly deign to see them as well, so that they may be honoured in like manner."

He proposed a time for the visit when he was confident that all the prepared food would have been consumed. None would be left for unforeseen visitors. The sage, who enjoyed constantly putting people to the test, agreed to comply with Duryodhana's request.

Duryodhana was confident that the Pandavas, who themselves struggled to survive in the jungle, wouldn't be able to accommodate the sage and his group. They would instead face some terrible curse from the impatient guest. When the sage offered a boon, this would bring him more joy than any advantage he could have wished for himself.

As requested by Duryodhana, Durvasa visited the Pandavas while they were resting after their midday meal. The brothers greeted, saluted, and honoured the sage. The wise man continued, "We will be back shortly. Because we will be hungry, our meals must be ready." And he went to the river with his followers.

The Sun god had given Yudhishthira the Akshayapatra vessel at the start of their sojourn as a reward for his austerities. The god had promised when giving the gift, "Through this, I shall put at your disposal for twelve years all the food necessary for your daily usage. The cup won't be completely empty for the day until everyone has been served, and Draupadi herself has consumed her fair share."

The brahmanas and other visitors would therefore be served first. The Pandava brothers would then have their dinner after that. Draupadi would then receive her portion.

All of them, including Draupadi, had finished their meals by the time Durvasa arrived. The vessel was empty and devoid of all of its power for the day. Draupadi was at a loss as to where to find sustenance. She fervently pleaded to Sri Krishna to intervene on her behalf and spare her the sage's anger.

Sri Krishna suddenly appeared before her. He said, "Bring immediately something to eat since I am quite hungry, and then we can talk about other things."

"Alas!" she screamed. "O Krishna, why do you test me in this way? The Sun's vessel has used up all of its power for the day. Durvasa, a wise man, has arrived. So what do I do? As if this weren't enough, you've arrived at this time claiming to be hungry. The sage and his students will be here in a short while."

"I am incredibly hungry and want food, not justifications," declared Sri Krishna. "Bring the vessel so I may inspect it for myself."

It was delivered to him by Draupadi. A grain of rice and a small piece of cooked vegetable were stuck to the vessel's rim. Sri Krishna accepted them as Sri Hari, the Soul of the Universe, and ate them with satisfaction.

Draupadi felt terrible about how shabbily she hadn't thoroughly cleansed the vessel of any leftovers. Vasudeva had eaten the remaining portion that was left!

After finishing his one grain, Sri Krishna called Bhima, instructed him to proceed to the river, and informed the esteemed sage that the meal was ready and waiting for them. He then appeared to be filled with satisfaction.

Bhimasena hurried to the river where Durvasa and his disciples were taking a bath. He was very perplexed yet full of faith in Sri Krishna. They were shocked to see that their insatiable hunger had given way to contentment. They exuded the same cosy joy of those who have enjoyed a satisfying meal. "We have come here after asking Yudhishthira to prepare food for us, but we feel well-fed and satisfied and cannot eat any more," the disciples said to the sage.

Durvasa informed Bhima of what had occurred and said, "We have eaten. Please ask Yudhishthira to pardon us. The celebration then dispersed."

The explanation is this. As Sri Krishna is the centre of the universe, his happiness with a single grain of rice temporarily allayed everyone's hunger, even the sage.

The Enchanted Pool

THE twelve years of sojourning were now drawing to a close.

One day, a deer rubbed on a poor brahmana's fire-kindling mortar. The mortar got caught in the animal's horns, and it ran into the forest. In ancient days, fire was kindled with wood by friction.

"Alas! The deer stole my fire-kindler. How can I make a fire sacrifice?" The Brahmana cried for aid and ran to the Pandavas.

The Pandavas pursued the animal, but it was a magic deer that rushed away into the jungle. Under a banyan tree, the Pandavas sat dejected. Nakula grumbled, "We can't even help the brahmana. How we have fallen!"

Bhima agreed. "We should have slain those wretches who dragged Draupadi into the assembly. If we had done that, we would not have to suffer these sorrows."

Arjuna said "I listened to that charioteer's son bragging and did nothing. We deserve our pitiful status."

Yudhishthira observed that they had lost their cheer and courage. He assumed they'd be happier working. Being thirsty, he told Nakula to climb a tree and look for a pool or river.

Nakula ascended a tree and saw water plants and cranes. "Surely there's water there."

Yudhishthira dispatched him for water. When Nakula arrived, he saw a pool. He decided to quench his thirst first. But as soon as he dipped his hand in the water, he heard a voice say:

"Be careful. This is my pool. Answer my inquiries and drink the water."

Nakula was astonished, but careless of the warning, drank the water. At once, overcome by overpowering drowsiness, he fell down, appearing dead.

Yudhishthira despatched Sahadeva to find Nakula. Sahadeva noticed his brother laying on the ground and wondered if he was hurt. But he ran to the water instead.

"O Sahadev, answer my inquiries to quench your thirst." But Sahadeva ignored the warning like Nakula. He too drank and fell.

Disturbed now at his brothers' absence, Yudhishthira despatched Arjuna to check on his siblings. He continued, "Bring water; I'm thirsty."

Arjuna found his siblings by the pool. He was shocked and thought they were killed by a hidden enemy. Though heartbroken and seeking retribution, he was driven to the fateful pool by a tremendous thirst.

Again, someone said, "Answer my question before you drink. If you disobey me, you will follow your brothers."

Arjuna was furious. "Who are you? Come challenge me, and I'll kill you," he said, firing arrows at the voice.

"Your arrows only wound air," laughed the unseen figure. "Answer my questions and you can drink. Without it, you'll die."

Arjuna decided to find and fight this elusive foe, but first he had to fill his thirst. His first enemy was thirst. So he drank and fell dead.

Yudhishthira told Bhima, "Dear brother, Arjuna, the great hero, hasn't returned either. Quickly find them. And bring water, I'm dying of thirst." The anxious Bhima hurried away without a word.

Imagine his sadness and wrath as he saw his brothers murdered. "Yakshas did this," he thought. "I'll hunt and kill them, but I'm so thirsty I'll first drink water to fight." Then he dove into the pool.

"Bhimasena, beware. Answer my questions before drinking. You'll perish if you ignore me."

Bhima drank water voraciously and glared defiantly. As he did so, his enormous power seemed to ebb away, and he fell dead among his siblings.

Yudhishthira moaned in fear and thirst alone. "Are they cursed, scouring the forest in search of water, or have they fainted or perished of thirst?" Unable to tolerate these thoughts, and driven mad by an uncontrollable thirst, he headed out to hunt for his brothers and the pool.

Yudhishthira followed his brothers and found a magnificent green meadow with a pool of clear water. Unable to control his anguish as he saw his brothers laying there, he wailed.

"Was this the end of all our promises?" he asked Bhima and Arjuna as they lay quiet and silent. "You've been taken just when our exile is ending. Even the gods have abandoned me!"

He was mystified at this occurrence. The world had no warriors who could defeat his siblings. They had no scars, and their faces were those of men who slept in peace. This was some great magic, indeed. Was it Duryodhana's trick? Perhaps he poisoned the water.

Yudhishthira too dived into the pool, consumed with thirst. As before, the formless voice warned:

"Your brothers perished because they didn't listen. Answer me questions, then drink. This is my pool."

Yudhishthira understood these were yaksha words and guessed what happened to his brothers. He saw a way out.

"Ask your inquiries," he said the bodyless voice.

The speaker asked quickly. "What causes daily sunshine?"

Yudhishthira responded, "Brahmanism."

"What saves a man?"

"Courage saves in peril."

"What science makes man wise?"

"No sastra makes man intelligent. He gains wisdom from the wise."

"What is more noble than the earth?"

Yudhishthira responded, "A mother who raises her offspring is nobler than the earth."

"What's higher than the sky?"

"Father."

"What's swifter than wind?"

"Mind."

"What's worse than wilted straw?"

"An anguished heart."

"What befriends travellers?"

"Learning."

"Who's a homebody's friend?"

"The wife."

"Who accompanies a man in death?"

"Dharma alone accompanies the soul in its lonesome journey after death."

"Which vessel is the largest?"

"The earth, which contains all within itself, is the biggest vessel."

"What is happiness?"

"Good conduct brings happiness."

"What is it that all love a man for abandoning?"

"Pride—for forsaking that, man will be adored by all."

Thus, Yudhishthira answered the yaksha's questions and many more.

"O king, one of your dead brothers can be revived," the yaksha said. Whom do you want revived?"

Yudhishthira considered for a time and then replied: "May the cloud-complexioned, lotus-eyed, and broad-chested Nakula appear."

The yaksha was happy and asked, "I've heard Bhima is your favourite and as strong as sixteen thousand elephants. Arjuna's prowess in arms is your safety. Why Nakula?"

Yudhishthira replied: "O yaksha, dharma is the only shield of man and not Bhima or Arjuna. Kunti and Madri were the two spouses of my father. I am surviving, a son of Kunti, and therefore she is not fully bereaved. In order that the balances of justice may be even, I ask that Madri's son Nakula may revive."

The yaksha praised Yudhishthira's impartiality and brought back all his brothers.

It was Yama, the Lord of Death, who had taken the appearance of the deer and the yaksha. He did this so that he would see his son Yudhishthira and test him. He blessed Yudhishthira.

Yama said: "Only a few days left to finish the stipulated duration of your banishment in the jungle, and the period of your exile in the forest. The thirteenth year will pass too. You will successfully perform your undertaking," and with this, he disappeared.

The Pandavas had to pass through all sorts of tribulations during their exile, but the advantages were not inconsiderable. It was a period of rigorous discipline and deep probation through which they emerged stronger and nobler men.

Section IV

Virata Parva

Domestic Service

"O Brahmanas, we have been robbed out of our empire and put to poverty by the sons of Dhritarashtra. Still, we spent these years in the forest cheerfully.

"It's time to say goodbye to you. We must remain covert for the ensuing twelve months as we enter our thirteenth year. God knows when we can all be together without fear. Bless us before we leave, and keep us hidden from those who might want to turn us into the Dhritarashtra sons."

Thus Yudhishthira spoke to the brahmanas who had been living with the Pandavas up until that point, trembling with emotion.

He was comforted by Dhaumya. "Parting is hard, and there are many, tremendous dangers. But you are too intelligent and knowledgeable to be scared or daunted," he counselled. "You must present a false identity. The finest souls in history have revered disguises when they are used for good. Likewise, you will triumph over your adversaries and get success."

The Pandavas retired to a remote area of the forest where they planned their course of action. "Arjuna, you are well versed in the ways of the world," Yudhishthira said. "Where would be the ideal location for us to spend the next year?

"O great monarch, you know Yama, the Lord of Death, has rewarded us," Arjuna responded. "We can easily get through the next twelve months. We have a lot of nations to pick from for our sojourn. In my humble view, the rich and endearing Matsya nation of king Virata is the best."

"Virata, the king of Matsya, is very strong and he loves us very much," Yudhishthira responded. "He has sound judgement and is committed to upholding virtue. He won't be intimidated or won over by Duryodhana. I concur that it would be best to remain anonymous in Virata's realm."

"Well then," said Arjuna. "What employment would you seek in his court, O King?" Arjuna wept bitterly at the idea that the noble and honourable king Yudhishthira would have to pose as someone else and perform servitude.

Yudhishthira responded, "I shall ask Virata to hire me as a courtier. I will dress as a sanyasin and use my aptitude for interpreting omens and knowledge of astrology, the Vedas, Vedangas, ethics, politics, and other sciences to keep him amused. I will tell him that I had the honour of knowing Yudhishthira well and had the opportunity to learn these things from him.

"What tasks would you undertake for Virata, O Bhima? You are brimming with bravery and courage. What mask can conceal your powerful personality and allow you to live anonymously?" As he asked this of Bhima, Yudhishthira was in tears.

"O king, I consider accepting employment as a cook in the palace of Virata," Bhima chuckled in response. "You are aware of my voracious appetite and my prowess in the kitchen. I will prepare such delicate meals that Virata has never had in order to delight him. I will also make the king happy by defeating the wrestlers that visit his court."

This worried Yudhishthira since he worried that if Bhima participated in wrestling matches, disaster would befall them. Bhima immediately said in an effort to allay his anxieties, "I may deliver a nasty jolt to any wrestler who deserves it, but I shall not murder anyone. I'll control wild creatures like buffaloes, bulls, and other animals to amuse King Virata."

Following that, Yudhishthira asked Arjuna, "What profession do you intend to pursue? How can you conceal your overwhelming bravado?" Yudhishthira could not help but recount Arjuna's amazing achievements when he posed this query.

"Revered brother, Urvasi cursed me with loss of manhood when I rejected her seductive advances. However, by Indra's grace, the curse would only last for a year, and the time would be up to me. I'll now finish the year in which I lost my manhood.

"I will perform menial labour in the interior chambers of Virata's queen while wearing bangles made of white conchs, wearing my hair in a bun, and dressing as a lady. I'll ask for help and claim that I already assisted Draupadi at Yudhishthira's court."

"Alas! Has fate ordained that he, who is comparable to Sri Krishna himself in glory and bravery, must go and look for work as a eunuch with Virata?" Yudhishthira spoke sadly. He asked Nakula what kind of employment he would do.

"I'll work in King Virata's stables. I enjoy training and caring for horses. I understand their hearts and am familiar with their problems and treatments. I am skilled at harnessing and driving horses in a chariot. I'll mention that I had taken care of the Pandavas' horses, and I have no doubt Virata will hire me."

"You, with the intelligence of Brihaspati, the priest and preceptor of the gods, and the knowledge of Sukra, the instructor of the asuras, what work would you undertake?" Yudhishthira questioned Sahadeva.

"I will protect Virata's cattle from sickness and savage attacks by wild animals."

"O Draupadi—" but Yudhishthira was at a loss for words to inquire about her plan. It was blasphemous to discuss serving her because she was more precious to him than life itself and deserving of every respect and protection. Shame and despair suffocated Yudhishthira.

When Draupadi witnessed his sorrow, she bravely said, "O finest of kings, do not mourn or have anxiety because of me. I will serve as Virata's queen Sudeshna's Sairandhri, a friend and attendant. I will claim that I assisted princess Draupadi in Yudhishthira's court in order to apply for a job with the queen. A princess's attendant and companion has this right, and is able to exercise it. I will thus maintain my independence and virginity."

Draupadi's bravery was lauded by Yudhishthira, who added: "O auspicious one, you speak as befits one of your family."

Dhaumya thanked the Pandavas and gave them the following advice once they had made their decision. "Those who are engaged in duty under a king should always be vigilant. They may only offer advice when requested and must never impose it. The monarch, who is a true fire in human form, must be informed before doing anything, no matter how tiny. Do not approach him too closely or attempt to run away from him.

"A person should constantly act as if they would be fired right away, even if they are trusted by the monarch and have a lot of power. A ruler shouldn't be trusted too much. That would be unwise.

"A king's servant should always be self-controlled and energetic. He shouldn't let the king's honour or dishonour cause him to feel overly happy or miserable. He is not permitted to divulge the information given to him or accept gifts from the populace. He shouldn't harbour resentment toward other servants. One should never even imply that their behaviour toward the ladies of the court is impolite.

"Live so in patience for one year, serving the monarch Virata, and you will live the rest of your days in happiness, reclaiming your lost throne." Dhaumya then wished the Pandavas.

Virtue Vindicated

YUDHISHTHIRA dressed in sanyasin-style clothing. Arjuna changed into a eunuch. Others also disguised themselves, but nothing could mask their inherent grace, dignity, and charm. They appeared to King Virata to be born to rule and command rather than to serve. Although he initially hesitated to employ them, he eventually bowed to their requests.

Virata's army was commanded by Kichaka, the monarch Sudeshna's brother. The monarch owed his influence and stature to Kichaka. He commanded such sway that some believed him to be the legitimate ruler of the Matsya nation. Kichaka was arrogant about his power and his ability to sway the king.

He fell in love with Draupadi's attractiveness. He had no idea that she had the capability to defy him despite being just a maid servant. He made her feel uncomfortable by his constant advances.

Draupadi revealed that her husbands were gandharvas who would murder those who attempted to defame her in a strange manner. Everyone bought into her story because of her good behaviour and attractiveness. But Kichaka was not one to be intimidated easily. His persecution finally grew harsh enough for her to complain to Queen Sudeshna and request her protection.

Kichaka naturally had more influence over his sister. He blatantly confided in her about his affection and asked for her help in carrying out his desire. He confessed, "I am so full of agony that I do not get any sleep or rest from the time I met your maid. You must make her accept my approaches in order to preserve my life."

When the queen failed to convince Kichaka to change his mind, she eventually bowed down. They came up with a scheme to capture Draupadi.

In Kichaka's home, a large feast was set up one evening. Sairandhri was summoned to her side by Sudeshna. She asked her to fetch her some wine from Kichaka's residence.

Draupadi resisted going to the house of the smitten Kichaka at that time and pleaded vehemently for another of her numerous attendants to be dispatched, but Sudeshna did not hear her and sternly told her: "Go, you must. I have to send someone else." Draupadi had no choice but to comply.

Draupadi's worries were valid. When she got to Kichaka's residence, the wretch started bugging her with frantic pleas and requests. He was drunk and enraged from lust.

"Why do you, who belong to a high royal family, seek me, born of a low rank?" She thus rebuffed his requests and asked, "Why do you approach me, a married lady? My guardians, the gandharvas, will slay you."

Kichaka grabbed her by the arm and drew her around. She tore herself free, and ran while being closely pursued. She ran screaming to the court, but even there, Kichaka pursued her and hit her in front of everyone while using nasty language, further inebriated by his influence and authority.

Draupadi's intense sorrow caused her to lose sight of the threat posed by the Pandavas' early discovery. That evening, she went to Bhima and told him about

Kichaka's vicious pursuit and treatment of her, pleading with him for protection and retaliation.

She cried out inconsolably, saying, "I can't take this anymore. I work in a menial position for your benefit and to assist you in keeping your promise, even though I have only ever served you or Mother Kunti, whom I love and respect. But now I'm serving these wretches, and live in constant terror of some scandalous outrage. I do not mind working hard—see my hands."

She then displayed her hands, which were tarnished and damaged from doing menial duties. Bhima dried her tears as she politely brought her hands to his face and eyes. He finally found his voice and uttered, "I do not care about what Yudhishthira promised or what Arjuna suggested. I will follow your instructions. Here and now, I'm going to kill Kichaka and his crew."

Bhima was cautioned by Draupadi not to act hastily. After much deliberation, they determined that Kichaka should be persuaded to arrive alone at night to a vacant location in the dancing hall where Bhima would be waiting for him, assuming the role of Draupadi.

The following morning, Kichaka turned on his malicious attentions once more and boastfully addressed Draupadi.

"O Sairandhri, I kicked you in front of the king. Did anyone offer to assist you while you were there? I am the true ruler of this Matsya nation. Virata is simply its nominal ruler. Now, don't be a fool. Instead, come and live a life of royalty with me. I'll work hard to be your loyal servant." He cried, pleaded, threatened, and devoured her while his eyes were blazing with lust.

Draupadi pretended to submit and declared, "Kichaka, I'm at your mercy. However, none of your friends or brothers ought to be aware of our relationship. I will grant your request if you vow that you will scrupulously keep the information hidden from others."

Kichaka enthusiastically accepted the requirement and pledged to travel by himself that very night to an assigned location.

"The women go to their dancing sessions throughout the day and return to their accommodations at night," she said. "At night, nobody will be in the dancing room. Come there this evening. I will be looking for you."

Kichaka luxuriated in his joy. He dressed elegantly, and entered the dining room with care. He noticed Sairandhri resting on a couch in the extremely low light. He made his way through the darkness and placed his hands softly on the sleeping person.

Alas! He didn't touch Sairandhri's delicate body. Instead, Bhima's steely bulk pounced on him like a lion on its prey and threw him to the ground.

Kichaka was surprised, but despite this, he wasn't a coward, and he was now fighting for his life. They grappled brutally, with Kichaka perhaps believing he was one of the gandharva husbands. They weren't mismatched because Bhima, Balarama, and Kichaka were known to be of comparable strength and wrestling prowess at the time.

Kichaka was ultimately murdered by Bhima, who worked his body into an amorphous mass by crushing and kneading it. After telling Draupadi with joy of Kichaka's punishment, he took a bath, covered himself in sandal paste, and went to bed feeling content.

"Kichaka came to molest me, but as I had warned him, the gandharvas, my husbands, made short work of him," Draupadi told the palace guards as she roused them. "Observe him." She also displayed Kichaka's corpse, which had been transformed to an amorphous mass with no discernible human features.

The people of Virata began to fear Draupadi as a result of what happened to Kichaka. "This woman is so stunning that she wins everyone's hearts. But the gandharvas defend her, making her as dangerous as she is beautiful. It's advisable to send her away from the city." As a result of their reflections, the people went to Sudeshna and appealed to her to drive Draupadi away.

"You are without a doubt a very virtuous woman, but kindly leave our city," Sudeshna said to Draupadi. "I've had it with you."

Only one more month remained of the required period of secret living. Draupadi pleaded fervently to be allowed to remain for only one more month, by which time she said her gandharva husbands would be prepared to take her with them. Sudeshna couldn't refuse because of her fear of the gandharvas.

Matsya Defended

AS of the start of the thirteenth year, Duryodhana's spies had been actively looking for the Pandavas. They reported their failure to Duryodhana after months of fruitless searching and noted that it was likely the Pandavas had died of privations.

Then word spread that a gandharva had killed the formidable Kichaka in single combat over a woman. Bhima was one of only two people who had the ability to kill Kichaka. Duryodhana also believed that Draupadi might have been the person responsible for the murder.

He declared, "I have a suspicion that the Pandavas are in the city of Virata. He is currently one of the kings who is too obstinate to pursue our alliance. It would be wise to attack his nation and take his cows. If the Pandavas are there, they will undoubtedly join us in battle to thank Virata for his hospitality. They will have to spend another twelve years in the wilderness if we find them. On the other hand, if the Pandavas are not present, nothing is lost."

Trigarta's king, King Susarma, backed him. He declared, "My enemy is the king of Matsya, and Kichaka has caused me a lot of difficulty. Virata must have suffered a great deal from Kichaka's passing. Now give me permission to attack Virata."

They all agreed that Susarma should attack Matsya from the south and send the Virata army in that direction for defence. Then, from the relatively undefended northern side, Duryodhana and the Kaurava army would assault Virata by surprise.

Susarma invaded Matsya from the south. He took the livestock with him and destroyed the farms and gardens he passed through. The cowherds rushed to Virata in great panic. The king now wished Kichaka was still alive because he undoubtedly would have put the raiders out of business.

He declared as much to Kanka, Yudhishthira's courtier Virata's assumed name. The latter responded, "O king, be not alarmed. I may be a recluse, but I know how to fight. I'll expel your adversaries. According to what I've heard, your butler Valala, stable-keeper Dharmagranthi, and cowherd Tantripala are all skilled combatants. Please issue orders so that we may receive the requisite chariots and weaponry."

Virata was more than happy to accept the proposal. With the exception of Arjuna, all the Pandavas joined the army. The armies of Virata and Susarma engaged in a bloody battle that resulted in significant casualties on both sides. Virata was taken prisoner by Susarma and imprisoned in his chariot.

Then Yudhishthira gave the order to Bhima to attack Susarma, liberate Virata, and rally the dispersed Matsya forces. But the army of Matsya lost heart and started to scatter in all directions.

Upon hearing these comments, Bhima was going to cut down a tree and fight. Yudhishthira intervened and warned him not to use any pranks or battle cries because his identity would then be known. Instead he counselled him to use his bows and arrows to battle like any other person would.

In response, Bhima boarded the chariot, released Virata, and apprehended Susarma. The scattered Matsyan forces came together, formed fresh charges, and routed Susarma's army. People in the city were ecstatic when they heard that Susarma had been defeated. To welcome their victorious monarch home, they bedecked the city.

The large army of Duryodhana descended upon them from the north as they were putting the finishing touches on receiving king Virata. They immediately started collecting up the cows on the cattle ranches.

The cowherds' leader rushed to the city and informed Prince Uttara that the Kauravas were taking their cows. "In order to battle the Trigarta, King Virata has travelled to the south. Nobody is there to keep us safe. We turn to you for protection since you are the son of the king. Please, for the sake of your family's honour, come and retrieve the cows."

The prince confidently responded, "If only I can get someone to be my charioteer, I shall reclaim the cows alone. People will be impressed by my military prowess and realise that choosing between Arjuna and I is not very difficult."

Draupadi was in the inner apartments when Uttara said these remarks, and she must have smiled to herself. "O princess, the Kaurava army is advancing on our city from the north and has captured cattle ranches and animals on the perimeter," she said as she hurried to princess Uttara. "I learned that Brihannala had been Arjuna's charioteer. She had received instruction in archery from Arjuna while I was in the service of queen Draupadi. Send Brihannala to drive the prince's chariot right away, per your instruction."

The princess hurried to her brother to share what she had discovered and received his approval. The princess immediately hurried to the dancing hall to alert Brihannala, who was Arjuna in disguise, that she was needed as a charioteer.

"The wealth and the cows of my father are leaving with the Kauravas," she declared. "These evil people have arrived to profit from the king's absence. You served as Arjuna's charioteer, according to Sairandhri, and you have gained dexterity in combat. Drive the prince's chariot, and don't be scared; he will guard you."

Arjuna agreed while maintaining a serious expression of doubt and uncertainty. He also giggled awkwardly while wearing the armour while pretending to be unfamiliar with it. His anxieties were mocked by the royal ladies, who also assured him that Uttara would take care of him.

However, it was evident that he was a skilled charioteer when he harnessed the horses. And the horses seemed to love and obey him when he held the reins.

The last words of Brihannala to the women of the palace before the chariot quickly carried the prince off into combat were, "The prince will triumph. We shall despoil the enemy of their embroidered robes and distribute them to you as the reward of victory."

Prince Uttara

UTTARA, the son of Virata, eagerly departed the city in his chariot with Brihannala serving as his charioteer. Uttara instructed Brihannala to travel to the location where the Kauravas had gathered the cows.

The horses were worked hard, and soon the Kaurava army could be seen. As Uttara got closer, he could see the vast army being led in combat by Bhishma, Drona, Kripa, Duryodhana, and Karna. His mouth got dry, and his hair stood on end as he saw it. His courage, which had been progressively evaporating during the quick run to the field, was completely gone.

"How can I attack an army by myself?" he asked. "My father, the king, has gathered all of the available forces, therefore I have no soldiers. It is ridiculous to believe that one man can defeat an army led by a renowned fighter who is well-equipped! Oh Brihannala, send the chariot back."

"O prince, you started from the city, full of furious determination," Brihannala said in amusement. "Additionally, the people have faith in you. If we go back and don't get the cows, we will be insulted. I won't send the chariot back. Let's fight and stand our ground. Do not be afraid." Brihannala then started to steer the chariot towards the direction of the foe.

Uttara was in appalling discomfort. He uttered in a trembling voice, "I simply cannot do it. If the women laugh, let them; I do not care. Let the Kauravas march off with the cows. Fighting those who are enormously stronger than we are makes no sense. Do not act foolishly! Reverse the chariot. If not, I will run back and leap out."

And Uttara, who was in a panic, threw away his bows and arrows, got out of the chariot, and raced in the direction of the city. Running after the prince, Arjuna yelled at him to stop and act like a kshatriya.

Drona was perplexed to see Brihannala, who, despite being clothed magnificently, appeared to be a man disguised as a woman and somehow reminded him of Arjuna. Karna commented on this and asked, "How can this be Arjuna? What difference does it make if he is? What can Arjuna do to us on his own? The king has abandoned his son to battle Susarma alone in the city. The young prince has as his charioteer the attendant of the women of the palace. And that's all."

Poor Uttara was pleading with Brihannala to release him and offering the king infinite riches in exchange. "I was raised on my mother's lap as a child," he said, making a plea for sympathy. "I'm terrified to death."

However, Brihannala wouldn't let him go since she wanted to save him from himself. She pursued him, grabbed him, and then forcibly hauled him to the chariot.

"What a fool I was to boast," Uttara sobbed as he murmured, "Alas! What will happen to me?"

Kindly, Arjuna said, "Do not be alarmed. I will battle the Kauravas. Assist me by driving the chariot and taking care of the horses, and I will take care of the rest. Flight, I assure you, has never resulted in good. We'll defeat the opposition and get your cows back. The glory will all go to you." After saying these remarks, Arjuna helped the prince board the chariot and gave him the reins, instructing him to steer the vehicle toward a tree close to the cemetery.

Drona, who was attentively observing everything, informed Bhishma that the extravagantly attired charioteer was Arjuna. "Why should we be concerned about who he is?" Duryodhana asked, turning to face Karna. "If he is Arjuna, he will only be strengthening our position because the Pandavas will be exiled in the jungle for an additional twelve years if he is found out."

As soon as they approached the tree, Brihannala commanded the prince to dismount, climb the tree, and remove the concealed weapons.

"People claim that the body of an elderly huntress hangs on this tree," the prince murmured in panic and anguish. "How am I supposed to touch a corpse?"

"It's not a corpse, prince. I know it has the Pandava weapons inside," Arjuna remarked. "Bring them down by scaling the tree fearlessly. Do not wait."

Uttara scaled the tree, grabbed the bag that was fastened there, and came down with much displeasure. He spotted sun-bright weaponry when the leather bag was unlocked. Uttara stood transfixed by the scene and worked up the nerve to reach out and touch them. He felt as though hope and great courage were being poured into him by the contact.

He fervently said, "O charioteer, what a wonder! You claim that the Pandavas own these bows, arrows, and swords. I am familiar with them. Do you recognize them? Where are they?"

Then Arjuna gave him a brief explanation of how everyone was at Virata's court.

"Kanka, who serves the monarch, is Yudhishthira," he declared. "It is none other than Bhima who cooks such lovely meals for your father as Valala. The person Kichaka was killed for insulting, Sairandhri, is Draupadi. Tantripala, the caretaker of the cows, and Dharmagranthi, who tends to the horses, are Nakula and Sahadeva, respectively. I am Arjuna. Do not fear. O prince, you shall soon witness my victory over the Kauravas and recovery of the cows in front of Bhishma, Drona, and Aswatthama. Additionally, you will become well-known, and you will learn from it."

Then Uttara lowered his hands and addressed Arjuna, saying: "O Arjuna, what a blessing it is to see you in person! Arjuna is the conquering hero whose very presence has given me heart and bravery. Please pardon the errors I made due to my ignorance."

Arjuna told Uttara some stories about his bravery as they got closer to the Kaurava host so that he wouldn't lose his newly found courage. He walked up to the Kauravas, knelt down, prayed to God, took off his conch bangles, and put on leather gauntlets.

He then entered the chariot after tying a handkerchief around his flowing hair and thinking about his armour. He strung his Gandiva bow, twiddled the string three times, and the loud noise it produced caused an echo from all directions.

The heroes of the Kaurava army exchanged the following words after hearing the sound: "This is definitely Gandiva's voice." The Kaurava army was startled as Arjuna appeared on the chariot in full godlike size and blew his conch Devadatta. There was a frantic cry that the Pandavas had arrived.

Promise Fulfilled

THE sound of the Gandiva bow twang made the Kauravas' hearts tremble. "Our army must be carefully and expertly positioned. Arjuna has arrived," a worried Drona announced.

The honour Drona bestowed upon Arjuna by way of this worry did not sit well with Duryodhana. "The thirteenth year has not yet come to a conclusion," he said to Karna. "Arjuna has already made himself known. Why should we succumb to our fears? The Pandavas will have to visit the forest once more. Drona is afflicted by the too-icy learned's feet. Let's move toward the combat and leave him behind."

"Our guys are shaking with fear," Karna agreed. "They claim that Arjuna is the man who triumphantly rides a chariot toward us while holding a bow in his hand. But even if it's Parasurama, why should we be afraid? Even if everyone else retreats, I will stop the warrior who is moving toward me, keep my pledge to you, and engage him in combat." Karna then started to extol his own virtue as usual.

The moment Kripa heard Karna's comments, he said, "This is genuine tomfoolery. Arjuna must be attacked by all of us at once. Our only hope of victory would be that. Therefore, refrain from boasting about your ability to oppose him by yourself."

Karna became enraged. "The acharya always takes pleasure in chanting Arjuna's praises," he continued. "I'm not sure if he behaves in this way out of fear or excessive affection for the Pandavas. While others who are true to the salt they have consumed participate in battle, those who are terrified need not fight. I will stand here and fight, for one. What business do folks have here learning from the Vedas that love and glorify their foes?" He said mockingly.

Drona's son and Kripa's nephew Aswatthama was unable to remain unmoved by this contempt directed at the revered instructors. "The battle still needs to be won," he admonished Karna. "Your boast is empty arrogance. We are members of the class that recite the Vedas and sastras but are not kshatriyas, and I have not been able to find any sastra that says it is honourable for kings to conquer kingdoms by tricking dice.

"Even people who battle and take kingdoms do not boast about it too much. I don't see anything you've accomplished to be proud of. In what conflict did your warriors beat the Pandavas, O Duryodhana, O Karna? A dice roll and a fight with Arjuna are entirely different things. Sharp arrows rather than fours and twos as in a dice game will be sent forth by the Gandiva. You conceited swine, do you really believe Sakuni can win you a battle by nothing more than cheating?"

The Kaurava army's leaders started a verbal battle. The grandsire, who was distressed to see this, remarked, "The wise man does not insult his teachers. Battles should only be entered into after careful consideration of the time, place, and circumstances. Even the typically sane Duryodhana, overcome with rage, is unable to recognise that the warrior standing and facing our army is Arjuna. His anger has clouded his intellect. Aswatthama, Drona, and Kripa should all forgive and forget.

"Now is not the time to foster animosity or sow discord. Where else in the world can the Kauravas find heroes who are more valiant and knowledgeable about the Vedas than Drona, the preceptor, and his son Aswatthama? There is no one else that we are aware of who can compare to Drona. Only if we all band together and battle Arjuna can we win. Let's get to work on the assignment at hand."

As the grandsire continued, his noble words helped to calm the crowd's irate emotions.

"The thirteen-year period specified in the contract came to an end yesterday," Bhishma continued, turning to Duryodhana. "Men knowledgeable in the science of planetary movements will tell you that your calculations are incorrect. When Arjuna blew his conch, I realised the time had come to an end. The time has come for you to make peace with the Pandavas. Which do you prefer: a war that both sides lose in, or a just and honourable peace? Think it over carefully before choosing."

"Revered sire, I have no wish for peace," Duryodhana responded. "I won't even give the Pandavas a village. Let's prepare for battle."

"Let prince Duryodhana take away a fourth of the army to guard him and return to Hastinapura," Drona ordered. "Let someone else take the cows; failing to do so would be an admission of defeat. The five of us will engage Arjuna in combat along with the rest of the army."

The Kaurava forces set up their battle formation accordingly.

"O Uttara, I do not see Duryodhana's chariot or Duryodhana," declared Arjuna. "Bhishma is standing there and is wearing armour. I believe Duryodhana is chasing the cows to Hastinapura; let's go after him and get the cows back."

As soon as Arjuna uttered these words, he turned away from the Kaurava army and pursued Duryodhana and the cows. He drew his Gandiva bow and sent arrows to fall near his teachers' and the elderly grandsire's feet as he approached them with respect.

Arjuna arrived at the location where the cows had been gathered and positioned to drive the invading forces away. He then asked the cowherds to lead the cows to the byres as he turned to face them. Then Arjuna went after Duryodhana. When they noticed this, Bhishma and the other Kaurava warriors ran to Arjuna's aid and began tossing arrows his way.

Arjuna engaged in a fantastic battle. He attacked Karna first and expelled him from the battleground. He then attacked Drona and vanquished him. When Aswatthama joined the battle and attacked Arjuna after seeing Drona standing exhausted from fighting, Arjuna had the chance to allow Drona to leave the field. Aswatthama and Arjuna then got into a heated argument. Kripa also lost, and the entire army was dispersed and bound by fear.

Though rallied and brought back to the attack by Bhishma, Drona and others, there was no fight left in them; and finally, they left the field, after a glorious fight between Bhishma and Arjuna, which reportedly came to witness.

Arjuna soon approached Duryodhana and violently attacked him. After losing, Duryodhana briefly left the battleground. He spun around like a serpent and continued the battle after Arjuna mocked him for being a coward.

Arjuna fought, Bhishma and the others surrounded and protected him, and then he used a magic weapon to cause everyone to collapse unconscious on the battlefield. He snatched away their clothing while they were in that state. In those days, capturing the enemy's clothing was a sure sign of victory.

He was sent back to the city by Bhishma when Duryodhana arrived. After this embarrassing loss, the entire army marched back to Hastinapura.

"Our cows have returned," Arjuna said. "Our adversaries have left. Return to your kingdom, prince, decked out in flowers and covered in sandal paste."

Arjuna put the weapons back where they belonged on the tree on the way back and put on his Brihannala disguise once more. In advance, he dispatched messengers to the city to announce Uttara's glorious victory.

Virata's Delusion

SUSARMA, king of Trigatta, was vanquished by Virata, who then went back to his palace. The womenfolk joyfully informed him that Uttara had set out to subdue the Kauravas. They had no doubts that their dashing prince could rule the entire planet. But the king's heart sank at the news since he was aware of the prince's daunting assignment.

He screamed, "My dearly loved son must be gone by now." He commanded his ministers to dispatch the largest force they could muster to save Uttara.

Dharmaputra attempted to console Virata while posing as the sanyasin Kanka. "You are ignorant about Brihannala," he said. "I know her well. Anyone fighting from a chariot pulled by her is guaranteed to win. Additionally, the Kauravas must have departed after hearing of Susarma's defeat."

Messengers returned from the battlefield then. They brought the happy news that Uttara had vanquished the Kaurava soldiers and retrieved the cows. Even to the loving father, this seemed too good to be true, but Yudhishthira reassured him with a smile.

"Have no doubts, O king," he said. "The message must be accurate. Success was assured as Brihannala set out as charioteer. Nothing remarkable about your son's triumph stands out. I am aware that Brihannala is superior than even Indra's or Krishna's charioteer."

Virata thought this was ridiculous, but he was too joyful to care. He lavishly bestowed precious stones and other riches on the messengers who brought the good news and commanded widespread celebration. He declared, "My victory over Susarma is nothing. The actual victory is the prince's. At all places of worship, may special prayers of thanksgiving be given. All major thoroughfares should be flag-draped, and the populace should march to triumphant music. Make all necessary preparations to receive my lion-hearted kid in a proper manner."

To welcome his son, Virata dispatched ministers, warriors, and maidens. Sairandhri was ordered to bring the dice when the king withdrew to his suites. "I cannot control my delight," he exclaimed to Kanka. "Come, let us play," he said, inviting Yudhishthira to join them in a game.

Naturally, the king extolled the majesty and prowess of his son. "Behold my son's splendour. He has dispatched the renowned Kaurava soldiers."

Yudhishthira said with a smile, "Yes. How else would your son have managed to get Brihannala to pull his chariot? Your boy is indeed fortunate."

Virata was enraged by the ongoing exaltation of Brihannala. He yelled, "Why do you refer to the eunuch? You keep talking about the charioteering prowess of the eunuch as if that were of any relevance. I am talking about my son's victory!"

When Kanka protested, the king's rage only grew. "I know what I'm talking about. Brihannala is not like other people. Anyone riding in the chariot she drives is guaranteed success and can never see loss."

Virata could not tolerate this perverted mockery. He threw the dice at Yudhishthira's face and then struck him in the cheek. The face of Yudhishthira was soon covered in blood. Sairandhri, who was close, squeezed the blood into a golden cup after wiping it with the edge of her gown.

"What is the problem?" The still-furious king screamed. "What are you doing collecting the blood into a cup?"

"The blood of a Sanyasin may not be spilled on the ground. O king," Sairandhri responded. "For as many years as there are blood droplets split on the earth, the rains will not fall in your land. I gathered the blood in this cup for that reason. I worry that you are unaware of Kanka's grandeur."

"Uttara and Brihannala have come," the gatekeeper said just then. "The prince is anticipating meeting the monarch."

"Ask him in, ask him in," shouted Virata as he stood up.

"Allow Uttara to enter by herself," Yudhishthira said to the sentinel. "Brihannala ought to stay put."

He took this action to avert a disaster. He anticipated that Arjuna wouldn't be able to contain his rage when he saw the damage to his brother's face. He could not bear to witness Dharmaputra being injured by anyone other than in a just conflict.

Uttara entered and honoured his kingly father as required. He was frightened to see Kanka's injured face when he turned to pay respect to him, because he now understood that Kanka was the great Yudhishthira.

"Who was it who injured this magnificent one, O king?" he cried.

"Why do you fuss about it?" Virata asked his son as he turned to face him. "I slapped him for criticising you inadvertently and with envy. This unfortunate brahmana always praised your charioteer, the eunuch. He gave him the victory whenever I mentioned you. Although I am sorry, it is not worth discussing."

Uttara was paralysed by terror. "Alas! You've made a terrible mistake. Father, you must immediately kneel at his feet and beg for mercy or we will perish."

Virata, who found the whole situation puzzling, stood there unsure of what to do. But Uttara was so impatient and insistent that he gave in and knelt down before Yudhishthira, pleading for forgiveness.

After that, Virata made his son sit while embracing him and praising him as a true hero. "I'm waiting for the details with a fever of eagerness. How did you disarm the army of the Kaurava? How did you get the cows back?"

Uttara sat hunched over. He declared, "I defeated no army, and I saved no cows. All of that the work of the god-prince. He championed our cause, saved me from annihilation, dispatched the Kaurava warriors, and led the herd home. I remained silent."

The king could not believe his ears. He inquired, "Where is that god-prince? I must thank the hero who saved my son and defeated my enemies, and I must visit him. My daughter Uttara will be given to him in marriage. Go and bring him inside."

The prince responded, "He has vanished for the time being, but I suspect he will come back either today or tomorrow." Arjuna was in fact a godly prince who had temporarily vanished into Brihannala.

All the important inhabitants of Virata had gathered in the hall of assembly to rejoice over the triumph of the king and the prince. Arriving with them were Kanka, Valala the cook, Brihannala, Tantripala, and Dharmagranthi, who had been in charge of the triumphs. To everyone's surprise, they sat among the princes without being invited to do so. Some justified the behaviour by arguing that these more modest people had provided crucial assistance at a crucial moment and truly deserved acknowledgment.

Entering the court was Virata. The king lost his cool and expressed his annoyance loudly when he noticed the others occupying seats intended for princes and aristocrats.

To the shock of everyone there, the Pandavas revealed their identity once they believed they had had enough fun. When Virata realised that Panchali and the Pandava princes had been serving him covertly all these days, he was ecstatic. He gave Kanka an embrace and formally abdicated control of his entire realm to him. Additionally, Virata insisted that he give Arjuna his daughter in marriage.

However, Arjuna responded, "No, that would not be appropriate. The princess learned music and dancing from me. I am in the role of her parent since I am her teacher." But he consented to take her in as his son Abhimanyu.

In the meantime, messengers from the evil and cunning Duryodhana arrived with a letter for Yudhishthira. "O Kunti's son," they cried. "Duryodhana is despondent that you must return to the woods once more as a result of Dhananjaya's rash action. You must remain in the forest for an additional twelve years because he made himself known before the conclusion of the thirteenth year."

"Messengers, tell Duryodhana to make additional inquiries," Dharmaputra chuckled. "Without a doubt, the revered Bhishma and others will inform him that a full thirteen years had passed when your warriors once more heard the twang of Dhananjaya's bow and fled in terror."

Section V

Udyaga Parva

Taking Counsel

THE Pandavas departed Virata's capital and made an open settlement in Upaplavya, another location in Matsya territory, as they were no longer required to remain in secrecy. They then dispatched emissaries to call on their friends and family.

Balarama and Krishna arrived from Dwaraka along with many Yadava troops and Arjuna's wife Subhadra and her son Abhimanyu. As the Pandavas and the Matsya prince travelled to meet Janardana, a loud and prolonged trumpet conch blare could be heard.

At Upaplavya, Indrasena and numerous others who had abandoned the Pandavas in the forest joined them with their chariots. The Saibya king and Kasi prince arrived with their armies. With three divisions and the sons of Draupadi, Sikhandin, Dhrishtadyumna, and Drupada, Drupada was also present.

In front of that illustrious assemblage of allies, Abhimanyu and princess Uttara were married in accordance with Vedic customs. Then they convened in Virata's assembly hall. Balarama and Satyaki were placed next to Drupada, while Yudhishthira, Virata, and Krishna were seated next to each other. All eyes were focused on Krishna, who was now rising to speak as the commotion subsided.

"You are all aware of the great deception—how Yudhishthira was tricked at the game board, stripped of his throne, and banished to the forest," Krishna spoke to the silent crowd. "The sons of Pandu have patiently endured their hardship for thirteen years. Think carefully and suggest a course of action that will be in accordance with dharma and promote the glory and well-being of both the Pandavas and the Kauravas. Keep in mind the dishonourable magnanimity of the Pandavas as well as the deceit and cruelty of the Kauravas. I believe that in order to convince him to come to a peaceful resolution through the restitution of half the kingdom to Yudhishthira, we should send a capable and honourable messenger to him."

Then Balarama stood up to address the crowd.

He said, "You just heard Krishna. He offers a just and wise solution. I support it as beneficial to Dharmaputra and Duryodhana alike. Nothing could be better for everyone involved if Kunti's sons were to reclaim their kingdom through a peaceful resolution. The nation will only experience joy and serenity after that. Someone who carries the weight and has the capacity to promote peace and good understanding must go to Duryodhana to convey Yudhishthira's wish for a peaceful resolution and deliver an answer.

"The emissary should obtain support for Kunti's sons by enlisting the assistance of Bhishma, Dhritarashtra, Drona and Vidura, Kripa and Aswatthama, and even Karna and Sakuni if possible. He ought to be someone who would never give in to rage.

"In spite of friends' protestations, Dharmaputra obstinately staked his kingdom while well aware of the repercussions and lost it. The fulfilment of the exile's requirements can only provide the Pandavas their own freedom; they are not entitled to their kingdom's restoration. Now, he is only able to supplicate for his rights rather than make complaints.

"A suitable envoy would be one who is committed to bringing about a peaceful resolution yet is not a warmonger. Princes, I ask you to diplomatically approach Duryodhana and seek his peace. By every means necessary, let's try to avert a war. Only peace-related gains are worthwhile."

When Satyaki, a Yadava warrior, overheard Balarama say this, he was unable to control his emotions. "Balarama's statements do not strike me as in the least bit just," he roared, rising in rage. "Any argument can be made convincingly if one is skilled enough, but no amount of talent can change wrong into right or injustice into justice.

"Yudhishthira was defrauded by the Kauravas of his part of the kingdom, there is no question about that. Allowing them to keep it would be just as unfair as confirming a thief's ownership of his stolen goods. Anyone who criticises Dharmaputra does so out of cowardly fear of Duryodhana rather than for a valid reason.

"O princes, please pardon my stern words. The untrained and reluctant Dharmaputra played that dangerous game with a sharper not of his own free will but because the Kauravas pressured and invited him to. Why should he grovel and pray to Duryodhana now that he has kept his promises? Duryodhana and his allies are doubting the performance despite the fact that they have maintained their word. In any event, how can a just war be wrong? Killing adversaries who take up arms and fight is not sinful. It would be foolish to spend time because Duryodhana will not cede territory without a fight. Let's begin the preparations now."

Satyaki's unwavering comments warmed Drupada's heart. "Satyaki is correct," he said as he stood up. "Soft words won't convince Duryodhana to see things rationally. Continue preparing for battle while giving our allies prompt notice so they can mobilise their forces. Undoubtedly, we must dispatch a suitable representative to Dhritarashtra. It is safe to send the erudite brahmana to Hastinapura to perform the religious rites in my court. Give him thorough instructions on what to say to Duryodhana and how to tell Bhishma, Dhritarashtra, and Dronacharya what needs to be done."

Vasudeva (Krishna, the son of Vasudeva) rose when Drupada finished speaking and addressed him, saying: "What you offer is doable and follows the kingly law. I and Baladeva share equal emotional ties with both the Kauravas and the Pandavas. We travelled here for Princess Uttara's wedding and are now leaving for our hometown.

"You are respected among the kings of the realm, equal in age and knowledge, and qualified to give us all advice. You are highly respected even in Dhritarashtra. You've known Drona and Kripa since you were young. Therefore, it is only fitting that you guide the Brahmana envoy in his quest for peace. Send news to us and get ready, my friends, for the inevitable confrontation if he is unable to convince Duryodhana to see his wrong."

"You are aware of both the virtues of the Pandavas and Duryodhana's mental bent," Drupada stated to his brahmana when he summoned him. "As the Pandava emissary, go to him. Show the old, feeble king the way of dharma and wisdom. He is being led astray by his son. Vidura will be a valuable ally for you in this endeavour. It might happen that the war-lords and the elder statesmen like Bhishma, Drona, and Kripa disagree as a result of your quest, and it might take some time before such disagreements are resolved.

"The Pandavas will use this extra time to finish their military preparations. Your rhetoric of peace in Duryodhana's capital will hinder their efforts to prepare for battle. Better still if, by some miracle, you can return with amicable conditions of peace. Duryodhana is not likely to consent to a peaceful resolution, in my opinion. But it will benefit us to send one on a peace mission."

Arjuna's Charioteer

THE Pandavas sent word to the princes likely to support them, to gather their forces and hold themselves in readiness for battle. At the same time, they sent Drupada's brahmana on a peace mission to Hastinapura. Arjuna travelled alone to Dwaraka.

Duryodhana and his brothers were active in the meantime. They started planning for the clash and told their allies to prepare their troops ready for battle.

The regular, quick journeys back and forth of princes produced a huge commotion everywhere. Word of these preparations on both sides quickly circulated across the nation. The poet claims that the earth trembled under the weight of the legions that were marching.

Duryodhana also took action after he realised the course that events were taking through his spies. Vasudeva (Krishna) accelerated his chariot toward Dwaraka as quickly as his fastest horses could carry him after learning that he was back in his hometown. Arjuna and Duryodhana arrived in Dwaraka on the same day as a result.

Krishna was dozing off. Arjuna and Duryodhana had access to his bedroom because they were his close kin. They both waited there for Krishna to awaken. Arjuna continued to stand at the bed's foot in a polite manner. Duryodhana, who entered first, sat himself on a gilded throne-chair.

Arjuna was standing in front of Mahadeva when he awoke, and he received a hearty greeting. He then turned to greet Duryodhana and inquired as to what had brought them both to Dwaraka.

It was Duryodhana who spoke first.

"It appears that war will soon break out between the two of us. In that case, you must back me. We are both equally adored by you, Arjuna and I. It is impossible for you to claim that one of us is closer to you than the other. I arrived here prior to Arjuna. According to custom, preference should be given to the person who arrived first. Because you are the best of the best, Janardana, you have a responsibility to lead by example. Remember that I came first and uphold the traditional dharma in your behaviour."

Purushottama (Krishna) responded, "Son of Dhritarashtra, it's possible that you arrived here first, but the first person I saw when I awoke was Kunti's son. Therefore, even in this regard, your claims on me are equal, and as a result, I am required to support both sides. The customary method for allocating favours is to start with the recipient with the least seniority. Therefore, I would let Arjuna make the decision first.

"My tribesmen, the Narayanas, are on par with me in combat and make up a powerful, nearly unstoppable host. They will be on one side of the aid I provide, and I will be on the other, but I won't use any weapons or engage in any physical combat."

He added, "Partha, give it some serious thought. Would you rather have the strength of the Narayanas or me, unarmed and alone? Use the first-choice privilege that tradition grants you as the younger man."

Just as Krishna was about to finish, Arjuna uttered the following words reverently and without hesitation: "I would be pleased if you were with us, though you may not bear any weapon."

Duryodhana could hardly contain his happiness at what he perceived as Arjuna's unwise decision. Vasudeva's troops were happy to assist him, and his request was granted. Duryodhana went to Baladeva and told him the tale after being pleased with his acquisition of a powerful army.

The powerful Balarama said, "Duryodhana, they must have told you what I stated at the time of the marriage of Virata's daughter. I advocated for you and said everything I could to help. I've tried to convince Krishna several times that we are on an equal footing with the Kauravas and the Pandavas. I have no power. I cannot support someone who Krishna disagrees with. I can't support you against Krishna and I won't assist Partha. So, if battle is necessary, conduct yourself in accordance with the kshatriya code," he said.

"Arjuna has embarrassed himself," Duryodhana thought to himself as he made his way back to Hastinapura. "Along with Balarama's good intentions, the vast army of Dwaraka will fight for me. An army has been abandoned for Vasudeva."

When they were alone, Krishna asked Arjuna with a smirk, "Dhananjaya, why did you select so foolishly, preferring me alone and unarmed to my fully prepared and heroic forces?"

"My goal is to earn glory even equal to yours," Arjuna responded. "All of the country's princes and their armies can be defeated by you on your own. I also believe I can succeed. I hope to defeat you when you are in the driver's seat of my unarmed chariot. You have granted my wish today, something I have long desired."

"Are you trying to outdo me?" Vasudeva asked with a blessing as he grinned once again. "May you prosper," he wished, as he approved of Arjuna's choice.

The holy tale of how Krishna came to serve as Partha's charioteer is told here.

Salya Against His Nephews

THE head of Madradesa, Salya, was Madri's brother. Madri was the mother of Sahadeva and Nakula. He learned that the Pandavas were setting up camp in Upaplavya and getting ready for battle.

He assembled a sizable army before setting out to join the Pandavas. The army was so enormous that its encampment stretched for more than fifteen kilometres.

When Duryodhana learned of Salya and his advancing army, he ordered his officers to provide them lavish hospitality. This was an effort to encourage Salya to join his cause. Accordingly, a number of exquisitely designed rest houses were built along the way, and Shalya and his troops received wonderful hospitality. Food and beverages were abundantly available.

Salya was overjoyed to receive the attention, but he suspected that Yudhishthira had planned it all. The ground trembled beneath the army's heavy steps as they marched forward. He called the servants one day, saying to them, "I must compensate you all for treating me and my warriors with such affection and attention. I was very happy with the hospitality. Please fetch Kunti's son, and tell him to bring me his permission to do this."

As required, the servants notified their lord, Duryodhana, who was constantly moving covertly with the group, keeping an eye on Salya and his warriors. He used this chance to introduce himself to Salya and express his gratitude for his acceptance of the Kaurava hospitality.

Salya was astounded by this because he was unaware of what was going on up to that point. He was also moved by Duryodhana's valour in treating a Pandava supporter to kingly hospitality.

He was deeply impressed, saying, "How honourable and generous of you! How can I give you back?"

"You and your forces should fight on my side," Duryodhana responded.

Salya was taken aback.

"You are the same to both of us. You must value me on par with the Pandavas. You must consent to helping me," Duryodhana said.

Salya responded, "Let it be so."

Thus Salya left the Pandavas, who were deserving of his love and respect, and swore an oath to fight alongside Duryodhana. This illustrates the perils that might arise from accepting the hospitality of rulers.

Salya then turned to Duryodhana and said: "Duryodhana, trust me. It would not be appropriate to return without first meeting Yudhishthira. You have my word that I will honour it. But I have to go see Yudhishthira and tell him what I did."

"Go see him and quickly get back to me. And keep in mind the commitment you made to me," Duryodhana said.

The Madra king was warmly welcomed by the Pandavas. Sahadeva and Nakula were ecstatic beyond words to see their uncle, to whom the Pandavas had recounted all of their tribulations.

Salya told them the tale of his commitment to Duryodhana when they started discussing getting his assistance in the looming conflict. Yudhishthira realised right away that he had made a mistake by taking Salya's help for granted and allowing Duryodhana to thwart them.

Yudhishthira said to Salya, doing his best to hide his disappointment, "Great warrior, you are bound to uphold the vow you have made. Vasudeva is no match for you, and Karna will use you as his charioteer when he goes looking for Arjuna on the battlefield. Will you allow Arjuna to perish or will you intervene to save him? I am aware that asking you to do this is unfair, but I still do."

"My child, I was duped into offering Duryodhana my promise," Salya responded. "However, if I were Karna's charioteer and he started attacking Arjuna, you may assume that he would be discouraged and Arjuna would be saved. Be at ease. The pains and insults that were inflicted upon Draupadi and all of you will soon be nothing more than a distant memory. Your future will be filled with luck. What fate has predetermined cannot be stopped or changed by anyone. I made a bad decision. Bear with me."

Sanjaya's Mission

PEOPLE travelled in groups from all over the nation to the Pandavas' camp at Virata's domain, Upaplavya. The Pandavas soon possessed a formidable force of seven divisions. Similar to the Pandavas, the Kauravas gathered an army of eleven divisions.

In accordance with standard military procedure, all arms were grouped together to form a division back then, as they do today. One division had 21,870 chariots, an equivalent number of elephants, three times as many horses, and five times as many foot soldiers. They also had a variety of weapons and other military supplies. Chariots served as the equivalent of modern-day "tanks" in ancient combat, and specially trained elephants served as the "armoured automobiles" of that era.

The brahmana envoy of Drupada arrived at Dhritarashtra's court. Following the customary ceremonial introduction and questions, the messenger spoke to the crowd on behalf of the Pandavas.

"Law has inherent validity and is eternal. You already know this, so I won't have to remind you. As the sons of Vichitravirya, Dhritarashtra and Pandu are equally entitled to their father's wealth. Despite this, Pandu's sons are not receiving their fair portion of the common inheritance, and Dhritarashtra's sons have assumed control of the entire country. This cannot be justified.

"The Pandavas, descended from the Kuru dynasty, seek peace. They are willing to put their past struggles behind them and let go of the past. They realise that war only produces damage, thus they are unwilling to utilise it. Give them what is owed to them by doing so. This would be in line with both the pre-existing agreement and the justice system. Let there be no delay."

The messenger's plea was followed by a thoughtful and courageous speech from Bhishma. "By God's favour," he declared, "the Pandavas are secure. Despite having the backing of numerous princes and having the strength to win a fight, they are not war-oriented. They continue to seek peace. The only moral thing to do is return their property to them."

Bhishma was still speaking when Karna rudely interrupted and said to the messenger: "Is there anything new in what you said, O Brahmana? Why does it continue to tell the same old tale? How does Yudhishthira go about recovering the items he misplaced at the gaming board? Yudhishthira must beg for gifts if he wants anything! He makes this ridiculous claim with conceited confidence in the power of his allies, especially Matsya and Panchala.

"Threats won't work on Duryodhana, I can assure you of that. The Pandavas must retire to the forest for another twelve years and then return because the prophesied word that they would remain hidden during the thirteenth year has been shattered."

"Son of Radha, you speak foolishly," Bhishma intervened. "If we don't follow the instructions that this message gives us, war will break out, in which we will undoubtedly lose, and we will all be destroyed."

Dhritarashtra had to step in because of the chaos and commotion among the crowd. "I have decided to send Sanjaya to the Pandavas," he continued to the messenger, "having in mind the wellbeing of the world and considering their welfare. Return right now and inform Yudhishthira of this."

Sanjaya was then pulled aside by Dhritarashtra, who gave him the following instructions: "Sanjaya, go to the sons of Pandu and all the assembled princes and communicate to them my heartfelt regards and my kind inquiries regarding Krishna, Satyaki, and Virata. Go there on my behalf and make amiable remarks to ensure the averting of conflict."

Sanjaya undertook this peace mission in Yudhishthira. Following the formal greetings, Sanjaya addressed Yudhishthira in the middle of his court as follows:

"Dharmaputra, I am fortunate to be able to see you with my own eyes once more. You display the image of Indra himself while being surrounded by royalty. My heart is cheered by the sight. King Dhritarashtra offers you his warmest greetings and hopes to hear from you soon. Ambika's son abhors any discussion of conflict. He yearns for calm and your companionship."

Dharmaputra was pleased to hear Sanjaya mention this and responded as follows:

"If that is the case, Dhritarashtra's boys have been preserved, and we have all avoided a terrible catastrophe. I despise fighting and only want peace. We will erase all memory of the anguish we endured if our kingdom is restored to us."

"The sons of Dhritarashtra are perverted," Sanjaya said once more. "They continue to be just as evil as they always have, disobeying their father's counsel and their grandsire's good counsel, but you shouldn't lose patience. You have always stood up for moral behaviour, Yudhishthira. Let's avoid the terrible horror of war. Can material goods acquired by combat provide happiness? What benefit can we derive from a kingdom we conquered by murdering our own family members?

"Let us not resort to fighting. Even if one were to acquire the entire ocean-bound world, old age and death are unavoidable. Even though Duryodhana and his brothers are idiots, you shouldn't compromise your moral principles or lose patience. You should not give up on the noble dharmic road, even if they refuse to return your country."

Yudhishthira responded: "What you say, Sanjaya, is true. The best possession is rectitude, but are we acting improperly? Krishna is aware of the nuances of morality and dharma. He wishes both parties success. I'll follow Vasudeva's instructions."

"I want the Pandavas' welfare," Krishna declared. "I also want Dhritarashtra and his sons to be content. This is a challenging situation. I believe I can resolve this matter on my own by travelling to Hastinapura. Nothing would make me happier than to be able to negotiate peace with the Kauravas on conditions that do not jeopardise the wellbeing of the Pandavas. The Kauravas will be saved from the jaws of death if I am successful. Additionally, I'll have accomplished something positive and worthwhile.

"The Pandavas will remain faithful to Dhritarashtra even if they receive what is rightfully theirs through a peaceful resolution. They have no other desires, yet they are also equipped to wage war if necessary. Dhritarashtra may select whichever of these two options, peace or war, he pleases."

"Sanjaya, go back to the Kaurava court and tell the son of Ambika this from me," Yudhishthira said. "Was it not through your kindness that we were able to get a share of the kingdom when we were young? You made me a king once; don't rob us of our portion now and force us to live like beggars off the kindness of others. There is space in the world for the Kauravas and both of us, dear uncle. Therefore, let there be no hostility between us.

"Please convey my love and best wishes to the grandfather and beg him to find a method to guarantee that his grandchildren are content and at peace. Send Vidura the same message as well. Vidura is the greatest at recognising what is in our best interests as a group and giving us advice in that vein.

"Explain the situation to Duryodhana and inform him on my behalf that you forced us to live in the wilderness while wearing animal skins as princes of the realm, and that you humiliated and tormented our sobbing wife in front of the other princes. We endured everything patiently. Give us what is rightfully ours back, at least for the moment. Do not envy someone else's possessions.

"We are just five in number. Give at least five villages to the five of us in exchange for peace. We'll be happy, then. Sanjaya, tell Duryodhana this. Both peace and conflict are something I am ready for."

Sanjaya left Kesava and the Pandavas when Yudhishthira had finished speaking and returned to Hastinapura.

Not A Needle-Point Of Territory

DHRITARASHTRA was overcome with worry after sending Sanjaya to the Pandavas and was unable to sleep at all that night. He sent for Vidura and talked to him all evening.

The most secure strategy, according to Vidura, was to give the Pandavas their fair portion of the throne. "Only this can benefit both parties. Give your own sons and the Pandavas the same amount of love. The intelligent course is also the right one in this situation."

In considerable detail, Vidura advised Dhritarashtra in this way.

Sanjaya returned to Hastinapura the following morning and provided a thorough description of what had happened at Yudhishthira's court.

"Chiefly, Duryodhana ought to be aware of what Arjuna declared, 'Krishna and I will obliterate Duryodhana and his adherents from root to branch.' There is no doubt about that. The Gandiva is eager for battle. Even without me straining my bowstring, arrows are restlessly protruding eagerly from my quiver. Sanjaya, bad stars cause the bumbling Duryodhana to want to fight Krishna and me in battle. We are unbeatable, not even by Indra and the gods."

Dhritarashtra was advised by Bhishma not to stand in the way of Arjuna and Krishna's united power. "Karna is not equivalent to a sixteenth part of the Pandavas, despite his frequent boasts that he will kill them. When your sons hear what he has to say, they will head for ruin. What was Karna able to accomplish when Arjuna successfully repelled your son's assault on Virata's capital and deflated his ego? Where did the unbeatable Karna hide himself when the gandharvas captured your son? Did Arjuna not drive the Gandharvas back?" Bhishma taunted Karna in this way and forewarned the Kauravas.

Dhritarashtra said, "The only right thing to do is what the pater familias recommends. All knowledgeable folks advice seeking peace, and I know this to be true. What, then, can I do? No matter how loudly I protest, these fools will continue on their course."

After hearing everything that had been spoken, Duryodhana got up. "Father, do not be alarmed and shaken about our security. We are aware of our strength. It is a given that we will prevail. Yudhishthira is aware of it as well because he is just pleading for five villages today after giving up all chance of building a kingdom. Does this not indicate that he is already afraid of our eleven divisions? What could the Pandavas possibly have against our eleven divisions? Why do you doubt our victory?"

Dhritarashtra urged his son to refrain from starting conflict. "Settle for half the kingdom. If we manage that even half as well, that is plenty."

Duryodhana reached his breaking point. He cried out and left the court, saying, "The Pandavas will not obtain even a needle-point of territory." The court dispersed as a result of the general agitation.

Now, let's discuss what the Pandavas were saying to one another.

"Vasudeva, Sanjaya is Dhritarashtra's alter ego," Yudhishthira informed

Krishna when Sanjaya departed Upaplavya for Hastinapura. "I was able to deduce Dhritarashtra's thoughts from his discourse. Dhritarashtra is attempting to establish peace without ceding any land to us. When I first heard Sanjaya speak, I was naively happy. But it soon became apparent that my happiness was unjustified. He talked with a desire for peace and struck a medium ground, but the last words of his message seemed to recommend meekness to us even when our rightful rights were rejected.

"Dhritarashtra has not treated us fairly. I proposed that we limit ourselves to only five villages. Even this will be refused by the evil Kauravas. How can we put up with such blatant intransigence? In this emergency, you are our only advisor."

In response, Krishna remarked, "I have made the decision to travel to Hastinapura for the benefit of you both. I'll go to Dhritarashtra's court and make peaceable efforts to uphold your rights. My mission will benefit the entire planet if it is successful."

"Krishna, please don't go," pleaded Yudhishthira. "What benefit does it serve you to visit your adversaries right now? The evil Duryodhana will continue to act foolishly. I object to you hanging out with those dishonest men. We can't allow you put your safety in danger because the Kauravas won't stop until they have their way."

"Dharmaputra, I know how wicked Duryodhana is, but we should still try to find a peaceful solution, so that the world has no reason to blame us of not trying hard enough to prevent war," Krishna replied. "No matter how remote the possibility of success, we must not neglect anything. Do not worry about my safety; if the Kauravas threaten to harm me or my messenger of peace, I will annihilate them!"

"You are all-knowing," said Yudhishthira. "You are aware of both ours and their hearts. There is no one better than you in explaining things and in persuasion."

"Yes, I understand both of you," replied Krishna. "Their minds are constantly entrenched in bitterness, envy, and animosity while yours consistently clings to righteousness. I will exert every effort to achieve the outcome that I know is important to you—a warless settlement, even if it offers little in the way of benefits to you. The warning indicators point to impending conflict. However, our responsibility compels us to try to bring about peace."

Krishna then bid the Pandavas farewell and departed for Hastinapura in his chariot.

Krishna's Mission

BEFORE beginning his journey, Krishna spoke with the Pandavas in-depth. Surprisingly, even the powerful Bhima chose a peaceful resolution. "Don't let the race be wiped out. Peace is definitely desirable," he said.

Draupadi, however, was unable to forget her humiliation. Standing before Krishna while holding her hair in her hand, she cried out to Madhusudana.

"Madhusudana, look at these tresses of mine and do what honour demands. With honour, peace is impossible. My father, even my children, with Subhadra's son Abhimanyu at their head, would battle the Kauravas even though Arjuna and Bhima are opposed to war. For the past thirteen years, I have repressed my wrath in order to protect Dharmaputra. I have run out of patience." She began to cry as she recalled the terrible outrage.

"Weep not," Krishna said, moved by pity. "The sons of Dhritarashtra won't heed my pleas for peace. Their bodies will tumble to the ground and become food for jackals and wild dogs. You will live to see us triumph, and you will soon receive just compensation for the insult you suffered." Draupadi was thus content.

The city was ecstatic to learn that Krishna would soon be visiting. Dhritarashtra gave the go-ahead to decorate the city, and preparations for welcoming Janardana were well under way. Duhsasana's palace's size and beauty was greater than Duryodhana's. Dhritarashtra gave the order that it be prepared and made available to Krishna and his company. Along the path that Krishna's chariot was supposed to traverse, shamianas were erected at a number of locations outside the city.

Vidura was consulted by Dhritarashtra. "Make plans to present Govinda with chariots and elephants," he instructed him. "Other types of presents should also be prepared."

However, Vidura remarked, "Govinda cannot be acquired with gifts. Give him what he is coming to the Kurus homeland to receive. He came here looking for a peaceful resolution. Make that a reality. Madhava cannot be appeased by other presents."

When Govinda arrived in Hastinapura, the populace had gathered in the festive streets in such great numbers that his chariot could only go very slowly. He started off at Dhritarashtra's palace before moving on to Vidura's home.

When Kuntidevi met him there, she was overcome with emotion as she sobbed as she thought of her sons' suffering. After giving her some consolation, Krishna bid her farewell and headed for Duryodhana's palace.

Govinda was welcomed by Duryodhana, who also extended an invitation to dine, but Krishna smiled and responded, "Emissaries eat only once their job is accomplished. When my job here is over, you are welcome to host a feast." He returned to Vidura's house where he rested after turning down Duryodhana's invitation.

Together, Vidura and Krishna sought advice. Vidura was sure that Duryodhana believed he was undefeatable as long as Bhishma and Drona were by his side. And they owed it to him morally not to desert him. Govinda would make a mistake even if he entered the wicked man's court. Everyone who knew Duryodhana and his siblings expected them to plan an attack on Krishna's life through deceit and trickery.

"What you say about Duryodhana is true. I didn't come here hoping to bring about a peaceful resolution. Rather, I did it so that the world wouldn't hold me responsible. My life is not in danger," remarked Krishna.

Dhritarashtra was waiting for Krishna when Duryodhana and Sakuni visited him the following morning. Along with Vidura, Govinda went to court.

Vasudeva entered the court, and the vast assembly of kings rose. Krishna took a seat after bowing to the seniors and greeting the others with a remark or a smile. After the introductions, Govinda got up from his seat and turned to Dhritarashtra to explain what he was there to do.

"Dhritarashtra, spare your people from disaster. You view as good what is awful, and what is healthy for you as bad. It is your responsibility to control your sons. The Pandavas want peace, but are ready for battle. They want to live happily under your rule. Treat them as your own sons as well and come up with a just solution, and the world will praise you," said Krishna.

"My friends are aware that I am not at fault," Dhritarashtra declared. "I want exactly what Madhava said, but I have no control over it. My sinful sons don't pay attention to me. I beg you, Krishna, to counsel Duryodhana."

"You come from a noble line," Krishna added as he turned to face Duryodhana. "Follow the dharma path. Your current thoughts are unworthy and are only appropriate for lowly men. This great statement is in danger of being lost because of you. The Pandavas themselves will appoint Dhritarashtra as king and you as the heir apparent if you pay attention to logic and justice. Give them half the kingdom to make peace with them."

Additionally, Bhishma and Drona pressured Duryodhana to hear Govinda out. But Duryodhana's heart was immovable.

"I feel bad for Dhritarashtra and Gandhari, whom Duryodhana is condemning to misery and loss via his wrongdoing," Vidura said.

Dhritarashtra warned his son once more, "Our race will vanish if you do not heed Govinda's counsel."

Everyone's pressure to accept a peaceful resolution infuriated Duryodhana. He stood up and said, "You mistreat me, Madhusudana, because you admire the Pandavas. The others in this room blame me as well, although I don't believe I am at all to fault. The Pandavas put their country on the line of their own free will, and when they lost, they rightfully forfeited it. They left the field after losing because they had a duty to their honour. They now desire battle and want to kill us, but what fault of mine is that? Threats won't compel me to relent.

"When I was a child, the elders committed a grave injustice against us by granting the Pandavas, for some reason I cannot explain, a portion of the kingdom to which they possessed no legal claim. I then consented. But at the game, they lost their kingdom. I won't give it back to them. I'm completely innocent. I'm not going to give the Pandavas even a tiny bit of land—not even a needle-point!"

As he reminded him of the other injustices he had committed against the Pandavas, Govinda laughed and said, "The play was fraudulently arranged by you in conspiracy with Sakuni, and you afterwards insulted Draupadi in an assembly of princes. Yet you have the impudence to say that you have committed no wrong."

"Brother, it appears that these people have a plot to bind you with ropes and give you over to the Pandavas," said Duhsasana as he observed Bhishma and others adopting Krishna's accusation of Duryodhana.

"Let's leave this place," said Duryodhana as he and his brothers left the court.

"Sires, the Yadavas and Vrishnis live blissfully now that Kamsa and Sisupala are dead," Govinda remarked in a second address to the court. "Sometimes a person must be sacrificed in order to save an entire people. Is it not occasionally necessary to abandon a village in order to rescue the nation? If you wish to rescue your race, I'm afraid you'll have to sacrifice Duryodhana. The only option is that."

"Bring visionary Gandhari here," Dhritarashtra commanded Vidura. "She has a chance of getting Duryodhana's attention."

Duryodhana was requested, and Gandhari was requested when she arrived at the court. When Duryodhana returned, his eyes blazing with rage, Gandhari used every tactic at her disposal to try and reason with him. Duryodhana declined and left the room once more.

He then planned to kidnap Krishna with his friends. The court learned about this. Govinda chuckled and revealed his divinity since he had already foreseen this.

By Krishna's favour, Dhritarashtra briefly gained his sight, enabling him to view Krishna in all of his Visvarupa forms. "Pundarikaksha," he said, "I don't want to view anything else after I've seen your Visvarupa. I ask that I should be blind again."

"All of our efforts were in vain," Krishna informed Govinda. "Duryodhana was obstinate."

As Satyaki and Vidura stood on either side of him, Krishna stood up and left the court. When Krishna left Hastinapura, any possibility of a peaceful resolution vanished, and war was declared to be inevitable.

Attachment And Duty

KRISHNA went straight to Kunti after leaving the court. She requested him to give her sons her blessings after hearing what had happened and he informed her of it.

She declared, "The moment has come for that for which a kshatriya woman bears boys. May you keep my sons safe!"

(A kshatriya mother gives birth to children who would be killed during battle.)

When Kunti discovered that it would be a battle to the death, she was overcome with grief.

"How do I express my ideas and tell my sons to bear the insults?" Kunti pondered? How can my sons agree to anything that goes against kshatriya tradition?"

At the same time, she pondered what the war's mutual killings may achieve and what enjoyment the extinction of the race could bring. She was plagued by the potential for complete annihilation and the assertions of kshatriya honour.

"How are my sons going to beat the trio of Bhishma, Drona, and Karna? These three are the only warriors in the Kaurava army that have a chance of defeating the Pandavas in battle. Dronacharya might choose not to harm my children out of love or a reluctance to engage one's own students in combat. Without a doubt, the grandsire won't want to murder them.

"Karna, however, is the Pandavas' main foe. He wants to kill my sons so that he can appease Duryodhana. Karna is a superb man-at-arms. My heart is torn apart like a faggot in the fire when I picture him fighting my other sons. I need to find Karna right away and tell him the truth about how he was born because once he does, he will undoubtedly turn against Duryodhana's cause."

She was tormented by these worry-filled thoughts for her children. Kunti travelled to the Ganga River's banks, where Karna typically made his daily prayers. Karna was lost in his thoughts while practising meditation until he felt the sun's scorching beams on his back. Behind him, Kunti patiently waited.

After finishing his prayers, Karna turned around to see Kunti behind him holding the hem of his upper garment over her head to protect it from the scorching sun. He was greatly perplexed and amazed that Pandu's queen and the mother of the Pandava princes could be there, waiting for him to complete his prayers.

"I, son of the charioteer Adhiratha, bow before you." In accordance with the customary protocols of respectful address, Karna questioned the queen, "What can I do for you, O queen?"

"Karna," said Kuntidevi, "You are not the charioteer's father, nor are you Radha's son. Do not believe that you belong to the caste of chariot drivers. You were conceived by Pritha of royal lineage, also known as Kunti, and are the son of Surya. May fortune be with you!"

She continued by telling the tale of his birth. "The Pandavas are your brothers, but you were born with all the adornments and golden earrings. As a result, you joined Duryodhana and have grown to despise them. Dependence on Dhritarashtra's sons is not appropriate for you to live in. Become one of the realm's kings with Arjuna.

"May you and Arjuna slay evil! You'll have the entire globe at your disposal. Like the brothers Balarama and Krishna, your fame will spread widely. Your radiance will be like Brahma's among the gods when you are surrounded by your five brothers. In difficult circumstances, one must act in a way that pleases their loved parents. According to our teachings, this is the ultimate kind of dharma."

Karna felt a sign in his heart that the Sun god approved of Kunti's request, as his mother said this to him at the conclusion of his devotions to the sun. But he checked himself and assumed that the Sun god was testing his loyalty and mental fortitude. He shouldn't be judged insufficient.

He exerted willpower to overcome both the urges of natural affection and the temptations of self-interest.

"What you have said, dear mother, is antithetical to dharma," he replied soberly but firmly. "If I deviate from my duty, I will have wounded myself far more than I could have been hurt by an adversary on the battlefield. When you dumped me, a defenceless baby, into the river, you deprived me of everything that was my inheritance as a kshatriya. Now you talk to me about my responsibilities as a kshatriya. In order to protect your other children's interests, you have since told me this story despite having denied me the maternal love that blesses all life.

"Will the world declare that I joined the Pandavas out of fear if I do so now? I have consumed the salt of Dhritarashtra's sons, gained their trust as their protector, and benefited from all the compassion and kindness they showed me. I am seen by the sons of Dhritarashtra as the ark that would carry them through the flood of war.

"Despite that, you want me to be unfaithful and side with the Pandavas just as the fight is about to begin. They were pushed into this battle by me personally. How can I just leave them now? Could there be a viler form of gratitude and treachery? What would be worthwhile at that price in life or elsewhere? Mother, if necessary, I will pay off my obligation with my life Otherwise, I will be no better than a common thief. In the upcoming conflict, I will undoubtedly employ every tool at my disposal against your sons. I cannot deceive you. Please pardon me."

But nonetheless, he added, "I cannot let my mother's plea go in vain. Arjuna or I must perish in this conflict. Even if they kill me, I will not kill your other sons. You will still have five sons, mother of warrior sons. You will still have five sons because one of Arjuna or I will survive this conflict, along with the other four."

Kunti's heart was filled with conflicting and tumultuous emotions as she listened to her first-born speak so firmly and in accordance with the kshatriya code. She hugged him and walked away silently because she lacked the confidence to speak.

"Who can defy what has been decreed?" She pondered. "At least he has promised not to hurt my four sons. I have said enough. May God bless him," she said before going back home.

The Generalissimos

GOVINA informed the Pandavas of what had occurred in Hastinapura when he arrived at Upaplavya.

"I asked people to do what was right and beneficial to them as well. However, it was for nothing. Right now, the only option left is to go to war. The wise assembly elders tried to counsel the ignorant Duryodhana, but he did not heed their words. War preparations must start right away."

Addressing his brothers, Yudhishthira declared that there was "no longer any chance of peace" and gave them instructions to prepare their forces for combat.

They divided the army into seven divisions, with the leaders of each division being Drupada, Virata, Dhrishtadyumna, Sikhandin, Satyaki, Chekitana, and Bhimasena. They then debated who ought to be made generalissimo.

Yudhishthira spoke to Sahadeva and said: "One of these seven should be chosen to serve as Supreme Commander. He should be someone who can defeat the powerful Bhishma, who can burn opponents to ashes and who is able to deploy his armies as needed. Who do you believe is the best qualified to carry out this duty?"

Prior to speaking with older people, it was customary to get younger people's perspectives. The younger people developed enthusiasm and confidence as a result. If the elders were consulted first, no one else would be able to speak freely, and even sincere disagreements could come across as disrespectful.

Sahadeva responded, "Let us take the king of Virata who assisted us when we lived in secrecy and with whose backing we now claim our part of the kingdom."

"Since Drupada is superior in terms of age, wisdom, courage, birth, and strength, it seems appropriate in my opinion to make him the Generalissimo," remarked Nakula. "He is highly regarded by all rulers and has long awaited a meeting with Drona. He is helping us much like he would his own boys."

Then Dharmaputra sought Dhananjaya's view.

"I believe that Dhrishtadyumna, the hero who is in control of his senses and was created to put an end to Drona, should be our commander on the battlefield. Only Dhrishtadyumna is capable of withstanding Bhishma's arrows, whose mastery of the bow caused even the legendary Parasurama to shrink back. The only one qualified to serve as our leader is him. There is nobody else that I can think of," Arjuna said.

"O king, everything Arjuna says is accurate. However, the rishis and elders have declared that Sikhandin has entered the earth in order to slay Bhishma," Bhimasena said. "My natural tendency would be to order Sikhandin, whose bright visage resembles that of Parasurama. Nobody else, in my opinion, can triumph over Bhishma."

Finally, Yudhishthira requested Kesava's judgement.

"The warriors described are all deserving of selection," Krishna said. "The fear of any of them would grip the Kauravas. Considering everything, I would support Arjuna's decision. Therefore, install Dhrishtadyumna as your Supreme Commander."

Dhrishtadyumna, Drupada's distinguished son, was appointed Supreme Commander of the Pandava army as a result. He had escorted Draupadi to the swayamvara and handed her to Arjuna. Arjuna was pondering over the slight his sister had received in Duryodhana's court and waiting for a chance to right the wrong.

The air was rent by soldiers' lion roars, conch and shell blowing, and elephant trumpeting. The Pandava army marched into Kurukshetra in battle formation, accompanied by warlike yells that made the earth quake.

The leader of the Kaurava army was Bhishma. Duryodhana bowed to him with respect and said: "May you guide us to success and fame, just as Kartikeya did for the gods. As calves follow the sire-bull, so will we follow you."

"So be it," The grandfather said. "But you must realise that my choice cannot be changed. To me, you, sons of Dhritarashtra, are the same as the sons of Pandu. I will command the army and carry out my duties as promised to you. In the fight, my arrows will daily kill tens of thousands of warriors. However, I am unable to slay Pandu's sons. I did not consent to this conflict. I will finish out my duties in this war, barring slaying the Pandavas.

"One more thing. The son of Surya, whom you revere, opposes my leadership and disapproves of my ideologies. I will not object if you ask him to command the army from the start of the conflict, should you be so inclined," said the grandsire.

Karna and his ways didn't sit well with Bhishma. "I will refrain from fighting as long as Bhishma is still alive and join only after he has passed away. Then I will fight against Arjuna and kill him," said Karna. Even among powerful men in the past, envy and jealousy exist.

Bhishma's condition was accepted by Duryodhana, who appointed him Generalissimo of his armies as they poured into Kurukshetra like a huge torrent.

Balarama

THE renowned brother of Krishna, Balarama, paid the Pandavas a visit at their camp. He entered the room while wearing a blue silk robe, like a lion. Yudhishthira, Krishna, and others greeted the broad-shouldered warrior with joy. The guest bowed to Drupada and Virata before taking a seat next to Dharmaputra.

“I arrived in Kurukshetra after discovering that the Bharata descendants had allowed greed, rage, and hatred to overcome them, that the peace negotiations had collapsed, and that war had been launched.”

He hesitated briefly, overcome by passion, and then continued: “Dharmaputra, terrible destruction is coming. The planet will become a bloody wasteland covered in dismembered bodies! The kshatriya world has gathered here to meet its end because of a dreadful destiny. I frequently remarked to Krishna, ‘Duryodhana is the same to us as the Pandavas; we may not take sides in their stupid disputes.’ His intense love for Dhananjaya misled Krishna, and now he is supporting you in the conflict that he appears to have approved of.

“How can Krishna and I belong to different factions? Both Bhima and Duryodhana are my pupils, and I value and cherish them equally. How am I supposed to support one over the other? I also cannot stand to see the Kauravas wiped out. Therefore, I won’t participate in this conflict. I have lost all interest in the world as a result of this catastrophe, so I will roam in sacred locations.”

After speaking out against the tragic battle in this manner, Krishna’s brother departed the area, his heart heavy with grief and his mind seeking solace in God.

Rukmini

VIDARBHA'S monarch Bishmaka had five sons and one daughter, the stunning Rukmini, who was also charming and strong-willed. She longed to wed Krishna because she had heard about him and his fame. All of her family members supported the plan, with the exception of her eldest brother Rukma, the heir apparent, who had no interest in Krishna.

Rukma urged his father to wed Rukmini to Sisupala, the king of Chedi, rather than giving her in marriage to the monarch of Dwaraka. Due to the king's advanced age, Rukmini appeared to be forced to wed Sisupala as Rukma's opinion gained sway.

Because she was Lakshmi's incarnation, Rukmini had Krishna's heart in her entirety. She was worried that her father wouldn't be able to stop the unpleasant marriage since he would be powerless in the face of her tyrannical brother. Rukmini decided to find a way out of her situation by using all of her mental might. She sought advice from a brahmana, whom she despatched as her ambassador to Krishna, instructing him to inform her beloved of the situation and ask for assistance.

As a result, the brahmana travelled to Dwaraka. He delivered to Krishna Rukmini's heartbreaking situation and her plea, as well as the letter she had written.

The letter stated, "My heart has already acknowledged you as lord and master. I thus want you to assist me immediately before Sisupala forcibly removes me. There can be no further delay. You must be here in one day. You will face resistance from Sisupala and Jarasandha's soldiers, which you will need to defeat in order to obtain me. May you succeed and catch me!

"I am heading to the temple with my retinue to worship Parvati as part of the wedding festivities because my brother has chosen to wed me to Sisupala. The ideal time for you to arrive and save me would be then. I'll terminate my life if you don't show up so that I can at least be with you in my next life."

After reading this, Krishna jumped on his chariot.

The Vidarbha capital Kundinapura was exquisitely decked at the king's request, and planning for the princess's nuptials to Sisupala was in full gear. The prospective bridegroom and his group, who were all ardent foes of Krishna, had already gathered in the city.

Balarama learned about Krishna's unexpected and covert departure. He knew it had to do with the Vidarbha king's daughter. Fearing that Krishna would be surrounded by enemies who were hankering for his blood, he quickly gathered a sizable army and moved to Kundinapura.

Rukmini left her apartments and entered the temple, where there was a sacred service, in procession with her entourage. Rukmini begged Devi in a prayer for her help, "Oh Devi, I grovel before you who are aware of my devotion. Please permit Krishna to support me."

As she exited the temple, Rukmini saw Krishna's chariot and, like a magnet drawn to a needle, she immediately ran to him and boarded it. To everyone's surprise, Krishna took off with her.

Rukma, the heir apparent, was informed of what transpired by the servants who had run to him. Rukma vowed, "I will not go without slaying Janardana," and he and his army set out to find Krishna.

However, Balarama had already arrived with his army. Therefore a massive fight between the two opposing forces took place in which the enemy was completely beaten. Balarama and Krishna triumphantly made their way back to their ancestral house, where Rukmini and Krishna were married according to the customs.

The defeated Rukma was ashamed to return to Kundinapura. He constructed Bhojakata, a new city under his control, right where he and Krishna engaged in combat.

When he learnt about the Kurukshetra battle, Rukma sent a massive troop to the Kurukshetra fight. He extended assistance to the Pandavas in the hope that he could gain Vasudeva's favour in this way.

He addressed Dhananjaya and said, "Oh Pandavas, the opposing armies are exceedingly strong. I'm here to support you. If you give me the command, I will assault the desired area of the opponent formation. I can defeat Drona, Kripa, or even Bhishma since I have the power to do so. Just let me know what you want."

Dhananjaya chuckled and then turned to Vasudeva.

"Oh, Bhojakata ruler, we are not frightened by the bulk of the opposing army. We don't need or really want your assistance. You are free to leave or remain however you like."

Rukma was furious and ashamed at this point, so he led his troops to Duryodhana's camp.

He told Duryodhana, "The Pandavas have rejected my promised assistance. My forces are available for your use."

Duryodhana cried, "Is it not after the Pandavas denied your assistance that you have come here? I am not in such severe need yet, as to welcome what they have discarded."

Rukma was humiliated by both sides as a result and went back to his kingdom without engaging in combat.

Non-Co-Operation

IT was the day before the commencement of the great battle. The grandsire, now the Kaurava Generalissimo, was with Duryodhana, seeking to inspire him with his own heroic spirit and cheerfulness. Bhishma spoke of the strength, skill and prowess of the warriors ranged on the Kauravas' side, and Duryodhana was cheered up.

Presently, Karna became the subject of their talk. "Karna has earned your affection," said Bhishma. "But I do not think much of him. I do not like his great hatred of the Pandavas, and he is too boastful. I would not place him in the highest rank among the warriors of the land. Besides, he has given away the divine armour with which he was born. He is not therefore likely to be of great help to me in this battle. The curse of Parasurama is on him too. The battle that will ensue between him and Arjuna will prove fatal for Karna."

Thus spoke Bhishma without mincing matters, and this was exceedingly unpalatable to Duryodhana and Karna. To make matters worse, Drona agreed with the grandsire and said:

"Karna is full of pride and overconfidence. This will cause him to be neglectful of the finer points of strategy. Through his carelessness, he will suffer defeat."

Enraged by these harsh words, Karna turned to the grand-sire with flaming eyes. "You, sir," said he, "have always slighted me through mere dislike and envy. You have never neglected an opportunity of humiliating me, and needlessly too. I bore all your taunts and thrusts for the sake of Duryodhana. You have said that I would not be of much help in the impending war. Let me tell you my settled conviction: it is you—not I—who will fail the Kauravas.

"Why hide your real feelings? The fact of the matter is that you have no genuine affection for Duryodhana, but he does not know it. By hating me, you seek to come between me and Duryodhana and poison his mind against me. And to advance your wicked design, you have been belittling my strength. This behavior is unworthy of a kshatriya. Age alone does not confer a title to honor and respect among warriors, but prowess does. Desist from poisoning our relationship."

Turning then to Duryodhana, Karna said: "Illustrious warrior, think well and look to your own good. Do not place too great a reliance on the grandsire. He is trying to sow dissension in our ranks. His appraisement of me will injure your cause. By running me down, he seeks to damp my enthusiasm.

"He has become senile and his time is up. His arrogance does not let him have regard for anyone else. Age must be respected and experience is useful, but as the sastras warn us, there is a point when age becomes senility and ripeness falls into rottenness and decay. You have made Bhishma your Generalissimo who will, I have no doubt, earn some fame from the heroic deeds of others, but I will not bear arms while he is in command. Only after he has fallen will I do so."

Controlling his anger, Bhishma replied: "Son of Surya, we are in a crisis and that is why you have not ceased to live this very moment. You have been the evil genius of the Kauravas."

Duryodhana was in distress. "Son of Ganga, I need the help of you both," he said. "I have no doubt you will both do deeds of great heroism. At break of dawn, the battle joins. Let there be no fighting among friends, with the foe in full force before us!"

But Karna was adamant in that he would not take up arms so long as Bhishma was in supreme command. Duryodhana eventually yielded to Karna and suffered him to carry out his threat. Karna kept out during the first ten days of the battle, though all his men participated in it.

At the end of the tenth day, when the great Bhishma lay on the battlefield covered all over with arrows, Karna went to him and bowed reverently and asked for forgiveness and blessings, which he received. Thereafter, Karna co-operated and himself proposed Drona for the command of the Kaurava forces in succession to Bhishma.

When Drona also fell, Karna took over the command and led the Kaurava forces.

Krishna Teaches

EVERYONE was prepared for the fight. Together, the warriors from both sides sincerely pledged to uphold the customary laws of war.

The rules of engagement and tactics used in battle can change from time to time. We can only understand the epic if we keep in mind what laws were popular at the time of the Mahabharata battle. Otherwise, parts of the plot would be confusing.

The reader may get a general picture of the laws of warfare used in the battle of Kurukshetra from what follows. At dusk each day, the conflict was over, and the adversaries began to interact amicably. Only equals may engage in single combat, and tactics contradictory to dharma are prohibited. As a result, those who quit or retired would not be criticised.

Only a horseman, not a person on foot, could be attacked. Similarly, only their opposite numbers in the opposing ranks might engage in battle, including charioteers, elephant troops, and infantrymen.

Those who asked for quarter or gave themselves up were spared from death. Neither could anyone who was not already involved in fighting point his weapons at another person who was. Slaying someone who had lost his armour, was retiring, was disarmed, or whose attention was diverted was wrong. Additionally, non-combatants who were serving as attendants or who were blowing conchs or banging drums were not to be the target of any shafts.

The Kauravas and the Pandavas swore firmly that they would abide by these guidelines.

Even in the Mahabharata conflict, established conventions occasionally went too far. The account makes it obvious that there were a few instances of transgression for a variety of reasons. But overall, all sides in the Kurukshetra conflict adhered to the accepted norms of honourable and compassionate war, and the few exceptions were viewed as wrong and humiliating.

"Heroes, yours is a great opportunity," Bhishma declared to the princes under his leadership. "The gates of paradise are wide open in front of you. You will like living with Indra and Brahma. Follow the kshatriya dharma and walk the path of your ancestors. Fight with joy to become famous and great."

The princes replied, ordering their trumpets to be sounded, "A Kshatriya does not seek to die of disease or old age in his bed, but prefers to die on the battlefield," and they cried triumph to the Kauravas.

The palm tree and five stars on Bhishma's flag were brilliantly illuminated. The lion tail on Aswatthama's moved in the air. The ascetic's bowl and bow sparkled in Drona's golden standard, and the snake from Duryodhana's fabled flag triumphantly danced with its hood outstretched. While Jayadratha's banner featured a wild boar, Kripa's featured a bull. Others did the same, and the battlefield subsequently displayed a pageant of flags.

Yudhishthira instructed Arjuna after spotting the Kaurava army arrayed in battle, "The opposing force is quite large. Due to the size of our force, our strategy should be concentration rather than deployment, which would only make us weaker.

Therefore, arrange our forces in a needle configuration."

Arjuna became concerned when he saw men lined up on both sides for mutual murder. Krishna talked to him to calm his anger and allay his worries. The Bhagavad Gita, which is revered in millions of hearts as the Word of God and is regarded by mankind as one of the greatest treasures of human literature, is Krishna's advice to Arjuna at this point.

Yudhishthira Seeks Benediction

FOR the start of the conflict, everything was prepared. During this crucial moment, Yudhishthira, the tenacious and valiant son of Pandu, abruptly removed his armour and laid down his weapons. Both armies watched in shock as he descended from his chariot to approach the leader of the Kaurava army on foot.

"What is Yudhishthira doing?" questioned those who watched him, perplexed by the Pandava's unexpected and silent action.

The other brothers and Krishna joined him as they hurried in confusion toward Yudhishthira. They worried that Yudhishthira, giving in to his natural propensity, had resolved to seek peace on any terms and was moving forward to announce this.

"King, why are you making your way to the enemy's trenches in such an odd way? The adversary is prepared for fight, with soldiers wearing armour and holding raised weapons. But you have taken off your armour, set aside your weapons, and are walking forward unaccompanied. Tell us about your intentions," Arjuna instructed Dharmaputra.

But Yudhishthira moved silently in deep contemplation.

Then Vasudeva, who was adept at reading men's intentions, smiled and declared, "He is going to the elders to get their blessing before beginning this horrible war. He believes that starting such a serious process without seeking official blessing and consent is improper. He visits the grandsire to receive Dronacharya's and his blessing. He should go unarmed, that is true. He is aware of propriety. Only then will we have a chance of winning this conflict."

The soldiers in Duryodhana's army thought, "Here comes the Pandava coming to sue for peace scared at our strength," as they saw Yudhishthira moving forward with his hands clasped in a modest manner. "This individual in fact casts shame upon the kshatriya race. Why did this coward come into the world?" They criticised Dharmaputra while laughing at the idea of winning without using force in their conversation.

After passing through the lines of warriors, Yudhishthira went directly to Bhishma and saluted him by bowing low and touched his feet. He said, "Grandsire, let's start the fight now. We've dared to engage in combat with you, our unbeatable and unparalleled grandsire, but we first ask for forgiveness."

The grandsire said, "Child, born in the race of the Bharatas, you have behaved honourably and in accordance with our code of behaviour. I find it uplifting to see this. Fight, and you will succeed. I do not have any recourse in this matter. I am required to support the Kauravas in battle because of my duty to the king. But you will not give up easily."

Yudhishthira travelled to Drona and bowed to the acharya in accordance with form after getting the grandsire's approval and blessings in this manner. The acharya then gave his blessings by saying, "O son of Dharma, I have unavoidable responsibilities to the Kauravas. Our personal interests enslave us and take control of us. But the triumph will be yours."

Similar to how Yudhishthira did, he went to get the blessings of uncle Salya and Kripacharya before heading back to the Pandava lines.

[Bhishma and Partha, Satyaki and Kritavarma, Abhimanyu and Brihatbala, Duryodhana and Bhima, Yudhishthira and Salya, and Dhrishtadyumna and Drona were thus engaged in great battles according to the rules of war of those days. Similarly, thousands of other warriors fought severally in accordance with those days' customs.

The Kurukshetra battle witnessed many such "sankula" fights wherein countless men fought and died in the mad lust of battle.

Bhishma led the Kauravas for ten days, followed by Drona, who took over when Drona passed away, and Karna, who died near the end of the seventeenth day's fighting. On the eighteenth and last day, Salya led the Kaurava army.]

Section VI

Bhishma Parva

The First Day's Battle

THE Kaurava armies were commanded by Duhsasana, and the Pandava forces were commanded by Bhimasena. The air was torn apart by the sounds of battle. The clamour of the kettledrums, trumpets, horns, and conchs made the welkin ring. As the elephants charged, horses neighed, and the warriors let out their "lion-roars." In the air, arrows appeared to be flaming meteors. Uncles, nephews, and fathers killed one another, disregarding their familial ties and long-standing affection. It was a horrific and insane massacre.

The Pandava army suffered significant damage on the morning of the first day of combat. Everywhere Bhishma's chariot travelled, it resembled the destroyer's dance. Angered by this, Abhimanyu struck the grandsire.

Thus, the gods came to see the battle between the eldest and the youngest warriors. The golden Karnikara tree was depicted on Abhimanyu's banner, which was proudly waved by his chariot.

One of his arrows struck Kritavarma, and Salya was struck five times. Abhimanyu's shafts struck Bhishma nine times in all. One of Abhimanyu's arrows with a sword edge struck the charioteer of Durmukha, and the severed head fell to the ground. One more shattered Kripa's bow.

As the gods watched, Abhimanyu's exploits poured down showers of flowers. "Indeed, a worthy son to Dhananjaya," said Bhishma and the warriors standing behind him.

The brave young man was then attacked by all of the Kaurava warriors, but he resisted them all. All of the shafts that Bhishma fired were parried by him.

The grandsire was quite happy to observe the young hero's bravery. One of Abhimanyu's carefully placed arrows knocked the grandsire's palm tree flag to the ground. Bhimasena was ecstatic and let out a loud yell that further enthused his brave nephew.

Unwillingly, Bhishma was forced to confront the boy with all of his might. When the young hero needed to be relieved, Virata, his son Uttara, Dhrishtadyumna, and Bhima arrived and attacked the grandfather, who then turned his attention to them.

Uttara, son of Virata, rode an elephant and led a ferocious assault against Salya. After Salya's chariot horses were crushed and killed, he threw a javelin at Uttara.

It struck him in the chest with unerring aim. He let go of the goad he was holding and collapsed to the ground. However, the elephant did not leave. It persisted in charging until Salya severed its trunk and shot it numerous times with his arrows. At this point it let out a piercing scream and died. Salya then boarded Kritavarma's vehicle.

Sveta, the son of Virata, witnessed Salya kill his younger sibling. His rage grew, like a fire fuelled by butter libations. He turned his chariot toward Salya.

Salya instantly received help from seven chariot warriors who shielded him on all sides. Sveta was doused in arrows as the rockets flew by like lightning in the skies.

Sveta gave an amazing defence of himself. He hacked down their javelins as they rushed towards him and parried their shafts with his own. The soldiers in both armies were astounded by Sveta's prowess.

As soon as possible, Duryodhana dispatched troops to Salya to relieve him, which sparked a fierce conflict. Numerous chariots were destroyed, horses and elephants were killed, and thousands of warriors perished. After successfully forcing Duryodhana's troops to flee, Sveta advanced and attacked Bhishma.

Sveta took down Bhishma's banner. In turn, Bhishma killed Sveta's charioteer and horses. Then they continued to fight while hurling javelins at one another.

Sveta grabbed a mace and swung it towards Bhishma's automobile, which was destroyed. However, the grandsire had foreseen this tactic, and leaped down before the mace even hit the chariot. From the ground, he then pulled the bowstring up to his ear and shot a fatal arrow at Sveta.

And so Sveta died. Duhsasana joyfully danced and blew his horn. Bhishma then launched a massive assault on the Pandava army.

On the first day of the conflict, the Pandava army experienced severe losses. Duryodhana was ecstatic, and Dharmaputra was paralysed with fear. The brothers visited Krishna and held tense discussions with him.

"Chief of the Bharatas, do not be afraid," Krishna replied to Yudhishthira. "You have brave brothers, thanks be to God. Why should you give any doubts any thought? In addition to myself, there is Satyaki, Virata, Drupada, and Dhrishtadyumna. What gives you cause to feel disappointed? Do you disregard the fact that Sikhandin is awaiting Bhishma, his intended victim?" Krishna consoled Yudhishthira in this way.

The Second Day

DHRISHTADYUMNA, the Generalissimo of the Pandava army, came up with strategies to prevent a recurrence of the battle's disastrous first day. The army was carefully arranged on the second day, and every effort was made to inspire confidence.

Due to his triumph on the first day, Duryodhana became arrogant and stepped in the middle of his army to address his soldiers. "Heroes in armour, our victory is guaranteed," he exclaimed loudly. "Fight and give life no thought."

Bhishma's Kaurava army once more attacked the Pandava soldiers fiercely. Breaking their formation, he slaughtered many of them.

"If we carry on in this manner, the grandsire will soon completely decimate our army," Arjuna said, turning to Krishna, his charioteer. "I fear we cannot save our army unless we kill Bhishma."

"Dhananjaya, prepare yourself. The grandsire's chariot is here," said Krishna as he headed directly in his direction.

The chariot moved forward quickly. The challenge was welcomed by the grandfather, who dispatched his shafts. Duryodhana had commanded his guards to guard the grandsire with the utmost caution and to never let him put himself in danger. As a result, all of the warriors fighting for the grandsire immediately intervened and attacked Arjuna, who continued to fight unfazed.

It was widely acknowledged that only three men on the Kaurava side had any chance of defeating Arjuna: Bhishma, Drona, and Karna.

The warriors who had interfered in support of Bhishma were easily dispatched by Arjuna. All the distinguished generals in the army watched in admiration at the manner in which he used his large bow on this particular occasion. His chariot moved so quickly that the eye strained to follow it as it shattered enemy ranks like forked lightning.

As Duryodhana witnessed this battle, his heart was racing. His faith in the great Bhishma started to wane.

"Son of Ganga, it looks as though Arjuna and Krishna would decimate our entire army even while you and Drona are still alive and engaged in combat," exclaimed Duryodhana. "Karna, who has the utmost dedication and allegiance to me, withdraws and does not defend me solely because of you. I worry that I'll be duped and that you won't act soon to destroy Phalguna."

The gods descended to observe Bhishma and Arjuna's battle. These two were among the world's best warriors. White horses pulled both chariots. There were innumerable arrows flying from both sides.

The blood gushing made Madhava more attractive than ever as he stood like a green palasa tree in full bloom with crimson flowers. As the shafts collided in the air and occasionally impacted Arjuna's and Madhava's breasts. When Arjuna saw his beloved charioteer hit, his anger increased, and he pulled out his bow and fired carefully-aimed arrows at the grandsire.

The conflict waged for a considerable amount of time between equal opponents. It was impossible to pinpoint Arjuna's and Bhishma's whereabouts due to the chariots' close proximity to one another and rapid manoeuvres. It was only possible to distinguish the flag.

While this magnificent drama was being played out in one area of the field, Drona and Dhrishtadyumna were engaged in a furious combat elsewhere.

Dhrishtadyumna was severely hurt by Drona's vicious attack. But the latter responded in kind, shooting arrows and other projectiles at Drona while grinning venomously.

Drona skillfully defended himself. With his arrows, he deflected the hefty maces and sharp missiles that were thrown at him, breaking them to bits even as they flew through the air. Dhrishtadyumna's bow frequently broke when Drona's arrows struck it.

The charioteer of the Panchala ruler was murdered by one of Drona's arrows. Dhrishtadyumna then grabbed a mace and leaped off the chariot to go on foot.

A Drona arrow knocked the mace to the ground. Then Dhrishtadyumna pulled out his sword and charged forward like a lion charging an elephant. But Drona once more rendered him incapable of moving on.

As soon as Bhima realised the Panchala's situation, he shot Drona with a hail of arrows and drove Dhrishtadyumna to safety in his chariot. Upon observing this, Duryodhana dispatched the Kalinga army to battle Bhimasena. The Kalinga warriors were massacred in large numbers by Bhima. He stalked his adversaries and brought them to the ground like Death itself.

Bhishma arrived to relieve the Kalingas when he witnessed this. Bhima was supported by Satyaki, Abhimanyu, and other warriors who rose up. Bhishma's charioteer was knocked to the ground by one of Satyaki's shafts, and Bhishma's horses fled, carrying him off the battlefield.

When Bhishma's chariot rushed out of the field in this manner, the Pandava army went into a frenzy of excitement. They profited from the circumstance and launched a ferocious assault on the Kaurava force.

Arjuna's valorous actions caused the Kaurava army to lose the war that day by a significant margin. The enthusiasm of the Kaurava army generals from the day before had completely vanished, and they were distraught. The conflict of the day would end at dusk, and they anxiously anticipated that moment.

"It's best that we cease fighting right now," Bhishma told Drona as the sun set in the west. "Our army is weary and demoralised."

Dhananjaya and other Pandava supporters cheered as they arrived back at their camp with bands playing. The Kauravas were in the same frame of mind as the Pandavas were the previous evening at the conclusion of the second day of combat.

The Third Day's Battle

THE third day began with Bhishma forming and leading his army in an eagle formation, with Duryodhana and his forces guarding the rear. Each detail had been planned with meticulous care. The Kauravas were confident that there would be no misfortune for them that day.

The Pandavas skillfully arranged their own forces. In order to more effectively counter the enemy's eagle formation, Dhananjaya and Dhrishtadyumna chose to organise their army into a crescent shape. Bhima and Arjuna were leading their respective divisions on the right and left horns of the crescent, respectively.

The conflict started. Blood poured from every weapon at once, and the sun was obscured by the dust that chariots, horses, and elephants had kicked up. Despite the might of Dhananjaya's attack, the adversary held firm.

The Kauravas launched a counterattack, focusing on Arjuna's location. In the air, javelins, spears, and other projectiles shone like forked lightning during a rainstorm. The arrow shafts covered Arjuna's chariot like a huge cloud of locusts. With astonishing ability, he erected a moving fortification around it with arrows shot from his renowned bow in an endless stream.

Another time, Sakuni commanded a sizable army in an attack on Satyaki and Abhimanyu. Satyaki's chariot was so badly damaged that he had to climb up Abhimanyu's, and they then engaged in combat from the same vehicle. They were successful in decimating Sakuni's army.

Together with their brother, Nakula and Sahadeva resisted Drona's attack on the Dharmaputra division while Bhishma and Drona attacked the division together.

When Bhima and his son Ghatotkacha attacked Duryodhana's division that day, the boy's bravery seemed to surpass that of his legendary father. Duryodhana was struck by Bhima's shafts and collapsed in his chariot.

His charioteer feared that the forces would be entirely demoralised if they learned that the prince had been injured. So he hastily steered the chariot away from the site. However, even this shift led to a lot of uncertainty. Bhimasena made the most of the situation and caused chaos among the Kaurava forces that were fleeing.

Drona and Bhishma soon arose in order to provide confidence after observing the discomfort and perplexity of the Kaurava army. Duryodhana was once more seen commanding the reunited armies after they had been dispersed.

Duryodhana asked the grandsire, "How can you stand here, watching as our forces are dispersed and forced into dishonourable flight? You treat the Pandavas far too nicely, I worry. Why didn't you come right out and say that you loved the Pandavas and couldn't harm or kill them? You need to have made your intentions clear to me. These men are undoubtedly inferior to you, and if you were so inclined, you could easily handle them. It would be great if you and Drona gave me a straight answer right away."

Duryodhana spoke bitterly because of his defeat and the knowledge that his grand sire disapproved of his behaviour, but Bhishma simply smiled and replied, "Wasn't I honest in my advice to you? When you chose to go to war, you disregarded that advice. I attempted to stop the conflict from happening, but now that it has, I am doing everything in my power to serve you."

The grandsire then continued his work after saying as much.

The happy Pandavas were now a little careless because the morning's turn of events had been so favourable to them. They did not anticipate Bhishma to gather his troops and launch another attack on them.

However, the grandsire raged across the field like a consuming fire after being pricked by Duryodhana's criticisms. He gathered his troops and launched the fiercest assault against the Pandava army yet. His movements were so swift that afternoon, it was almost as though the grandsire had multiplied into a number of Bhishmas who were battling at various spots. Those who opposed him were killed and burned to death like moths.

The Pandava army was completely dispersed after being severely damaged. Sikhandin, Partha, and Vasudeva made valiant attempts to regain confidence and order but were unsuccessful.

"Dhananjaya, the crucial moment has arrived," stated Krishna. "Maintain your will to carry out your obligation to kill Bhishma, Drona, and all the other family members and revered seniors in battle without wavering. You made a commitment to it, and now it is up to you to follow through. Otherwise, our army is irreparably damaged. Now you have to go after the grandsire."

"Keep going," Arjuna commanded.

The grandsire greeted Dhananjaya's chariot with a fiery reception and covered it with his arrows as it raced toward Bhishma. The grandsire's bow was broken by three shafts that Arjuna fired after bending his bow. Bhishma chose a different bow, but it suffered the same fate. When the grandsire observed Arjuna's proficiency with a bow, his heart was filled with joy.

"Salute you, courageous fighter!" The grandsire said as, drawing another bow, he skillfully aimed arrows towards Arjuna's chariot.

The manner Arjuna responded to the assault did not please Krishna. Despite the intense labour of the grandsire's bow, Arjuna's hands did not provide their best effort because his heart was not in it. He had too high of an opinion of his grandfather.

Krishna believed that if Arjuna continued in this manner, the army, which was already severely disheartened, would be completely decimated and all would be lost. Despite Krishna's expert chariot management, Bhishma's arrows repeatedly struck both him and Arjuna.

Janardana's ire increased. "No more of this, Arjuna. If you do not kill Bhishma, I shall do it myself!" he yelled, dropping the reins, picking up his discus and leaping out of the chariot, he raced over to Bhishma.

Bhishma wasn't at all bothered by this. On the contrary, overwhelming ecstasy filled his face.

He said, "Come, come, O Lotus-eyed One! You have my respect, Madhava. Have you really descended from the chariot, Lord of the World, for my benefit? I extend my life to you. I will be honoured in the three worlds if you kill me. Give that to me, please. May your hands end this life and keep me in your care forever."

When Arjuna saw this, he was distraught. He descended quickly and pursued

Krishna. He overtook him with much difficulty and pleaded with Krishna to turn around.

"Be patient with me, please." He urged Krishna to go back, promising not to flinch if he desisted.

Krishna was once more holding the reins of the chariot. Furiously attacking the Kaurava troops, Arjuna killed thousands of people.

The third day's nightfall saw a crushing setback for the Kauravas. They remarked to one another as they made their way back to their encampment by torchlight: "Who can equal Arjuna?"

The Fourth Day

THE conflict was essentially the same every day, and the story consists of repetitive combat and deaths. However, the big battle is the Mahabharata's main event, and if we ignore it, we won't be able to comprehend the epic heroes who fought there.

Bhishma reorganised the Kaurava army at dawn. The grandsire appeared to be none other than the great Indra, clutching his thunderbolt while accompanied by the devas, including Drona, Duryodhana, and others. The Kaurava army resembled a massive rainstorm with its chariots, elephants, and horses arranged in battle order and prepared for battle.

The grandsire issued directives in advance. From his chariot, Arjuna observed the hostile activity and prepared himself as well.

The conflict started. Around Abhimanyu, Aswatthama, Bhurisravas, Salya, Chitrasena, and the son of Chala assailed him. The fighter engaged five elephants in combat like a lion. As soon as Arjuna became aware of this coordinated assault on his son, he joined him and the conflict accelerated.

A sizable force was also brought in by Dhrishtadyumna. Chala's son was murdered. Now that Chala had joined, he and Salya launched a fierce assault against Dhrishtadyumna.

A sharp missile fired by Salya split the latter's bow in half. When Abhimanyu realised this, he shot Salya with a hail of arrows. Salya was put in such danger that Duryodhana and his brothers hurried to save him.

At this point, Bhimasena also showed up on the scene. The brothers of Duryodhana trembled as Bhima hoisted his mace in the air. When Duryodhana noticed this, he became extremely furious and instantly charged at Bhima with a sizable elephant force.

Bhima left his chariot with an iron mace in hand as soon as he noticed the elephants approaching. The Kaurava ranks were disorganised as a result of his vicious onslaught, which caused them to scatter in a frenzied stampede. The dead mammoths were spread out across the area like enormous hills. Those who managed to flee did so in a panic and wreaked havoc on the Kaurava army, trampling many troops underfoot.

Bhima was then targeted in a broad assault by Duryodhana, but he resisted like a rock, and eventually the Pandava warriors joined him. Bhima again ascended his chariot after being injured in the chest by several arrows from Duryodhana.

Bhima addressed his charioteer, saying, "Visoka, now is the happy hour. Several of Dhritarashtra's sons are standing in front of me, waiting to be beaten like ripe apples on a tree. Maintain a firm grip on the reins and continue driving. These wretches are going to be delivered to Yama's residence by me."

Those arrows from Bhima would have killed Duryodhana if it weren't for his armour. Bhima killed eight of Duryodhana's brothers in that day's battle.

Duryodhana battled valiantly. One of Duryodhana's arrows broke Bhima's bow. Bhima picked up a new bow and fired an arrow with a knife edge at Duryodhana, breaking his bow in two. Bhima was so violently struck on his chest that he reeled and sat down. Duryodhana was unperturbed by this and pulled out a new bow.

Now, Duryodhana was bombarded by a massive hail of arrows from the Pandava warriors. When Ghatotkacha noticed his father sitting dazed from the force of the blow, he became extremely enraged and attacked the Kaurava army, which was helpless to repel him.

To Drona, Bhishma said, "We can't take on this rakshasa right now. Our men are worn out. As dusk falls, the power of the rakshasas grows. It is almost time for sunset. Ghatotkacha can be handled tomorrow."

The grandsire gave the order to put his army to bed. In his tent, Duryodhana sat reflecting as his eyes welled with tears. In the battle that day, many of his brothers had perished.

Dhritarashtra exclaimed, "Sanjaya, you only give me bad news every day. Your story has always been one of sorrow—of loss of loved ones and defeat! This is getting too much for me. What tactic can I use to save my people? How will we prevail in this conflict? I do feel very afraid. It appears that fate has more influence than human effort."

Sanjaya responded, "King, isn't this all the result of your own foolishness? What good is sorrow? How can I make you the recipient of good news? You should listen to the truth firmly."

The blind old king, overcome by intense sorrow, exclaimed, "Ah! Vidura's words are coming true."

The Fifth Day

"I am like a man who has been shipwrecked and is trying to swim to safety in a stormy sea. In this sea of grief, I will undoubtedly drown." Thus Dhritarashtra would sob, unable to take his sorrow, whenever Sanjaya recounted the events of the important fight.

He declared, "Bhima will kill all my sons. I do not believe anyone in our army has the strength to save my sons from dying. When our army fled in fright, did Bhishma, Drona, Kripa, and Aswatthama stand by unconcerned? What exactly is their strategy? How will my sons avoid being destroyed?" The old, blind king sobbed as he said this.

"King, keep your composure," Sanjaya said. "The Pandavas rely on a just cause for support. So they triumph. Although your sons are valiant, they have evil thoughts. As a result, their luck is not in their favour. They have greatly harmed the Pandavas, and now they are paying for their transgressions. The Pandavas are engaging in combat in accordance with kshatriyan custom. They are strong because their cause is just.

"Although Vidura, Bhishma, Drona, and others tried to dissuade you from your foolish route, you did not pay attention and continued. You stubbornly refused to heed our advice, which could have saved your people. Instead you chose to follow the wishes of your misguided son, much like a sick person who is dumb enough to refuse to take harsh medicine. You are now in trouble. The same question that you are asking me now was posed to Bhishma by Duryodhana last night, and Bhishma responded in the same way that I will."

The fourth day's evening saw the end of the combat, and Duryodhana walked alone to Bhishma's tent. He bowed reverently and addressed Bhishma, saying, "Grandsire, the world knows that you are a warrior who knows not fear. Drona, Kripa, Aswatthama, Kritavarma, Sudakshin, Bhurisravas, Vikarna, and Bhagadatta are similarly affected. These veterans don't fear death. There is no question that these great fighters possess boundless skill, just like you. No one of the Pandavas can overcome you on their own. What therefore is the secret behind the everyday humiliation suffered by our troops at the hands of Kunti's sons?"

"Prince, pay attention to me," Bhishma said. "On every occasion, I have provided you advice and let you know what is best for you. However, you have consistently disregarded the words of your elders. I'll say it again: for your sake and the sake of the world, it is preferable for you to make peace with Pandu's sons. You all can enjoy this enormous land as your own because you are members of the same royal family. Krishna himself guards the Pandavas.

"Even today, it is not too late for making peace because that is the way to run your kingdom, making the Pandavas, your mighty brothers, allies instead of adversaries. How can you hope for victory? If you insult Dhananjaya and Krishna, who are none other than Nara and Narayana, destruction is in store for you."

Duryodhana left and went to his tent, but he had trouble falling asleep.

The following morning, the conflict was renewed. Both Dhrishtadyumna, the Pandava army, and Bhishma organised the Kaurava forces into a formidable organisation. As per usual, Bhima led the front lines. Sikhandin, Dhrishtadyumna, and Satyaki stood in behind, firmly guarding the main body with the assistance of other generals. The twin brothers and Dharmaputra held the back.

Bhishma released his shafts while bending his bow. The attack of the grandsire caused the Pandava army enormous harm. When Dhananjaya noticed this, he replied by hurling ferocious shafts at Bhishma.

As was his habit, Duryodhana went to Drona and complained vehemently. He received a strong reprimand from Drona: "Obstinate prince, you speak without comprehension. You don't know the power of the Pandavas. We are working hard."

Satyaki, who was defending Bhima and the Pandava army from Drona's tremendous attack, found it too much and turned his focus to Drona. The conflict intensified further. Together, Drona, Bhishma, and Salya attacked Bhima.

Sikhandin assisted Bhima by dousing Bhishma in arrows. Sikhandin was born a girl and according to Bhishma's ethics, he was not allowed to assault a woman. Bhishma turned aside as soon as Sikhandin entered. In the end, it was determined that the identical objection was what killed Bhishma. Drona viciously fought Sikhandin and forced him to retreat when he noticed Bhishma turning away.

The entire fifth day's forenoon was occupied with a fierce struggle. Duryodhana dispatched a sizable force to confront Satyaki in the afternoon. However, Satyaki fully destroyed it before moving on to assault Bhurisravas. Powerful adversary Bhurisravas forced Satyaki's warriors into battle and exerted such intense pressure on Satyaki that he became distressed.

The ten sons of Satyaki wanted to relieve their father of his suffering by mounting an offensive against Bhurisravas. But Bhurisravas was unfazed by their size and resisted the united assault, refusing to be moved. His well-aimed darts snapped their weapons and they were all killed. Their bodies were left sprawled across the field like so many towering trees hit by lightning.

Satyaki moved quickly to kill Bhurisravas as he was consumed with fury and despair. The two warriors' chariots collided and broke apart, leaving them to engage in desperate single combat while facing each other with sword and shield.

Bhima knew Bhurisravas was a master swordsman and he did not want Satyaki to be killed. He arrived and forcibly removed Satyaki into his chariot before fleeing.

That nighttime, Arjuna slew thousands of warriors. The warriors whom Duryodhana sent to attack him perished like moths in a fire. As the sun set, Bhishma gave orders to stop fighting. The princes of the Pandava army gathered Arjuna and greeted him with raucous yells of awe and victory. The worn-out horses and elephants retired to camp with the army on both sides.

The Sixth Day

DHRISHTADYUMNA arranged the Pandava army in makara formation for the combat on the sixth day in accordance with Yudhishthira's directive. The Kaurava army was positioned in heron formation. It was possible to determine which battle array was ideal for a given situation. Each depended on the demands of the offensive and defensive strategies of the moment.

A massive massacre occurred on the sixth day, even in the early hours of the morning. After the charioteer of Drona died, Drona assumed control of the horses by himself. He caused enormous destruction. He moved amid the cotton piles like a flame. The formations of both forces were quickly destroyed, and ferocious battle continued.

In order to locate and kill Duryodhana's brothers, Bhimasena broke through the enemy's lines. For their part, they rushed at him in a coordinated attack from all sides instead of waiting to be found. Duhsasana, Durvishaha, Durmata, Jaya, Jayatsena, Vikarna, Chitrasena, Sudarsana, Charuchitra, Suvarma, Dushkarna, and others all assaulted him at the same time.

Bhimasena got up and engaged them all as though he had no concept of fear. They too wanted to capture him so they could instantly kill him. The conflict was intense, resembling the earlier conflict between the gods and asuras. The son of Pandu abruptly lost patience, sprang from his chariot, grabbed his mace, and ran directly toward the sons of Dhritarashtra in a frenzy to kill them.

Dhrishtadyumna was worried and hurried to avert tragedy when he noticed Bhima's chariot vanishing in the enemy lines. When he got to Bhima's automobile, he saw that just the charioteer was inside and that Bhima was not.

"Where is Bhima dearer to me than life, Visoka?" he cried out to the charioteer. Naturally, Dhrishtadyumna believed Bhima had fallen.

Visoka bowed and addressed the son of Drupada, saying, "The son of Pandu asked me to stay here and raced forward on foot, mace in hand, into the enemy ranks without waiting for my reply."

Drishtadyumna drove his chariot towards the enemy lines in search of Bhimasena. His path was indicated by the remains of dead elephants, fearing that Bhima would be conquered and murdered. When Dhrishtadyumna discovered Bhima, he discovered him surrounded by foes engaged in battle from their chariots. With a mace in his hand and burns all over him, Bhima faced them all. Dhrishtadyumna embraced him, then placed him in his chariot and began to remove the shafts that had been lodged in his body.

Now, instead of waiting for them to fight or challenge, Duryodhana ordered his warriors to attack Bhimasena and Dhrishtadyumna. They therefore coordinated their attacks even though they had no desire to continue the conflict.

A secret weapon that Dhrishtadyumna had gotten from Dronacharya was used to paralyse the opposing army. However, Duryodhana later entered the conflict and unleashed weapons in response to Dhrishtadyumna's weapons of stupor.

At that precise moment, Yudhishthira's reinforcements showed up. Abhimanyu led a group of twelve chariots and their equipment to the area to reinforce Bhima.

When he noticed this, Dhrishtadyumna felt a profound sense of relief. By this time, Bhimasena had also slept and was prepared to resume the battle. He boarded Kekaya's chariot and took his place with the others.

But that day, Drona was dreadful in battle. He slashed Dhrishtadyumna's chariot and killed the charioteer and horses, forcing Drupada's son to seek refuge in Abhimanyu's vehicle. The Kaurava army praised Drona as the Pandava forces started to falter.

On that day, there was indiscriminate mass violence and slaughter. Bhima and Duryodhana had a face-to-face encounter. Following the customary heated discussion, there was a fierce archery duel. Duryodhana was struck and knocked out. He was skillfully freed by Kripa, who then drove him off in his own chariot.

Now that Bhishma had personally arrived, he took the initiative in the battle and dispersed the Pandava forces. Even though the sun was setting, the conflict raged on for another hour. Many people died in the violent fighting.

The day's conflict ended at that point. Yudhishthira rejoiced that Dhrishtadyumna and Bhima had survived their journey back to camp.

The Seventh Day

DURYODHANA went to Bhishma while severely hurt and said, "The battle had been going against us every day. Our lines of defence are disintegrating, and we are losing a lot of warriors."

Duryodhana was comforted by the grandsire with these words: "Why do you let yourself be disheartened? We are all gathered together in this place: Drona, Salya, Kritavarma, Aswatthama, Vikarna, Bhagadatta, Sakuni, the two Avanti brothers, the Trigarta chief, the king of Magadha, and Kripacharya. Why should you feel depressed when these mighty warriors are here and willing to sacrifice their lives for you? Get rid of this negative attitude."

After saying this, he gave the day's instructions. The grandsire told Duryodhana, "See there, these thousands of vehicles, horses and horsemen, magnificent war elephants, and those armed foot soldiers from different kingdoms. They are all ready to fight for you. Even the gods are no match for this magnificent army. Be at ease."

He gave a healing balm for his wounds to the dejected Duryodhana in order to cheer him up. It relieved Duryodhana as he rubbed it over his numerous wounds. Encouraged by the grandsire's words of assurance, he went to the field.

On that day, the army was arranged in a circle. Seven fully equipped chariots were towed by every war elephant. Seven horsemen rode in support of each chariot. Ten shield bearers were attached to each horseman. Indra-like radiant, Duryodhana commanded this vast and well-equipped army from the centre.

The Pandava army was organised into vajravyuha by Yudhishthira. The conflict of this day was fiercely fought simultaneously in numerous sectors. Arjuna's attacks were personally opposed by Bhishma.

At another point, Drona and Virata were conversing. At another sector, Sikhandin and Aswatthama engaged in a fierce battle. Duryodhana and Dhrishtadyumna clashed with one another. Uncle Salya was attacked by Nakula and Sahadeva.

After losing his own chariot, horses, and charioteer in the fight between Drona and Virata, the latter had to board Sanga's chariot. Sanga was also killed on this seventh day, just as his father approached his side.

Aswatthama defeated Drupada's son Sikhandin. When his chariot was destroyed, he leaped out and stood with his sword and shield. Aswatthama struck his sword with his shaft, shattering it. Aswatthama's arrow blocked Sikhandin's attempt to whirl the broken sword and hurl it at him with great force. After suffering severe injuries, Sikhandin boarded Satyaki's chariot and fled.

Duryodhana's horses were killed during the battle between him and Dhrishtadyumna, forcing him to leave his chariot. However, he kept fighting while holding his sword. The prince was then taken away by Sakuni in his chariot.

Kritavarma attacked Bhima hard, but he was defeated. He lost his chariot and horses, admitted defeat, and fled in the direction of Sakuni's car while Bhima's arrows stuck all over him, giving the impression that he was a porcupine speeding through the forest.

Ghatotkacha was attacked by Bhagadatta, who also drove away all of his supporters. However, Ghatotkacha stood alone and bravely fought, but ultimately, he too had to flee to save himself. This greatly delighted the entire Kaurava army.

Salya renewed his attacks on his nephews. Because his horses were destroyed, Nakula was forced to ride alongside his brother in his chariot. From the same car, both continued their fight. Salya swooned after being struck by Sahadeva's arrow. He was saved by the charioteer's deft manoeuvring.

Duryodhana's army lost heart when they saw the Madra king leaving the battlefield. In celebration, Madri's twin sons blew their conches, severely wounding Salya's army.

Yudhishthira led an assault on Srutayu at noon. Dharmaputra's missiles were deflected by the latter's carefully aimed arrows, and his armour was broken. Then, in a fit of rage, Yudhishthira launched a potent arrow that pierced Srutayu's breastplate. Yudhishthira was not his usual self on that day; he was enraged. Srutayu was forced to leave the field on foot after his charioteer, horses, and chariot were all killed. This brought the army of Duryodhana to a complete standstill.

Chekitana lost his chariot and charioteer during the assault on Kripa. He dismounted, attacked Kripa's charioteer and horses with a mace, and killed them. Kripa got down as well and shot his arrows. Chekitana was severely injured.

With swords drawn, they drew close to one another. When Bhima arrived and picked up Chekitana in his chariot, both were hurt and collapsed to the ground. In a similar manner, Sakuni drove Kripa's injured body away.

As Bhima had sworn to kill them, three of Duryodhana's brothers attacked Abhimanyu, who dealt them a severe defeat but spared their lives. Bhishma then launched an assault on Abhimanyu.

When Arjuna noticed this, he commanded Krishna to drive the chariot toward Bhishma.

The other Pandavas joined Arjuna at that point. But until the battle was called off for the day, the grandsire was able to hold his own against all five. The weary and wounded warriors of both sides retired to their tents for rest and to have their wounds treated.

After that, gentle music was played for an hour to lull the warriors to sleep. According to the poet, that hour was spent in heavenly bliss without a mention of war or hatred, and it was a joyful sight to behold.

The Eighth Day

BHISHMA arranged his army in tortoise formation when the eighth day broke. Dhrishtadyumna was informed by Yudhishthira that the enemy was located in Kurma Vyuha. "You must immediately respond with a formation that can topple it."

Dhrishtadyumna started working on his assignment right away. The Pandava army was positioned in a triangular formation. Satyaki led one prong, Bhima the other, and Yudhishthira the third, at the crest of the middle division.

Eight of Dhritarashtra's sons were killed by Bhima at the start of the battle that day. Before this, Duryodhana's heart trembled. He cursed in the assembly hall, but even as he did so, Bhimasena seemed to be carrying out his vengeance today, according to his friends.

During this day's battle, Arjuna experienced a significant loss. Iravan, his beloved son, was killed. This son of Arjuna by Naga wife's had travelled to Kurukshetra and joined the Pandava forces. Alambasa, a rakshasa friend of Duryodhana, was sent to battle the Naga warrior. Iravan was killed following a bloody battle.

Arjuna broke down when he heard this. "Vidura had indeed told us plainly that both sides would be plunged in grief unbearable," he said, turning to face Vasudeva. "Why are we inflicting such dreadful harm on one another? O Madhusudana, I now understand why the foresighted Yudhishthira remarked that he would be happy if Duryodhana gave us five villages. Men would otherwise view me as a coward who could submit tamely to wrong, so I only keep fighting for that reason. My heart is overcome with unfathomable agony as I observe the dead warriors lying on the battlefield. Oh, how sinful and wicked we are to continue in this miserable manner!"

After witnessing Iravan's death, Ghatotkacha shouted a war cry so loud it caused the assembled soldiers to quake. He then joined his division and ruthlessly attacked the Kaurava army. He caused such extensive damage that the Kaurava formation was broken numerous times.

When Duryodhana noticed this, he personally led an assault on Bhima's son. With his elephants, the king of Vanga joined Duryodhana. The eighth day of the battle saw Duryodhana fight with the greatest bravery. He eliminated many warriors who were on Ghatotkacha's side. A javelin thrown by Ghatotkacha would have ended Duryodhana's life had the Vanga chief not stepped in with one of his elephants. When the missile struck the beast, it instantly died, saving Duryodhana.

Bhishma sent a sizable force to support the Kaurava prince under the command of Drona because he was worried about Duryodhana. Veterans made up a large portion of the force that attacked Ghatotkacha. The battle was so chaotic and intense that Yudhishthira feared for Ghatotkacha's safety and sent Bhimasena to intervene on his behalf. The conflict then turned even more fierce than before.

On this day, sixteen of Duryodhana's brothers died.

The Ninth Day

DURYODHANA was meeting privately with the grandsire on the morning of the ninth day, prior to the start of the battle. He let out his resentment and disappointment in words like jagged spears, which deeply hurt the grandsire.

The latter, however, was patient and sadly remarked, "I am pouring out my life for you like ghee on the sacrificial fire. Why do you continue to make me look bad when I've been working so hard for you? You speak as though you lack understanding and don't know what is right and wrong. Your vision is clouded, so you don't see things as they actually are. You intentionally sowed the seeds of hatred, and now you are reaping the rewards.

"The best thing you can do is to keep fighting as hard as you can. It is impossible for me to fight Sikhandin because I can never raise my hand against a woman. This is also the obvious course of duty. I also can't kill the Pandavas with my hands because my mind rebels against it. With the exception of these two, I will take on all of your enemies and fight. Losing heart doesn't accomplish anything. No matter what happens, if you fight like a kshatriya, honour will be yours."

After telling Duryodhana this, Bhishma gave orders for assembling the troops for the day's battle.

Duryodhana felt encouraged. "Brother, put forth all of our strength in today's battle," he said to Duhsasana. "The grandsire is fervently fighting for us, I'm certain of it. He is only prohibited from using his weapons against Sikhandin. But even a wild dog can kill a lion if the latter scorns to defend itself. We should take care to ensure that he is not exposed to Sikhandin's attacks."

The conflict between Abhimanyu and Alambasa was intense. Abhimanyu proved that his bravery was equal to that of his legendary father. Alambasa had to escape on foot in order to survive.

Satyaki and Aswatthama engaged in violent combat, as did Drona and Arjuna. The grandsire was then attacked by all of the Pandavas, and Duryodhana sent Duhsasana to aid the veteran warrior. Bhishma put up a fierce fight and defeated the Pandavas. The Pandava forces had completely lost all motivation and were running around aimlessly like lost cattle in the forest.

"Partha, you and your brothers must have been looking forward to this day, after thirteen years," said Krishna as he stopped the chariot and addressed Arjuna. "Kill the grandsire without thinking twice. Keep in mind what a soldier must do."

Without looking up, Arjuna bowed his head and said, "I would have preferred to remain an exile in the forest than kill the grandsire and the teachers I love, but I shall obey you. Carry on."

Arjuna's heart was not in the fight. Unwillingly and in great distress of mind, he proceeded to the combat. Bhishma, on the other hand, burnt fiercely like the noonday sun.

When the army saw Arjuna's chariot proceed towards Bhishma, it regained courage and order once again prevailed. Bhishma's arrows came thick and fast and covered the advancing chariot so completely that neither horses nor vehicles could be seen. Krishna was unperturbed and drove on with circumspection and skill. Arjuna's shafts hit Bhishma's bow and shattered it many times. But the grandsire went on renewing his weapon.

"You are not fighting, as you should Arjuna!" exclaimed Krishna, and jumped down in a rage from the chariot and, taking up his discus, he advanced towards the grandsire.

Bhishma saw Vasudeva approaching. "Hail, O Lotus-eyed One!" he cried. "Blessed am I to be separated from the body by you! Come, come!"

Arjuna jumped down from the chariot and, rushing forward overtook and held Krishna, casting both his arms round him. "Stop, Krishna," he cried. "Do not break your pledge. You have promised not to use weapons in this battle. This is my duty. I shall not fail. I shall send my arrows and kill the beloved grandsire myself. Pray, mount the car and take the reins."

Arjuna took Krishna back and the battle was resumed. The Pandava forces had been handled roughly, but now the sun was down in the west and the fighting ended for the day.

Bhishma's Death

THE battle had been going on for ten days. Sikhandin was kept in front of Arjuna, who beat Bhishma.

The grandsire's eyes flashed as Sikhandin's daggers pierced his breast. The ancient warrior's rage briefly surged to the heights of burning fire, and his eyes seemed to be devouring Sikhandin. But the grandsire immediately exercised self-control. Sikhandin was born a woman, and he made the conscious decision not to be provoked into fighting her, as doing so felt unworthy of a warrior. But once he realised his demise was nigh, he relaxed.

Sikhandin continued to shoot his arrows, unconcerned by his opponent's internal struggle. Even while Bhishma's grandsire stayed still, Arjuna hardened his heart and Sikhandin fired arrows into the gaps in Bhishma's armour from behind.

As the arrows continued to rain down heavily on him, Bhishma grinned and exclaimed to Duhsasana, "Ah, these are Arjuna's arrows! These are not Sikhandin's, because they burn my flesh like crab babies tear apart their mothers' bodies."

The grandsire observed his beloved pupil's arrows in this way, and as he was telling Duhsasana this, he picked up a javelin and threw it towards Arjuna. Even as it was flying through the air quickly, Arjuna shot it with three arrows, which severed it in three.

Bhishma then made an attempt to descend from his chariot while holding his sword and shield in order to end the battle, but Arjuna's arrows struck his shield first, shattering it. Bhishma plunged headlong to the ground from his chariot with arrows sticking all over his body so thickly that there was not an inch of space between them.

The gods, who watched from above, folded their hands in a respectful greeting as he died. A soft breeze, fragrant with flowers and cool rains, flowed over the battleground.

The noble and upright Bhishma, Ganga's son, who had come to the earth to sanctify it and everything on it, was thus killed. This was the blameless hero who made the significant renunciation to bring his father joy, the unconquered bowman who had brought Rama's axe-wielding ego low, and the selfless worker for the cause of righteousness. He paid back Duryodhana's debt by lying wounded to death while sanctifying the battlefield with his life-blood. The Kauravas' hearts plummeted with the grandsire when he was brought low.

Because of the arrows that protruded from every part of Bhishma's body, his body did not contact the ground. His body was lying as though on a bed of honour, supported by the shafts that had pierced his flesh. It gleamed more brilliantly than ever before. All the warriors rushed to the great hero and gathered around him as the battle between the two armies came to an end. As the gods circled Brahma, the monarchs of earth stood around him with bowed heads.

The grandsire reportedly said, "My head hangs down unsupported." The nearby princes fled and brought cushions. With a smile, the elderly warrior turned to face Arjuna and said, "Dear son Partha, provide me a pillow befitting a warrior."

When Arjuna heard such comments directed at him, his arrows were already piercing the grandsire's flesh. He pulled three arrows from his quiver and arranged them so that the grandsire's head rested on their tips.

When speaking to the gathered chiefs, Bhishma stated, "Princes, Arjuna's arrows were indeed what my head needed to be balanced on. I feel satisfied after using this pillow. I now have to lay like this till the sun faces north. Until then, my soul won't leave this body. Those of you who may still be alive after I pass away are welcome to visit me."

The grandfather then turned back to Arjuna and declared, "I am tortured by thirst. Bring me some water to drink."

Arjuna immediately raised his bow, drew it to his ear, and fired a shaft into the ground close to his right-side grandfather. A torrent of pure, sweet water rushed up the arrow's hole, reaching the dying man's own lips. According to the poet, Ganga herself appeared to quench the burning thirst of her beloved son. Bhishma was content as he drank.

Bhishma addressed the Kaurava prince, saying, "Duryodhana, may you be intelligent! You saw how Arjuna brought me water to assuage my thirst, right? Who else in the world is capable of such an act? Make peace with him as soon as possible. May my departure end the war. Make peace with the Pandavas, son, and listen to what I say."

Duryodhana was not amused by the grandsire's remarks. The patient dislikes treatment even when they are near death. He doesn't like the bitter flavour.

The princes dispersed to their respective camps.

Section VII

Drona Parva

Karna And The Grandsire

KARNA came to the scene after learning that Bhishma was there, dying from his wounds. He bowed to him and said, "Radha's son, the oldest of the race, who without his fault caused you severe displeasure, humbly prostrates before you."

After a respectful greeting, Karna stood up. His grandfather, who had been deeply moved, gently laid his hand on Karna's head and gave him a blessing.

He said lovingly, "You are not Radha's son, young man. You are the first child born to Kuntidevi. Narada, who is aware of all the world's secrets, himself told this to me. Son of Surya, I genuinely harboured no ill feelings toward you. But even though the Pandavas didn't deserve your animosity, I was saddened to see it grow. I am aware of you and love your bravery and generosity. I am also aware that you are of the same calibre of prowess as Phalguna and Krishna. You deserve to be friends with the Pandavas. You, their brother, are on the right track if you follow that. May the chapter of your hostility close along with my involvement in this battle. This is what I want, Karna."

Karna respectfully acknowledged what was said before responding, "Grandsire, I know I am Kunti's son and not a charioteer-born. To be true to my own ancestry and Duryodhana, though, I must have consumed his salt. I'm unable to join the Pandavas at this time. If need be, you must allow me to pay back Duryodhana for his love and trust with my life. I made serious mistakes in both words and deeds. You must accept my apology and grant me your blessing."

After giving Karna some thought and reflecting on all the moral principles, the great acharya responded, "Do then as you wish, for it is the proper way."

The fight continued even while Bhishma lay dying and was gravely wounded. The Kauravas continued fighting despite the grandsire's advice.

When Bhishma ceased to be their leader, the Kaurava forces felt abandoned, like sheep without a shepherd. The men actually yelled while Bhishma was hurt, "Karna, you are the only one remaining to guide and safeguard us."

The Kaurava warriors believed that victory was inevitable if only Karna would agree to accept the command. As was previously said, Karna had reportedly remarked, "So long as you are fighting, I shall keep away. I will be pleased and go to the wilderness if you kill the Pandavas and give Duryodhana victory. However, if you lose and retreat to the home of the courageous, I shall ride my chariot and face off against everyone you believe to be stronger than me, defeating them to deliver victory to Duryodhana."

Karna had made the aforementioned oath and, with Duryodhana's approval, had abstained from the combat for the first ten days. He then went on foot to Bhishma, who was ready to die on his bed of arrows, and saluted him before addressing him as follows:

"You lie on the battlefield, veteran grandsire, conqueror of Parasurama, killed by Sikhandin. It is obvious that no one can achieve in this world what they deserve on the basis of merit if you, who had attained the pinnacle of moral life and was the very embodiment of purity, must lie wounded in this way. The Kaurava princes relied solely on you to help them get beyond the deluge of their problems. The Kauravas will suffer greatly as a result of the heavy blows that the Pandavas will now deliver to them. Arjuna and Krishna will decimate the Kauravas' army much like how the wind and tyres burn away the forest. Bless me, who have taken up the command of the forces in your kind eyes."

Karna received the blessing of Bhishma. "You are trustworthy and steadfast in your allegiance, like good soil to seedlings and rain clouds to living things. Save Duryodhana by serving him. For him, you defeated the Kambojas. You lower the Himalayan fastnesses' Kiratas for him. On his behalf, you engaged in battle with and overcame the Girivrajas. You've done much more for him. Now command the Kaurava army and keep it safe. May you successfully command Duryodhana's soldiers! May you be blessed with success! Go and fight your opponents."

After receiving the grandsire's blessing, Karna ascended his chariot and headed to the battle area. Duryodhana was ecstatic as soon as the brave Karna and his war chariot arrived on the scene. In some ways, his grief over losing Bhishma was lessened.

Drona In Command

IN order to decide who should be given ultimate command of the armies, Duryodhana and Karna conferred.

Karna answered, "Each of these royal warriors fighting on your side is great enough to be made supreme leader of our armies. The prowess, power, energy, skill, courage, valour, ancestry, and intelligence of all these rulers are equal. They cannot all be given joint command. And if any of them were chosen, the other candidates would feel offended and might not give their all. As a result, we risk suffering. My recommendation is that Dronacharya, who taught all of these princes and warriors, be appointed supreme commander. He possesses the qualities needed to command our army better than any other kshatriya."

This was chosen because Duryodhana concurred that it was the appropriate course of action.

In front of the assembled warriors and princes, Duryodhana proceeded to Dronacharya and bowed before hin. "Revered Master, you are unrivalled among all those assembled here in caste, ancestry, knowledge of sciences, age, intelligence, courage, and skill. I implore you to assume the absolute command. This army will triumph under your leadership."

This proposition was met with raucous applause and battle shouts from the assembled kings, which made Duryodhana happy. Drona was properly fitted to great applause. The Kauravas felt as though they had already defeated the adversary with the courtiers' adoration and the sound of trumpets that followed the ritual. Their enthusiasm and faith in Drona's leadership were at an all-time high.

The troops was arranged in a circle by Drona. Karna, who had been absent until that point, could now be seen pacing the battlefield in his massive chariot. The Kaurava troops felt renewed courage and delight as a result of this. In the army, it was said that the great Bhishma had not thrown his whole heart into the battle because he did not want to kill the sons of Pandu. They said that the Pandavas would be killed now that Karna was on the battlefield.

Dronacharya oversaw the fight for five days. Despite his elderly age, he stayed active throughout the battlefield and exuded the ferocity of a youthful warrior. The Pandava armies dispersed whenever he led an assault, much like clouds before a storm. Satyaki, Bhima, Arjuna, Dhrishtadyumna, Abhimanyu, Drupada, and Kasiraja were among the greatest fighters on the Pandava side, and he personally fought them and vanquished them on numerous times. The five days he was in charge, he tormented and severely punished the Pandava army.

Deliver Yudhishthira Alive

DURYODHANA, Karna, and Duhsasana met in council and came up with a plan as soon as Drona took control of the Kaurava army. Duryodhana then proceeded to Dronacharya to have the plan carried out.

"Acharya, we want you to find Yudhishthira alive and deliver him to us. Nothing more, not even a complete victory, is what we seek. We will all be really happy with the way you have handled the conflict if you succeed in doing this for us."

The acharya loved the sons of Kunti, especially the upright Yudhishthira, despite the fact that he loyally sided with the Kauravas in their conflict with the Pandavas. Drona was extremely happy to hear Duryodhana refer to him in this way because he detested the entire thought of killing the Pandava brothers.

The acharya said, "Duryodhana, may you be blessed! Would you also like to forgo killing Yudhishthira? How it makes me happy! Yudhishthira is undoubtedly a person without enemies. Your wise choice has vindicated the appellation Ajatasatru that Kunti's eldest son has been given by the populace. His unrivalled glory has grown ten times more when even you decide that he shouldn't be slain but rather be caught alive.

"I understand what you're trying to do, dear Duryodhana," Drona continued. "You want to win the struggle against the Pandavas, give them a piece of the kingdom, and then live in harmony and peace with them. Your determination to capture Yudhishthira alive makes this apparent to me."

But Duryodhana had very other reasons for wanting to catch Yudhishthira alive, and as soon as Drona agreed to his request and promised to use all of his resources to do so, Duryodhana started to disclose his true motivations.

Nothing would be achieved if Yudhishthira were killed, and the Pandavas' rage would be amplified. Duryodhana anticipated a fiercer battle and understood that it would result in his army's complete annihilation. Even if the battle raged unabatedly until both armies were wiped out. Krishna would still be alive. He would give either Draupadi or Kunti exclusive control of the kingdom. Why then did Yudhishthira need to be killed?

However, Duryodhana reasoned that if Yudhishthira were to be caught alive, the Kauravas would win the war more quickly. He could undoubtedly capitalise on Yudhishthira's goodwill and his adherence to the orthodox kshatriya code of conduct. He could be dragged back into the dice game and banished back to the woods at any moment. Duryodhana was convinced after ten days of battle that more conflict would only lead to the extinction of the race rather than the satisfaction of his goals.

The acharya was deeply unhappy and vowed to curse Duryodhana when he revealed his intentions to Drona. But, whatever the cause, he was happy that Yudhishthira wouldn't be put to death.

Their spies informed the Pandava army that Drona had informed Duryodhana in a solemn assurance that he would capture Yudhishthira. The Pandavas were aware that his committed word was a very serious matter due to his unmatched excellence in the art of battle and his bravery. They assembled the necessary forces to ensure that Yudhishthira never went alone.

The acharya amply displayed his remarkable skill and vigour throughout the first day's battle under Drona's command. The Pandava soldiers were destroyed as he walked around, burning them up like dry logs in a fire. The Pandava army experienced Drona's swift motions as if he were everywhere at once, dousing them in arrows that fell like rain and transforming the battlefield into a stage for the dance of the God of Death.

Where Dhrishtadyumna was, he split the Pandava army in half. There were a lot of solo battles between famous warriors. Sahadeva and Sakuni, who was expert in illusion-based combat, engaged in a furious battle. When their chariots fell apart, they descended to the ground and, like two bills set in motion, struck one another with maces before engaging in single combat.

Salya always grinned provocatively while fighting and tormenting his nephew Nakula. However, Salya ultimately had his car destroyed and his flag pulled down, and he withdrew, admitting defeat.

There was a duel between Kripacharya and Dhrishtaketu, and the latter came out on top. Virata and Karna, as well as Satyaki and Kritavarma, engaged in violent combat. Abhimanyu's bravery was also displayed when he defeated Paurava, Kritavarma, Jayadratha, and Salya by himself.

Then Salya and Bhimasena engaged in a fierce battle, which ended with Salya losing and being forced to retire. When the Pandava army noticed that the Kaurava forces were starting to lose their spirit, it attacked them with renewed vigour and tore apart their ranks.

When Drona noticed this, he made the decision to lead a direct assault on Yudhishthira in an effort to boost morale. Four noble Sindhu horses pulled his golden chariot as it moved toward Yudhishthira. Yudhishthira responded with eagle feather-tipped barbed arrows.

Drona did not care, though, and moved forward quickly. Drona was rapidly approaching as Yudhishthira's bow was being destroyed. Dhrishtadyumna unsuccessfully attempted to stop Drona. The entire army screamed, "Yudhishthira has been seized!" Drona came very close to succeeding.

The earth rumbled beneath Arjuna's chariot as it raced fast through the bloody field, over the bones and dead laying in heaps. Arjuna then abruptly emerged on the battlefield. Drona refrained since Arjuna had arrived on the scene.

Arrows were launched in a never-ending barrage from Gandiva. Nobody could observe the arrows being removed from the quiver or positioning them. It appeared as though an endless flow of arrows was released without pause from the great how. The soaring missiles cast a shadow across the battlefield.

Drona backed off. No one took Yudhishthira. The Kaurava warriors returned to their camp in a chastened tone after the combat was called off for the day. The Pandava army marched proudly to camp as Arjuna and Kesava followed behind them and engaged in conversation. The eleventh day of the conflict had thus concluded.

The Twelfth Day

THE effort to kidnap Yudhishthira alive was unsuccessful. Drona was conversing with Duryodhana about this.

"It is obvious that as long as Dhananjaya is close, our efforts to capture Yudhishthira will fail. I could break through the Pandava formations and seize Yudhishthira if we could get Arjuna to move to another area of the battlefield. If he does not flee the combat, renouncing honour, I swear to capture him and hand him to you. We will definitely win if he does that, will we not?"

They decided to take the samsaptaka pledge, confront Arjuna, and engage him in combat in an effort to sway him from Yudhishthira's side. As a result, they gathered in a sizable group, sat before the fire, dressed in matted grass. They went through funeral rites and gifts as if they were already dead, and then signed an oath.

"We won't turn around until we have killed Dhananjaya. May we be punished as for a grave sin if we run away from fight in terror!"

After preparing themselves in this manner in front of the holy fire, they marched in the direction of Death, which was to the south, and said, "O Arjuna!" in order to challenge him to a duel. It was a fantastic suicide squad set up to accomplish what Drona had emphasised as being necessary.

"King, the samsaptakas are summoning me to battle," Arjuna said as he turned to face Yudhishthira. "I promise to accept any challenge subsequently rejected. I'm being summoned to combat by Susarma and his soldiers. I'll annihilate them all and then go back. Please let me leave."

Yudhishthira responded, "Brother beloved, you know Drona's intents. Don't forget that, and act as you see fit. He has vowed to carry me out alive for Duryodhana. He is an unmatched warrior who is fearless, powerful, and proficient in all aspects of archery. Nothing eludes his vigilant eyes, and he is unaware of exhaustion."

Arjuna answered, "King, here comes Satyajit, supporting you. Nothing can happen to you as long as he is by you and alive." After stating this, Arjuna ordered Panchala prince Satyajit to keep watch by Yudhishthira's side before charging off to confront the Samsaptakas like a ravenous lion.

The Trigartas can be seen standing there, happy from the effects of their pledge, even though they are aware that they will die. In fact, they are giddy with excitement as Swarga approaches. Arjuna then made his way toward the sizable samsaptaka force after speaking to his great charioteer.

The big fight was on its twelfth day at the time. It was a bloody struggle. The Trigartas eventually succumbed to Arjuna's attack and fell before him in large numbers, but Susarma reminded them of their commitment.

"Heroes, we have sworn our allegiance in front of the fire and in the presence of the entire warrior army. It is disgraceful to falter after making horrible promises. Let's avoid being laughed at in public." The Samsaptakas applauded their leader and confronted Arjuna with the supreme bravery of willing deaths.

"Hrishikesa, they intend to battle till the very end. Continue on," urged Arjuna.

In the epic battle between the gods and the asuras, Arjuna's chariot, which was driven by Madhusudana, moved like Indra's automobile. Similar to the bloom of Palasa blossoms in a springtime woodland, the gush of blood in their serried ranks. Fighting was intense. The flagpole and car belonging to Arjuna were once completely obscured by the rain of arrows.

"Are you still alive, Dhananjaya?" cried out Krishna.

"Yes," Arjuna said, pulling the Gandiva's cord to release shafts that cut off the arrow downpour.

Drona gave the command for a brutal assault on the Pandava soldiers at the spot where Yudhishthira stood. Arjuna went on to oppose the samsaptakas. The Panchala prince Dhrishtadyumna was approached by Yudhishthira after he noticed this movement. "The brahmana is on his way to take me away. Vigilantly watch over the forces."

Instead of waiting for Drona to go ahead, Drupada's son marched in his car forward to meet Drona.

Dronacharya steered his chariot in the other direction where Drupada was leading his warriors in order to avoid Dhrishtadyumna. He was doomed to die at his hands but his time had not yet come. Drona dealt harsh punishment to Drupada's army, and the battlefield was covered with rivers of blood. Then Drona once more focused on Yudhishthira.

Drona's onslaught was met with arrow showers from the Pandavas as they stood their ground. When Satyajit charged Drona's vehicle, there was a furious battle in which Drona's form took on the ominous appearance of the Destroyer. He repeatedly killed numerous warriors. Both Satyajit and Vrika, a prince of Panchala, perished.

When Satanika, son of Virata, noticed this, he marched against Drona. The golden kundalas in Satanika's earlobes shone as her dismembered head rolled on the ground. Another chief, Ketama, pursued the attack but also perished. Then Vasudhana dashed forward to halt Drona's onslaught, but he too died.

Satyaki and Yudhamanyu. When Sikhandin and Uttamaujas attempted to force Drona back, they were repelled, forcing all of these legendary warriors to turn around. Yudhishthira was now almost able to approach Drona.

A second son of Drupada, Panchalya, raced frantically up to the acharya and fought fiercely. But like the falling star, he too was terribly wounded and lost his footing.

Then, in a state of ecstasy, Duryodhana exclaimed to Karna:

"Do you see the bravery of our powerful leader, Radheya? The Pandavas will no longer be drawn to combat. Watch how their army collapses under Drona's attacks."

Karna gave a head shake. "Do not be so sure of yourself," he said. "The Pandavas are not to be taken down so easy. Their mistreatment is too severe to be forgotten. You made an attempt to poison and murder them. You attempted to set them on fire. At the dice game, you grieved and degraded them, and you drove them outside to spend many years in the forest. They won't give up, they say.

"As you can see, their army has come together, and all of their soldiers are launching a coordinated assault on Drona. See how many warriors have gathered to defend Yudhishthira, including Bhima, Satyaki, Yudhamanyu, Kshatradharma, Nakula, Uttamaujas, Drupada, Virata, Sikhandin, Dhrishtaketu, and others, and how they are putting a lot of pressure on Drona. Given that we have placed such a large weight on the acharya, we should not be passively watching. Despite how great he is, even he has a maximum load he can handle. Let's move on. Leaving Drona unaided won't do any longer."

Brave Bhagadatta

DRONA thus made numerous unsuccessful attempts to capture Yudhishthira. Against Bhima, Duryodhana commanded a sizable elephant division. With carefully placed arrows, Bhima protected himself from his chariot. He sent forth shafts with crescent heads, tore down Duryodhana's banner, and destroyed his bow while it was still in his hand.

The Mlechchha king Anga witnessed the king being harassed. Mounted on a massive elephant, marched against Bhimasena. However, Bhima dispatched shafts that killed the Mlechchha monarch and brought down the elephant. That part of the Kaurava soldiers were scattered in panic and disarray. Thousands of foot soldiers were crushed under the elephants and horses' feet as they stampeded in fear, sending them flying in a frenzied frenzy.

The gallant Bhagadatta, king of Pragjyotisha, became furious upon seeing this extreme chaos and the dispersion of the Kaurava army in all directions. He mounted Supratika, his legendary elephant, and charged against Bhimasena.

The horses and chariot of Bhimasena were instantly transformed into an indistinguishable mess when the enormous beast, which had large ears and a whirling trunk, charged forward. However, Bhima managed to flee by leaping from the vehicle just in time.

He was an expert in elephants. When the large, ferocious elephant became enraged and began to spin around like a potter's wheel, Bhimasena, who was stuck to its legs and pursuing it from below, unleashed a barrage of blows on its critical places. It stooped down, grabbed Bhima by the trunk, and was about to crush him between its knees when Vrikodara managed to break free. He then retreated below, wedged himself in between the elephant's limbs, and caused the animal excruciating anguish.

As a result, Bhima was buying himself some extra time in the hopes that some elephant on the Pandava side would be persuaded to attack Bhagadatta's elephant so that he could escape. However, the troops believed Bhima had been killed when he vanished from view while he was concealed between the beast's legs.

"Bhima is dead!" they exclaimed. The shout was heard all over Kurukshetra. "Bhimasenal has been crushed by Bhagadatta's elephant."

When Yudhishthira heard the cries, he assumed Bhima had been killed and ordered the troops to kill Bhagadatta. Bhagadatta was attacked by the king of Dasarna. Supratika engaged in a furious struggle with Dasarna's elephant, which was also a fearsome animal. However, Dasarna's beast was punctured by Supratika's tusk in the side, and it died as it fell.

Bhima ran out safely from behind Supratika at that precise moment. The Pandava army applauded when they spotted him alive.

Bhagadatta was currently under attack from all sides, yet he remained courageous. He rode his elephant in Satyaki's chariot while resplendent, shining like a forest fire on a hill while he ignored the foes in his immediate vicinity. With its powerful trunk, the elephant grabbed the chariot, lifted it high, and flipped it over.

Satyaki managed to save himself by leaping off the chariot. After righting the chariot and saving both the horses and the vehicle, his charioteer drove the chariot to where Satyaki was standing.

The Pandava army was severely damaged by Bhagadatta's elephant, which terrorised everyone it encountered while tossing fighters around and murdering them in vast numbers. When Indra battled the asuras on Airavata, Bhagadatta stood on that animal's back. The gigantic beast tore into the Pandava army, trampling on innumerable horses, chariots, and men with its trunk extended and ears rigidly wide out in wrath.

Bhimasena renewed his assault on Bhagadatta after arming himself with a chariot once more. The horses of Bhima's chariot bolted in a mad flight and the charioteer was unable to stop them. The elephant extended out its trunk and blew out a tremendous shower of mucus.

A huge cloud of dust rose from the field where this fierce elephant conflict took place. Arjuna heard the commotion caused by Bhagadatta's elephant as well as saw it from where he was fighting the Samsaptakas. "Madhusudana," he said. "This is the cry of Supratika, Bhagadatta's elephant. I fear that things have gone wrong. This Pragjyotisha monarch is horrible with his elephant and is unmatched in that style of combat. He will undoubtedly fail and stump our men. We must act immediately to avert disaster. We have dealt these samsaptakas enough punishment. Go where Drona is battling Yudhishthira by driving there."

And Krishna directed the chariot in the direction of the main front of the conflict.

"Stop, stop," yelled Susarma and his siblings as they approached the chariot from behind. They launched shafts at Arjuna's chariot at the same time.

Arjuna was unsure of himself. "Susarma is here challenging me to a fight, and I hate to turn down this kind of offer, but there, to the north of us, our formation is fractured, and our troops are in need of rapid rescue."

Arjuna was thinking along these lines when two javelins came flying at him and one towards Janardana. Arjuna fired three precisely placed shafts at Susanna while furious, forcing her to turn around.

They wasted no more time and hurried to the scene of Bhagadatta's mayhem. The Pandava forces rallied as soon as they spotted Arjuna's automobile, and he soon arrived at the lines where Bhagadatta was.

Bhagadatta assaulted Arjuna on Supratika in the form of the Destroyer. The beast charged, but Vasudeva's skill kept the shock at bay each time.

Arjuna and Krishna received arrows from Bhagadatta. However, Arjuna's arrows damaged the elephant and broke through its armour. Bhagadatta threw a javelin at Krishna when he saw that his elephant was no longer able to withstand the assault. With a shaft from his bow, Arjuna engaged it and split it in half. The next javelin that Bhagadatta launched landed on Dhananjaya's helmet.

Arjuna adjusted his helmet and bowed while yelling, "Bhagadatta, take your final look at the world and get ready to die!"

Bhagadatta was a very old veteran. He had the courageous aspect of a lion thanks to his grey hair and the wrinkles on his noble old face. He was actually so ancient that his skin hung loosely down over his eyes. To prevent it from obstructing his vision, he had bound the folds of his skin over his forehead with a silk kerchief. One of the most famous and valiant men of his era, Bhagadatta was not so much known for his bravery as for his moral rectitude. He was so wonderful that men gave him the moniker "Friend of Indra."

This mighty man was told by Arjuna to "look around for the last time" before he launched arrows at him that destroyed his bow, splintered his quiver, and punctured the joints of his armour.

Bhugadatta threw his elephant goad at Arjuna when he was left without any weapons. It was fired with the Vaishnava mantra and dispatched with murderous intent. Arjuna would have been murdered, but Krishna stood in the way and offered himself as a target. It became a sparkling necklace that landed on his breast. Being charged with Vishnu's mantra, it was unable to harm him and instead served as the Lord's jewelled ornament.

"How come you have made yourself a target for the enemy's missile, Janardana? You promised to drive the chariot and let me handle all the combat. How are you able to do this?" argued Arjuna.

"My dear Arjuna, you do not comprehend. You would have died if this shaft had struck you, but it actually belongs to me and has returned to its rightful owner." Krishna chuckled as he spoke.

Then, like a serpent entering an anthill, Partha shot an arrow that struck Bhagadatta's elephant in the head. Bhagadatta attempted to prod his massive animal forward, but it remained steadfast and immobile. The elephant appeared to be a large hill for a brief period. Then it suddenly fell down, slamming its tusks into the ground and dying with an agonised shriek.

The loss of the noble animal and his inability to kill Bhagadatta without also killing the beast caused considerable sadness in Arjuna. The ageing king's forehead folds were wrapped up with a silken handkerchief that was torn by Arjuna's shafts, instantly rendering him blind. Soon after, Bhagadatta was struck in the breast by a pointed, crescent-shaped shaft. As he fell, his golden necklace shone like flowers on the uprooted tree.

The Kaurava army became completely disorganised.

Vrisha and Achala, the brothers of Sakuni, made every effort to defeat Arjuna by attacking him from the front and the back. However, their chariots were quickly destroyed, and they themselves were struck down and left lying on the ground like two lion cubs. They both had similar features and appeared just as noble.

When Sakuni saw his valiant and exceptional brothers laying dead on the field, he became furious. He employed all of the illusionary weapons at his disposal to viciously attack Arjuna. However, Arjuna's blows destroyed all the charms and made them ineffective, forcing Sakuni to flee the scene as quickly as his horses could carry him.

The combat on the twelfth day came to an end as the sun set after the Pandava forces had attacked Drona's army and caused immense destruction. The fighting was ordered to stop by Drona, and the heavily defeated Kaurava warriors withdrew sullenly to their camp. On the other side, the Pandava army was in good spirits, and its soldiers gathered around campfires to converse and sing praises to Arjuna and the other heroes who had guided them to victory.

Abhimanyu

EARLY the following morning, in the presence of several generals, Duryodhana went to Dronacharya in a bitter and angry state and addressed him as follows: "Esteemed brahmana, Yudhishthira was entirely within your reach yesterday. If you had genuinely wanted to seize him, no one could have stopped you. I do not understand why it's so difficult for you to keep your word to me. Indeed, great persons are incomprehensible."

This offensive implication angered Dronacharya. "I am putting up all of my might and expertise on your behalf, Duryodhana. You have thoughts that are unfit for a king. We are unable to capture Yudhishthira as long as Arjuna is present and standing by him. I have already told you that. I'm thinking of methods to accomplish this goal. We can only hope to carry out this plan as you wish if we can find a means to get Arjuna off the battlefield." Drona bravely overcame his justified rage in this way and sought to ease Duryodhana's suffering.

The samsaptakas once more challenged Arjuna to a duel on the thirteenth day, and he responded by going to attack them where they were positioned to the south of the main battlefront. The conflict between Arjuna and the Samsaptakas was the fiercest that anyone had ever seen or heard of up until that point.

Drona reorganised his army into a lotus formation and launched a strong attack on Yudhishthira after Dhananjaya left the main front to meet the samsaptakas. Many opposed him, but the brutality of Drona's attack seemed to paralyse their opposition.

Even though he was still a young man, Arjuna and Subhadra's son Abhimanyu had already established himself as a formidable warrior, standing on par with both of his parents and his uncle in combat. Yudhishthira informed Abhimanyu that Dronacharya was severely harassing their troops. "Arjuna is not with us, and if we should lose without him, he would be devastated. None of us have been able to defeat Drona's defences. Only you and nobody else can doubt your ability. Please take on this responsibility."

"I can do it," Abhimanyu affirmed. "My father taught me how to break through this configuration, so I know I can do it. However, I haven't yet received any instruction in extrication techniques. If I end up having to exit after pushing my way in due to tragic circumstances, I won't know what to do."

"Victorious youngster, pierce through this impenetrable formation and create a way for us. We'll all break in after you. There will be no doubt that you must emerge because we will be by your side to face any danger."

Bhimasena endorsed Yudhishthira's proposal. "I shall be directly behind you and enter when you succeed in breaking the enemy's formation. So also will Dhrishtadyumna, Satvaki, the Panchalas, the Kekayas and the army of Matsyadesa. Only disrupt the formation as you alone can do; we shall do the rest and defeat the Kaurava army."

Abhimanyu thought of his father and Krishna and, feeling encouraged by what had been stated by Bhimasena and Yudhishthira, and propelled by his own valiant nature, attempted the adventure.

"I shall gratify my wonderful father and uncle." he replied with passion. "Let my valour be placed on this."

"May your prowess blossom," murmured Yudhishthira and praised the youth.

"Sumitra, see Drona's flag fluttering there! Drive straight and swiftly to that point," urged Abhimanyu to his charioteer.

"Faster, faster!" yelled Abhimanyu as they drove along.

"May the gods protect you!" exclaimed the charioteer. "Think thoroughly before you pierce Drona's array and enter. The acharya is unequalled in ability and experience, but you, though his equal in ferocity, have not his long years to back it."

Abhimanyu grinned and replied: "Friend, I am Krishna's nephew and son of Arjuna, am I not? Which other has that advantage? Fear dare not approach me! These enemies here have not a sixteenth part of my strength. Drive fast towards Drona's division."

The charioteer obeyed.

As the golden chariot to which were yoked beautiful young horses approached, the soldiers in the Kaurava army shouted: "Abhimanyu is coming! He has come!" The Pandavas followed Abhimanyu close behind him.

The Kaurava warriors were perturbed as they saw Abhimanyu's chariot approach them with great speed. "Here is one greater in valour than Arjuna," they thought and began to lose heart.

Like a young lion on a herd of elephants, Abhimanyu rushed on. There was a ripple in the Kaurava ranks which bent under his headlong onslaught. The bend soon became a break and under Drona's very eyes, the formation was breached and Abhimanyu entered. But before the other Pandava warriors could force their way in according to plan, the breach closed by command of Jayadratha, king of the Sindhus—and Abhimanyu was alone!

Kaurava warriors opposed him, but they fell like moths in the fire, one after another. Abhimanyu's shafts searched the weak points in the armour of his enemies. The bodies of soldiers soon lay strewn on the field like Kusa grass on the sacrificial platform. Bows, arrows, swords, along with severed heads and limbs of slain warriors, covered the field.

Seeing the destruction wrought by Abhimanyu, Duryodhana was wrathful and rushed in person to oppose the youthful warrior. Drona, having learnt that the king himself was engaged in battle with Abhimanyu, became anxious and sent veterans to protect Duryodhana. With great difficulty, they managed to rescue the king from the boy-hero. Greatly disappointed at the escape of Duryodhana, he vented his anger on the warriors that had come to rescue him and put them to headlong flight.

Then, throwing away all sense of shame and chivalry, a large number of veteran warriors made a combined and simultaneous attack on the hero. He found himself alone, surrounded by enemies on all sides. But, even as on all sides a rock receives the rising tide of the sea, Arjuna's son withstood this united onslaught.

Drona, Aswatthama, and many other great warriors in their chariots, equipped with all arms, surged in attack on the young hero, only to be dashed back, baffled and broken. Karna's armour was pierced. Salya was badly wounded and sat, unable to move, in his chariot. Salya's brother came up in great wrath to avenge his brother's disgrace but he fell and his chariot was broken to pieces.

Thus did Abhimanyu, alone and unsupported, oppose a host of veteran warriors and show the skill in the use of arms which he had learnt from his illustrious father and from Vasudeva, his uncle. Seeing this, the poet says, Dronacharya's eyes were filled with tears of affectionate admiration.

"Was there ever a fighter to equal this boy Abhimanyu?" exclaimed Drona to Kripa, in the hearing of Duryodhana who could not contain his anger.

"The acharya's partiality for Arjuna prevents him from killing Abhimanyu," Duryodhana said, "And he sings his praises instead of fighting him. Indeed, if the acharya were minded to dispose of Abhimanyu, would it take him long to do it!"

Often did Duryodhana suspect and complain in this manner against Bhishma and Drona. Having undertaken a war of adharma, he was often led to speak in this manner and hurt the feelings of the acharyas who stood loyally by him, even when they saw the wickedness of his ways.

Duhsasana roared in anger and exclaimed, "This obstinate lad will perish now!" He led his chariot forward to attack Abhimanyu.

The chariots of Abhimauyu and Duhsasana made wonderful movements against each other and the battle raged long. Duhsasana was struck senseless in his car, and his charioteer just managed to drive away from the field saving Duhsasana's life.

Karna attacked Abhimanyu with his shafts and harassed him greatly. But one of Abhimanyu's arrows felled Karna's bow and the young warrior followed up this advantage so vigorously that he put Karna and his supporters to flight. The Kaurava forces, when they saw this were completely demoralised.

The army was in confusion and men fled in all directions, not caring for Drona's shouts of remonstrance, and Abhimanyu destroyed those that stood, as fire destroys a dry jungle in summer.

The Death Of Abhimanyu

THE Pandavas had, as intended, closely followed Abhimanyu as he entered the Kaurava formation. However, Jayadratha, the brave king of the Sindhus and the son-in-law of Dhritarashtra, swooped down upon the Pandavas with all of his forces. He enabled the gap in the formation to be effectively and firmly filled up. It was impossible for the Pandavas to barge in.

When Jayadratha's bow was cut off by a javelin thrown by Yudhishthira, the Saindhava quickly picked up another bow and fired unerring shafts at Dharmaputra. Bhimasena's arrows accomplished their deadly mission by toppling Jayadratha's car's canopy and flagstaff. When his equipment broke, the Saindhava was attentive and rearmed himself. He destroyed Bhima's chariot horses, forcing them to board Satyaki's vehicle.

In this way, Jayadratha withstood the Pandavas' attempts to follow in Abhimanyu's footsteps with valour and tenacity. As a result, the Kaurava forces encircled and isolated the young hero.

But Subhadra's son showed no sign of giving up. He assaulted every warrior nearby and slew a large number of them. The troops that were going to attack him vanished before his arrows, much like rivers disappearing into the ocean. The assaults of Abhimanyu caused the Kaurava army to tremble.

Then Lakshmana, a brave young warrior who was the son of Duryodhana, charged towards Abhimanyu. As soon as they noticed this, the troops who had been fleeing turned around and helped Lakshmana, shooting arrows at Abhimanyu like rain on a hill. Still, Arjuna's son was unfazed and sent Lakshmana through with a fast, brilliant shaft that looked like a freshly shed serpent. The Kaurava troops were overcome with sorrow when they saw the attractive young man, who had a lovely nose, brows, and hair, lying dead on the field.

The six mighty warriors, Drona, Kripa, Karna, Aswathama, Brihatbala, and Kritavarma, roared, "To hell with the wicked Abhimanyu!" and drew near to Abhimanyu.

Drona told Karna, "It is difficult to pierce this youth's armour. Take aim at his horses' reins and cut them off. That will disable him. Then sneak up behind him to attack."

Surya's son acted accordingly. A shaft fired from behind damaged Abhimanyu's bow. They slaughtered his charioteer and horses. The young warrior was now hampered and faced his adversaries while standing on the battlefield with a sword and shield.

The other warriors were in awe of him as he stood fearless, like Kshatriyadharma incarnate. He battled the several warriors who had surrounded him while whirling his blade with an ability that bewildered them. They had the impression that his feet were off the ground and that he was flying through the air on wings.

The shaft that Drona sent smashed Abhimanyu's sword. His shield was destroyed by Karna's pointed arrows.

Then Abhimanyu knelt down, picked up one of his chariot wheels, and spun it around like a discus before standing up and facing all of his foes. The poet claims that the young hero's innate attractiveness was amplified by the chariot wheel's dust that covered him. With the discus, he battled ferociously, like a second Vishnu.

He was quickly overcome by the united assault of the warriors who had surrounded him. The chariot wheel was completely destroyed. When Duhsasana's son appeared, they engaged in fatal struggle. Together, they collapsed, but Duhsasana's son got up and killed Abhimanyu by striking him with his mace as he struggled to stand.

Sanjaya informed Dhritarashtra that "Subhadra's son who, like an elephant in a lily pond, single-handedly wreaked havoc on the Kaurava army, was thus overrun by numbers and slain horribly. And after killing him, your people celebrated by dancing around his body like savage hunters with their kill. All the good soldiers in the army wept and were saddened. Even the raptors that were circling above and creating noise appeared to be yelling, 'Not like this!'"

Yuyutsu, the son of Dhritarashtra, disapproved of everything that was happening when conchs were being blown and victory screams could be heard across the Kaurava army. He screamed indignantly, "This is ignoble. Soldiers, you no longer remember your code. You should be humiliated, to be sure, but you instead shout cocky triumphant cries. You take pleasure in foolish joy after performing a most evil deed while being unaware of the peril that is approaching."

Yuyutsu turned away from the battle and threw his weapon in disgust. This young son of Dhritarashtra was afraid of sin. Although his statements were not pleasant to the ears of the Kaurava, he was a good man and spoke his thoughts.

A Father's Grief

YUDHISHTHIRA was overcome by grief. "He who defeated Drona, Aswatthama, and Duryodhana in battle and who was like a destructive fire to hostile armies has entered the sleep that knows no waking. Are you dead, warrior who caused Duhsasana to flee in terror? What do I fight for win for now? What consoling words can I say to Arjuna? What should I say to Subhadra, who is trembling like a cow that has lost a calf? How am I supposed to comfort them with meaningless words?

"Truly, men's understanding is destroyed by ambition. I forced this youngster, whose life was all before him in love and joy, to the front lines of battle out of my thirst for victory. I was like the fool who searches for honey and falls into a deep pit below and is destroyed. There is no fool in the world like me. Instead of guarding Arjuna's cherished son while his father was away, I killed him."

Yudhishthira was moaning in his tent as warriors sat silently all around him, reflecting somberly on the bravery of the young hero and his sad demise.

Vyasa had always made it a point to visit the Pandavas whenever they were grieving greatly. He was also their great-grandfather and instructor. He now made himself known to Yudhishthira.

The sage was greeted with respect. After forcing him to sit, Yudhishthira said. "I have looked everywhere for tranquilly, but I cannot find it."

Vyasa remarked, "You are wise and knowledgeable, and it is not proper that you should permit yourself to get lost in grief in this way. Knowing the nature of death, it is improper for you to grieve in an uneducated manner."

The distraught Dharmaputra was then comforted by Vyasa, who said, "When Brahma created living things, he was burdened with anguish. These lives will continue to grow, and soon the world won't be able to support all of them. There doesn't seem to be a way to handle this. This flame of Brahma's thought swelled until it threatened to extinguish the entirety of creation at once.

"Rudra then arrived and begged for the suppression of this terrible fire. The enormous fire was under Brahma's control, and he turned it into the law of Death, which is known to mortals. The creator's law, which regulates the balance between life and death, manifests itself in many different ways, including war, illness, and accidents.

"Death is a necessary law of existence that was put in place for the sake of humanity. Being impatient with death or expressing excessive grief for the deceased is not true wisdom. There is no justification for feeling sorry for the dead. We may have good reason to be sad for the people who are still here."

After offering these consoling remarks, Krishna-Dwaipayana left.

Following their victory over and killing of the samsaptakas, Dhananjaya and Krishna were making their way back to their camp.

Arjuna responded, "Govinda, I don't know why, but my mind is not at ease. My heart is tormented by a huge presentiment of loss, and my mouth feels dry. I wonder if Yudhishthira has experienced any tragedies. Krishna, I'm terrified of something."

"Yudhishthira shouldn't be a cause for anxiety," said Krishna. "He is secure, as are your other brothers."

They stopped along the route to offer evening prayers. They got back on the chariot and drove over to the camp. Arjuna began to have increasingly dire predictions of disaster as they neared the camp.

"Janardana, the camp is devoid of the customary opportune music. The troops lower their heads and turn away when they notice me from a distance. They are acting in an odd manner with this. O Madhava, I am quite frightened. Consider my brothers to be secure. I'm perplexed. How come Abhimanyu and his brothers don't come out to meet us today like they usually do?"

They walked into the camp.

"Why do you all have dejected expressions? I don't see Abhimanyu in this place. How come I don't see any happy faces? I recognised the lotus pattern in which Drona had set up his soldiers. As far as I know, none of you could breach it. Did Abhimanyu break through the breach? If that is the case, he has already passed away because I never showed him how to escape that structure. Has he really been killed?"

His worst suspicions were verified by their melancholy quiet and glum eyes that dared not meet his. The devastated father erupted into heartbroken wailing.

"Alas, has my beloved boy actually arrived as Yama's guest? Have you all, mighty Satyaki, Yudhishthira, Bhimasena, Dhrishtadyumna, let the enemy to kill the son of Subhadra? Alas! What solace should I offer Subhadra? How do I respond to Draupadi? What consolation can be given to Uttara, and to whom?"

Vasudeva addressed his ill friend. "Beloved Arjuna," he commanded, "Do not succumb to anguish in this manner. Those who have chosen the life of arms and enter war with the intention of staying put always have death close by. Kshatriyas must always be willing to pass away young. Even as a little child, Abhimanyu has reached the joyful places above that battle-weary veterans long to reach. The desired and required end for all kshatriyas is undoubtedly Abhimanyu's. Your brothers and other rulers will lose heart if you succumb to grief in such an excessive way. Instead of crying, encourage others to have strength and fortitude."

When Dhananjaya asked for the whole account of his valiant son's demise, Yudhishthira gave it as follows, "I encouraged Abhimanyu to enter the enemy's formation because I knew that he alone among us could achieve it. The young hero followed through and destroyed the enormous formation. As planned, we followed behind him. But at that precise moment, the evil Jayadratha arrived and effectively halted us. We were unable to follow Abhimanyu because he immediately closed up the opening in the formation. Oh, shame on kshatriyas who could do this! The Sindhu kept us out, and suddenly a swarm of valiant soldiers surrounded him, isolating him, and killing him."

Arjuna was once more overcome with sorrow upon hearing the entire tale, and he collapsed to the ground in a faint. After he had recovered, he swore, "I will kill this Jayadratha, who killed my kid, before the sun sets tomorrow. If Drona and Kripa stand in the way of him and me, these acharyas will likewise be overpowered and killed." He then twitched the Gandiva string while saying this, causing Krishna to blow the Panchajanya.

And Bhima remarked, "To the sons of Dhritarashtra, this twang of Arjuna's bow and this blare of Krishna's conch shall be the summons of Death!"

The Sindhu King

ARJUNA'S pledge to assassinate the Sindhu king before sundown the following day after was reported to the enemy. The spies told Duryodhana's friends that Arjuna had learned that Jayadratha was the reason for Abhimanyu's demise and pledged in this manner.

The great king of the Sindhus, Vriddhakshatra, was blessed with a son who he named Jayadratha. At the time of the prince's birth, a voice was heard saying, "This prince will gain great renown and he will attain the happy regions above, slain in battle. One of the most legendary fighters in history will cut off his head from his body on the battlefield."

None of the living things, no matter how intelligent or courageous they are, enjoy dying. When the voice announced the death of his son, Vriddhakshatra was devastated. He cursed, "He who causes my son's head to roll down on the ground, shall have his head shatter into fragments in that very instant," in his disturbed state of mind.

When Jayadratha reached adulthood, Vriddhakshatra transferred control of the State to him. He retreated to the forest, where he spent his days performing austerities in an ashrama close to the plain that would later serve as the site of the Battle of Kurukshetra. When Jayadratha learned of Arjuna's promise, he recalled the prophecy regarding his death and worried that his time was running out.

"I don't want to continue fighting in this conflict. Let me return to my nation," he pleaded with Duryodhana.

"Saindhava, have no fear," Duryodhana responded. These veterans and warriors are gathered here to protect you from harm. Since I am present, together with all of these legendary warriors, you cannot be in danger. My entire army will only be tasked with one mission today: protecting you from Arjuna. You must not depart at this time."

Jayadratha consented to stay. "Master, you educated me and Arjuna and you know us both well," he said as he approached Drona. "What do you think about the two of us?"

"Son, I did my job as your teacher and treated you both fairly. Arjuna succeeds because of his exceptional discipline and self-practice. However, this need not be a deterrent for you. You will be positioned behind a formidable army that Arjuna will find difficult to overcome. Everyone will die, and the warrior who perishes in combat enters the joyful regions easily while others must work very hard to do so. Put fear aside and fight."

After giving Jayadratha this advice, Drona went on to organise the troops for the following day.

Jayadratha and his detachment were positioned in a heavily fortified position twelve kilometres behind the main army. With all of their armies, Bhurisravas, Karna, Aswatthama, Salya, Vrishasena, and Kripa were present.

Dronacharya arranged the major Kaurava soldiers in a circular arrangement between them and the Pandava army. A lotus shape backed and supported this, and it was once more supported by a force with spiked heads. Jayadratha was located beyond this.

Drona rode majestically at the head of the encircling army on a chariot carried by horses with chestnut manes, his flag flying high. He exhorted the Kaurava army to supreme bravery and sacrifice. When Duryodhana observed the army's formation, his confidence returned.

One of the sons of Dhritarashtra, Durmarshana, led the main army forward with a force of a thousand armed chariots, one hundred elephants, three thousand horsemen, ten thousand foot soldiers, and fifteen hundred archers. He blew his conch and uttered his challenge: "Where is Dhananjaya of whose wrath and prowess men speak? Let him advance and smash himself into bits in front of the warriors, striking against us like a pot on a rock."

At a bowshot's distance, Arjuna halted his vehicle and responded by blowing his conch. Conchs then blew throughout the Kaurava army.

Kesava, head in the direction of Durmarshana, ordered Arjuna. "We're going to pierce the elephant line."

The army of Durmarshana was defeated. The Kaurava forces dispersed like clouds in a wind and fled in all directions.

Duhsasana became enraged when he noticed this. He surrounded Arjuna while in command of an enormous elephant force. Although Duhsasana was a very evil person, he was also brave. He engaged Arjuna in a furious battle, leaving a trail of dead people in his wake. He eventually surrendered, defeated, and returned to join Drona's forces. Drona was passed by Savyasachi's chariot as it moved forward quickly.

"Honorable one, I have come to exact revenge on the Sindhu king because I am mourning the loss of my son. In order to fulfil my commitment, I beg your blessings," Arjuna pleaded to the acharya.

"Arjuna, you must first battle and vanquish me before you can reach Jayadratha," the acharya said, smiling.

In response, Drona let loose a hail of arrows on Arjuna's vehicle. Partha responded with his own arrows, which the acharya easily parried and sent flying in the direction of Krishna and Arjuna. The Pandava then decided to break Drona's bow and bent his Gandiva accordingly.

Drona's shaft arrived and severed the string as he was still tugging on his bowstring. The acharya shot a hail of arrows at Arjuna, his horses, and his chariot while still smiling. Arjuna retaliated, but the acharya shot his arrows all over him, enveloping him and his chariot in darkness.

When Krishna realised how poorly things were going, he exclaimed, "Partha, stop wasting time. Let's move on. Fighting this brahmana who doesn't seem to recognise exhaustion is useless." Krishna then moved Arjuna's chariot to the left of the acharya while continuing to speak.

"Stop, you can't move forward without eliminating your adversary."

"O acharya, you are not my enemy. You are my master. You can think of me as your son. Nobody in the entire world can overcome you," declared Arjuna, and they rapidly passed Drona.

The Bhoja army was then pierced by Arjuna. The opponents of his passage,

Kritavarma and Sudakshina, were defeated. Srutayudha also made an effort to halt Arjuna's advancement. Srutayudha lost his horses in the hard combat and threw his mace at Krishna.

His mother had offered this mace, and it had been accepted. This is the mace's narrative. After performing penances that pleased Varuna, Parnasa received a blessing from the god ensuring that her son Srutayudha wouldn't perish at the hands of any foe.

"I'll give your son a supernatural weapon. Let him employ it in all of his conflicts. He won't be killed or defeated by an enemy. However, he shouldn't use the weapon on a non-combatant. The weapon will recoil and kill him if he does." The God Varuna threw a mace as he spoke this.

When Srutayudha was fighting Arjuna, he disregarded the command and threw the mace at Krishna, who was simply operating Arjuna's chariot and not engaging in combat. The missile struck Janardana in the chest before violently bouncing back to Srutayudha, killing him and leaving him lying dead on the ground like a large forest tree felled by a storm. It behaved like a demon turning back fatally on the magician who makes a mistake when casting the spell of power that enslaves it.

The Kamboja ruler then led his army against Arjuna. He was spread out lifeless on the field after a bloody battle, looking like a huge flagstaff.

The Kaurava soldiers were completely disoriented when they saw Srutayudha and the king of Kamboja, two powerful warriors, killed. As Partha attempted to control the situation, Srutayu and his brother Asrutayu attacked him from both sides and severely hurt him.

Arjuna was knocked out by his injuries at one point in this conflict and was leaning on the flagstaff. Krishna, however, gave him words of encouragement. Arjuna soon rallied and picked up the fight, killing the two brothers and their two sons who persisted in fighting.

Arjuna continued to march and eventually reached Jayadratha after killing numerous additional warriors.

Borrowed Armour

As he heard Sanjaya describe Arjuna's victory, Dhritarashtra said, "When Janardana arrived to Hastinapura looking for a solution, I advised Duryodhana that it was a fantastic opportunity and that he should seize it. Duryodhana ignored them, nevertheless. He thought that Karna and Duhsasana's suggestion was wiser than mine. He had a vision of The Destroyer and wanted his own destruction. Drona, along with Bhishma, Bhurisravas, Kripa, and others, disapproved of war. My son, though, was disobedient. Due to his excessive desire, he became embroiled in animosity and hatred and incited this destructive battle."

Sanjaya responded to Dhritarashtra's lamentations by asking: "Of what use are your regrets now? Now that the water that gives life has been completely wasted, you're trying to close the breach. Why didn't you stop Kunti's son from playing the lottery? All of this terrible suffering could have been avoided if you had acted responsibly at the time. This tragedy could have been prevented even later if you had been stern and dissuaded your son from his terrible deeds. You were aware of the bad, yet you disregarded your own good judgement and went along with Karna and Sakuni's misguided advise.

"You no longer have the respect of Kesava, Yudhishthira, and Drona. Vasudeva is now aware that your virtue is nothing more than hypocrisy. Despite the Kauravas' best efforts as warriors, they are unable to match Arjuna, Krishna, Satyaki, and Bhima's power. Duryodhana hasn't dispersed. He is exerting all of his strength. It is inappropriate for you to now accuse him or his loyal followers."

"Dear Sanjaya, I sincerely apologise for my negligence. Your assertion is accurate. Nobody has the power to alter fate. Tell me what is taking place, no matter how painful." Sanjaya completed his tale according to the ancient king's instructions.

When he observed Arjuna's chariot riding triumphantly in the direction of the Sindhu king, Duryodhana became very angry.

"Arjuna has caused a gap in the big army and has advanced on Jayadratha's position," he hurried to Drona and groused angrily. "The troops guarding the Sindhu king had thought Arjuna would never be able to pass; they will undoubtedly lose heart. You appear committed to aiding the Pandavas. I'm mentally quite distressed.

"Tell me, sir, how exactly did I offend you? Why are you disappointing me in this manner? I should not have asked Jayadratha to stay here if I had known you would do this. I made a big error by not allowing him to return to his native country as he had requested. He cannot escape death from Arjuna's onslaught, so please pardon me. I'm speaking carelessly because I'm upset. Don't hesitate to personally travel to help the Saindhava."

Drona responded to this frantic plea. "King, I shall not take offence at your careless and unworthy statements. I love you more than Aswatthama himself—you are like a son to me! I am required to be here in this area of the field, thus I am unable to accomplish that. We are under heavy attack from the Pandava army. Is this not the perfect opportunity since Arjuna is not supporting Yudhishthira here? As a result of the success of our scheme, I must now imprison Yudhishthira. I can't follow Phalguna right now because if I do, our battle array will be completely destroyed, and we'll be lost.

"Follow my instructions. Put on my armour, then go thwart Arjuna. Your body won't be able to take any blows. Wearing the armour provided by Brahma, Duryodhana should charge into war with the same assurance as Indra did. The victory be with you."

After regaining his confidence, Duryodhana went to fight Arjuna while clad in magical armour and escorted by a sizable army of troops.

In order to go to Jayadratha, who had been kept in safety, Arjuna had to traverse the Kaurava army. When the brothers Vinda and Anuvinda unexpectedly appeared and started to fight Arjuna, Krishna had just stopped the chariot and was about to unyoke the horses when he noticed that they were a little tired. Arjuna dispersed their forces after they were vanquished and killed both of them.

Krishna then released the chariot's yoke and gave the horses some time to rest. They then carried out their plan once more.

"Dhananjaya, look back! The reckless Duryodhana is approaching. This is good luck indeed! The person who started all of this trouble is now putting himself in your hands. You've been holding back your rage for a while; it's time to let it out. But keep in mind that he is an excellent archer, knowledgeable in bowcraft, and a skilled and powerful fighter." Krishna said as much, and they stopped to engage the Kaurava in combat.

Duryodhana came without hesitation. "They claim that you have performed prowess, Arjuna. I have not personally witnessed this. Let me see if your courage and your talent are indeed as great as your reputation."

In fact, the fighting was fierce, which astonished Krishna. "Partha, I'm amazed, how come your arrows don't seem to harm Duryodhana?" he asked Krishna. "For the first time, I saw the Gandiva's shafts striking their targets ineffectively. This is peculiar. Do your arms no longer have strength? Or has Gandiva's quality declined? Why do your arrows hit Duryodhana yet fail to pierce him, falling to the ground instead? This is quite mysterious."

"I understand," Arjuna said with a smile. "Drona has outfitted this man in enchanted armour. I was taught the key to this armour by the acharya, but this man wears it like a bullock might. Now you will enjoy yourself!"

Having said this, Arjuna started to shoot his arrows, first taking Duryodhana's horses, chariot, and vehicle away from him. Then Arjuna shattered his bow, effectively disarming him. Then, until Duryodhana could take it no more, he sent needle-like darts that wounded only the areas of his body that were not protected by armour. Duryodhana then turned and fled.

When Duryodhana became uneasy as a result, Krishna sounded his conch, which terrified Jayadratha's soldiers. The Sindhu king's guards were taken aback. Eight of them—Bhurisravas, Chala, Karna, Vrishasena, Kripa, Salya, Aswatthama, and Jayadratha—got ready right away in their chariots and deployed their forces against Arjuna.

Yudhishthira's Misgivings

WHEN the Pandavas noticed Duryodhana moving in Arjuna's direction, they launched a fierce assault on the Kaurava army to stop Drona from rescuing Jayadratha. The three fronts of combat severely reduced the Kaurava army.

Drona was viciously attacked by Dhrishtadyumna as he drove his chariot directly into his. The Panchala's dove-colored horses and Drona's chestnut horses were intertwined with one another. A beautiful scene reminiscent of the setting sun's clouds was created.

Dhrishtadyumna threw away his bow and charged Drona's chariot while brandishing a sword and shield. He assaulted Drona bewilderingly while shifting positions on the vehicle's shafts, the horses, and the yoke. The entire time he appeared to sear him with his baleful, bloodshot eyes.

This struggle lasted a very long time. In a fit of rage, Drona pulled his bow and launched a shaft that nearly ended the Panchala's life. Satyaki offered unexpected assistance by shooting an arrow that deflected the acharya's shaft

After that, Drona attacked Satyaki, allowing the Panchala soldiers to capture Dhrishtadyumna. Satyaki, one of the top warriors on the Pandava side, moved forward to accept the challenge. But then he saw Drona approaching, hissing like a black cobra and his eyes crimson with rage.

Satyaki replied to his charioteer, "This is the man who, putting up his job as a brahmana, has taken up the profession of fighting and is distressing the Pandavas. This individual is the main reason for Duryodhana's haughtiness. He is constantly brimming with vanity and thinks of himself as a very outstanding soldier. I have to make him pay for it. Fasten the chariot to the chariot."

In response, Satyaki's charioteer whipped the silver-white horses and accelerated toward the vehicle. The light was briefly obscured by Satyaki and Drona's rapid-fire arrows, leaving the battlefield in pitch-blackness. The steel shafts swung and shimmered, looking like snakes that had just shed their skin.

Both sides' flagstaffs and chariot hoods had been severely damaged. Both Satyaki and Drona were haemorrhaging heavily. The warriors on both sides of the duel watched it without blowing their conchs, raising their war cries, or roaring like lions.

The son of Bharadwaja had to take another bow after Satyaki's well-aimed shaft destroyed Drona's bow. Satyaki continued to shoot it down while he was stringing it. Drona attempted to use another bow, but it was also destroyed. And so it continued until Drona had lost 101 bows and was unable to fire an arrow.

The great acharya was pleased to face a foe who was equal to him and said to himself, "This man Satyaki is a warrior of the class of Sri Rama, Kartavirya, Dhananjaya, and Bhishma."

It was a craftsman's professional delight in seeing his talent demonstrated in the art he cherished. Long did this equal conflict go on, Satyaki having a ready answer of equal quality for every specially-charged shaft that Drona sent. After deciding to kill Satyaki, Drona, an archer of unmatched talent, blasted the fire into space. However, Satyaki immediately dispatched the Varuna astra to combat it after noticing this.

The Kaurava soldiers rejoiced and screamed in pleasure when Satyaki's strength started to wane at this point. Those around were instructed by Yudhishthira to head to Satyaki's aid.

"Drona is defeating our great and noble warrior Yuyudhana," he instructed Dhrishtadyumna, "You should go there right away. If not, Satyaki will be killed by the brahmana in a short while. Like a cat and a bird, Drona is playing with Satyaki. Satyaki is in fact in the Destroyer's hands." Yudhishthira gave the soldiers the command to launch a fierce assault on Drona.

Satyaki was just barely saved. Krishna's conch could be heard from the area where Arjuna was engaged in combat at that very moment.

Yudhishthira screamed, "O Satyaki, I hear Panchajanya, but the twang of Arjuna's bow does not accompany it. Forces are against Arjuna from both his front and his behind. Even though the majority of the day has passed, he still hasn't returned after cutting through the Kaurava ranks in the morning. I believe Dhananjaya has died, and as a result, Krishna has joined the fight.

"There is nothing you cannot do, Satyaki. Arjuna, the man who trained you, is in imminent danger. Arjuna has frequently praised my outstanding competence and prowess in his conversations with me. When we were in the forest, he told me, 'There is no other soldier like Satyaki.' Oh, there it is! On that side, the dust is rising. Arjuna has undoubtedly been encircled. There are numerous enemy warriors who have vowed to die in defence of Jayadratha, who is a strong warrior. Go right away, Satyaki." Dharmaputra expressed this in great apprehension.

After fighting Drona, Satyaki was worn out and responded, "Faultless among men, I shall obey your command. What wouldn't I do to help Dhananjaya? In my opinion, my life is a minor inconvenience. I am prepared to battle the gods themselves if you give the order.

"However, allow me to tell you what the sage Arjuna and Vasudeva informed me before they went. 'You must remain by Yudhishthira's side until we arrive after killing Jayadratha. We give you our trust in this. We only have fear for Drona, one fighter in the Kaurava army. You are aware of his sworn purpose. We depart, entrusting Dharmaputra's security to your care.'

"How am I supposed to ignore his order? Do not worry about Arjuna's security. Nobody can overcome him. The sixteenth part of Arjuna is too much for the Sindhu king and the rest to handle. Dharmaputra, if I must leave, to whom shall I commit the care of your safety? If Drona arrives to capture you, I don't see anyone in this room who can resist him. Never ask me to leave. Think carefully before ordering me to go."

"Satyaki," responded Yudhishthira urgently, "You must leave. I have weighed the risk and the need. You have my full consent to depart. Here is the strong Bhima to watch out for my security. Dhrishtadyumna is another, among a large number of others. You shouldn't be concerned about me."

After stating this, Yudhishthira loaded a box full of arrows and other weapons into his chariot and had new horses tacked to it. He sent Satyaki ahead with praise for him.

"Bhimasena, you are in charge of Yudhishthira. Be careful," Satyaki said before joining Dhananjaya.

As he dashed past the Kaurava army, Satyaki encountered fierce resistance, yet he did so while pressing down on all opponents. But the opposition was fierce, and he made little headway. Drona attacked the Pandava formation without stopping or pausing when he saw Satyaki separate from Yudhishthira/ Eventually it broke and started to retreat. Yudhishthira was perturbed.

Yudhishthira's Fond Hope

"NEITHER Arjuna nor Satyaki, who was despatched to look for him, have returned. Bhima, I get more nervous. I can hear the Panchajanya but not Arjuna's bowstring's twang. Satyaki, the bravest and most dependable of friends, has not returned with any news." In severe mental confusion, Yudhishthira replied to Bhima, "My uneasiness is growing every instant."

Bhimasena answered, "I have never seen you so agitated. Don't let your resolve erode. You are free to give me orders. Avoid letting your thoughts become bogged down in fear."

"Dear Bhima, I fear that your brother has been killed, and it appears that Madhava has now turned to violence. I can hear Madhava's conch, but I don't hear Gandiva's resonant twang. I worry that Dhananjaya, the unmatched hero on whom all of our aspirations were centred, has been killed. My thoughts are jumbled. If you follow my instructions, head straight towards Arjuna. Join him and Satyaki, do the necessary tasks, then return. I gave Satyaki the go-ahead to cut through the Kaurava ranks and move in Arjuna's direction. You go ahead and follow suit, and if you do in fact spot them alive, I will be alerted by your lion roar."

"My Lord, don't be upset." Bhima instantly turned to Dhrishtadyumna and said, "Panchala, you know quite well that Drona is striving, by some means or other, to grab Dharmaputra alive. I shall go and let you know they are safe. Our priority is to keep the King safe. But I also have to follow his instructions and obey him. I'm leaving him in your care while I travel."

"No need to worry, Bhima. Go with confidence in mind," the valiant son of Drupada, Drona's sworn enemy, declared. "Drona cannot capture Yudhishthira without first murdering me."

Bhima then sped off. He was encircled by the Kauravas in full force, and they tried to stop him from going to Arjuna's aid. But he drove his adversaries away, killing no fewer than eleven of Dhritarashtra's sons, much like a lion does when it scatters less noble animals.

Then Bhima went up to Drona alone. Drona screamed, "Stop! You must defeat me in order to move on. I allowed your brother Arjuna to enter. I cannot, however, let you go."

Drona said this in the hope that Bhima would extend the same politeness that he did to Arjuna. However, when Bhima heard Drona say these things, he was incensed and mocking in his response.

"Oh brahmana, Arjuna did not go with your consent. He forced his way through your defences and broke down your resistance, yet he did not harm you out of sympathy. But unlike Arjuna, I won't have pity on you. You used to be our preceptor and acted as a father figure to us. We held you in high regard. You have admitted that you are our adversary now. May that be true!"

In response, Bhima pointed his mace at Drona's chariot, which broke apart and forced Drona to board another vehicle. The second chariot was also completely destroyed. And Bhima overcame every resistance by pushing his way through.

That day, Drona lost eight chariots, and the Bhoja army that attempted to oppose Bhima was utterly decimated. He continued, destroying all opposition, and arrived where Arjuna was engaged in battle with Jayadratha's soldiers.

When Bhima spotted Arjuna, he roared like a lion. When Krishna and Arjuna heard the roar, they were overjoyed and shouted with delight. When Yudhishthira heard these roars, it allayed his worries and fears, and he gave Arjuna his blessings.

And he had the thought, "Arjuna's oath will be carried out before the sun sets today. He will kill the person responsible for Abhimanyu's demise and come back victorious. After Jayadratha's passing, Duryodhana might file a peace suit. It's likely that gullible Duryodhana will come to his senses after witnessing so many of his brothers killed. Will this actually occur? Bhishma, the great-grandson, has been sacrificed. Will this evil hostility stop along with it, and will we be rescued from more gruesome destruction?"

As a result, Bhima, Satyaki, and Arjuna were engaged in fierce combat while Yudhishthira was affectionately yearning and dreaming of peace.

Karna And Bhima

ON the fourteenth day, severe fighting broke out between Satyaki and the Bhurisravas in one area, Bhima and Karna in another, and Arjuna and Jayadratha in a third. At the main front, Drona continued to fight off the Panchalas and Pandavas while directing a counteroffensive against them.

At the point where Arjuna engaged Jayadratha, Duryodhana arrived with his men but was quickly routed.

As a result, the conflict raged fiercely and for a long time on several fronts. Each side was vulnerable to danger from behind because to how the armies were positioned.

"Arjuna, Bhima, and Satyaki have treated us with contempt and advanced successfully to Jayadratha's area, and they are pressing hard on the Sindhu king," Duryodhana said to Drona. "It is remarkable that, under your direction, our battle-array was destroyed and our goals were totally thwarted. Everyone wonders how the mighty Drona could have been so terribly outwitted. What should I say in response? You have betrayed me."

Thus, Duryodhana berated Drona once more. Drona responded unperturbed: "Duryodhana, your allegations are as contemptible as they are untrue. Talking about things that are damaged beyond repair will not benefit anyone. Consider what must be done right away."

"Sir, you should give me advice. Let me know what has to be done. Give the challenges of the scenario your best thought before deciding, and let's move rapidly." Duryodhana begged, baffled and puzzled.

"My child, the situation is undeniably serious," Drona responded. "Three powerful generals have moved forward and outwitted us. They have just as much cause for concern as we do, though, as their rear is now just as vulnerable to attack. They are not in a safe position because we are on both sides of them. Be encouraged. Approach Jayadratha once more, and offer him all the assistance you can. It serves no use to demoralise oneself by reflecting on past setbacks and struggles. I must remain here and maintain hostilities with the Panchalas and Pandava troops. If not, we will be completely decimated."

As a result, Duryodhana returned with additional troops to the area where Arjuna was aiming his attack at Jayadratha.

Bhima had no desire to fight or argue with Karna for very long. He was eager to get to Arjuna's location. Radheya, however, would in no way let him do this. He stopped Bhimasena from moving forward by shooting him with his arrows.

The difference between the two warriors was startling. Attractive Karna's lotus-like face was beaming with smiles when he attacked Bhima, yelling things like, "Do not show your back," "Now, do not flee like a coward," and other similar things.

Ridiculed in this way, Bhima was furious. The grins of Karna enraged him. While Bhima's face was glowing with wrath and his actions were ferocious, Karna handled the combat with a relaxed smile. Bhima would ignore the arrows and javelins that were raining down heavily on him and constantly attempt to close with Karna. Radheya, on the other hand, would maintain his distance and send his well-aimed shafts. He performed each task with calm and grace, whereas Bhimasena grew agitated and impatient as he displayed his incredible limb strength.

Bhima was scarlet with gushing wounds all over and presented the appearance of an asoka tree in full blossom. Yet he seemed unaware of them as he approached Karna, cutting bows in two and wrecking his chariot. When Karna had to rush for a fresh chariot, there was no longer a smile on his face. Fury swelled in him, like the sea on a full moon day, as he attacked Bhima. Both showed the power of tigers and the speed of eagles, and their anger was now like that of serpents in a fury.

Karna's bow was shattered and his charioteer reeled and fell. Karna then hurled a javelin at Bhima, but Bhima parried it and continued pouring his arrows on Karna, who had taken up a fresh bow.

Again and again Karna lost his chariot. Duryodhana saw Karna's plight and, calling his brother Durjaya, said to him: "This wicked Pandava will kill Karna. Go at once and attack Bhima and save Karna's life."

Durjaya went as ordered and attacked Bhima, who sent seven shafts which sent Durjaya's horses and his charioteer to the abode of Yama. Durjaya himself fell mortally wounded. Seeing his bleeding body wriggling on the ground like a wounded snake, Karna was overwhelmed with grief and circled round the hero, paying mournful honour to the dead.

Bhima did not stop but continued the fight and greatly harassed Karna. Karna once again had to find a fresh chariot. He sent well-aimed shafts and hit Bhima who in a fury hurled his mace at Karna. It crashed on Karna's chariot and killed his charioteer and horses and broke the flagstaff. Karna now stood on the ground with a bent bow.

Duryodhana sent another brother to relieve Karna. Durmukha went accordingly and took Karna on his chariot.

Seeing yet another son of Dhritarashtra come to offer himself up to death, Bhima licked his lips in gusto and sent nine shafts on the newly arrived enemy. Even as Karna climbed up to take his seat in the chariot, Durmukha's armour was broken and he fell lifeless. When Karna saw the warrior bathed in blood and lying dead by his side, he was again overwhelmed with grief and stood motionless for a while.

Bhima relentlessly continued his attack on Karna. His sharp arrows pierced Karna's coat of armour and he was in pain. But he too returned the attack at once and wounded Bhima all over. Still, the Pandava would not stop and attacked Karna furiously.

The sight of so many of Duryodhana's brothers dying for his sake one after another was too much for Karna. This, and the physical pain of his own wounds made him lose courage and he turned away defeated. But when Bhima stood up on the field of battle red with wounds all over like a flaming fire and emitted a triumphant yell, he could not withstand it but returned to the combat.

Pledge Upheld

HEARING about the murder of his boys and the payment made to Karna, Dhritarashtra was devastated. "Oh Sanjaya, my sons are burning up like moths in the fire. I've lost track of these children! The stubborn fool Duryodhana declared, 'Karna, unsurpassed among men for bravery and war success, is on our side. Therefore, who can defeat us? When Karna is on my side, not even the gods can defeat me. What could these Pandavas possibly do to me?' However, he had recently witnessed Karna fleeing after Bhimasena struck him. Has he at least now recognised wisdom? Unfortunately, Sanjaya, my son has gained the ferocious hate of Bhima, the Vayu family's son who possesses the power of the death god! Indeed, we are destroyed!"

Sanjaya responded, "O King, was it not you, listening to the words of your ignorant and headstrong son, who brought about this insatiable hatred? This greater catastrophe must be linked to you, in fact. You are currently reaping the benefits of disregarding Bhishma's and the other elders' recommendations. You are to blame, king. Don't hold Karna and the valiant warriors accountable. They gave it their all in combat."

Sanjaya then told the blind king what had happened after reprimanding him in this manner.

When they witnessed Karna being chased away by Bhima, five sons of Dhritarashtra immediately rushed on the latter. Karna was encouraged when he observed this and turned around to continue his assault.

Bhimasena first paid Karna more attention than the sons of Dhritarashtra. However, they escalated their violence to the point where Bhima became enraged and turned his attention to them, slaying all five of them.

Along with their horses and charioteers, they were soon all lying dead on the field. The young soldiers with their bleeding wounds looked like a forest with trees uprooted by a violent wind and lying flat on the ground with their lovely crimson bloom.

Karna battled more grimly than ever before when he witnessed another group of princes being killed for his benefit. As a result of all the harm that Karna had caused the Pandavas, Bhima was also more violent than usual. He fully disarmed Karna using his bow. His charioteer and horses were also killed.

At this point, Karna sprung from his chariot and threw Bhima with his mace. However, Bhima fended it off with arrows from his strong bow, doused Karna in arrows. Karna was forced to turn around and proceed on foot.

As he observed this battle, Duryodhana, who was deeply saddened, sent seven of his brothers to relieve Radheya. They engaged Bhima in combat with great skill and vigour. But they all perished as a result of Bhima's unstoppable attack and stirred desire.

Karna's face was moist with tears as he watched so many of Dhritarashtra's sons give their lives in his service. He then mounted a new chariot and started to attack Bhima with lethal might. Like clouds in a thunderstorm, the two combatants exchanged blows.

As they witnessed Bhima battling, Kesava, Satyaki, and Arjuna were overcome with admiration and happiness. Exclamations were also made by a large number of other Kaurava army soldiers who were astounded by Bhima's fighting style.

Duryodhana was enraged and felt like he had been stung to the core. Karna's situation made him quite concerned that Bhima would kill Radheya that day. He despatched seven more of his brothers, telling them to encircle Bhima and attack him simultaneously.

The seven brothers that Duryodhana ordered to fight Bhima were killed one by one by his arrows. The last person to die, Vikarna, was much loved. After a valiant struggle, Bhima saw him collapse to the ground and was moved to tears.

He cried out, "Alas, O Vikarna, you were righteous and knew what was dharma! You carried out your responsibility to fight honourably. Even you had to die for me. The fact that men like you and the grandsire Bhishma had to be killed in this conflict is a curse on us."

Karna was devastated with grief when he witnessed Duryodhana's brothers, who had come to aid him, being killed one after another in this manner. He closed his eyes and leaned back on his chariot seat because he could not take what he saw. After regaining emotional control, he hardened his heart and resumed his onslaught on Bhima.

Bhimasena's shaft dismantled bow after bow, yet Karna continued the conflict. He had to pick up a new bow eighteen times. Karna had lost his smile a long time ago, and both he and Bhima could see the ferocious rage on each other's faces. They were now squabbling while exchanging vicious glares. Now when Bhima's roar could be heard over the din of battle, Yudhishthira was encouraged and battled Drona harder.

Bhima lost his horses and charioteer in the furious conflict that erupted between him and Karna once more. His chariot was soon destroyed as well. Then, as Karna, who was riding in his chariot, parried the spear with his shaft, Bhima advanced with his sword and shield. Karna, however, instantly destroyed the shield with his arrows.

Then, Bhima spun and threw his sword, which split Karna's bow in two and hit the ground. But Karna picked up another bow and launched a ferocious new arrow attack on Bhima. In a frenzy of irrational wrath, Bhima attacked Karna. Radheya hid behind his flagstaff to prevent being destroyed.

After then, Bhima leaped out of Karna's vehicle and into the battlefield. Lacking any weapons, he used the dead elephants that were lying there to shield himself from Karna's arrows and carried on with the battle. Karna was kept busy nonstop by Bhima picking up anything he could get his hands on and flinging it at him. But this could not last for very long and Bhima soon found himself in a precarious position.

"Foolish glutton, you do not know the science of combat. Why do you engage yourself in battle here?" exclaimed Karna with joy. "Visit the jungle, gorge yourself on fruits and roots, and gain weight. You are an animal, unfit for kshatriya combat. Run away!"

He insulted him and incited fury in the defenceless Bhima, but out of respect for Kunti, he refrained from killing him.

"That's it, Arjuna! Watch how Karna is harassing poor Bhima," said Krishna.

When Dhananjaya saw the predicament of his brave brother, his eyes flared crimson with rage. Karna eagerly switched his focus from Bhima to Arjuna after he bent his Gandiva and shot his arrows at him. He had promised Kunti that he would not murder more than one Pandava, and he left the choice up to the peerless Arjuna.

Bhurisrava's End

THE charioteer Krishna exclaimed to Dhananjaya, "Here comes the brave Satyaki. Your student and friend is approaching, triumphantly piercing the defences of the adversary."

"Madhava, I do not like it," Arjuna replied. "He shouldn't have left Dharmaputra and came here to be with me. Drona is constantly looking for a chance to take Dharmaputra. Satyaki ought to have remained at his place to watch over him. He has instead arrived here. Satyaki has been intercepted by Old Bhurisravas. Yudhishthira made a big error by sending Satyaki away."

Between Bhurisravas and Satyaki, there existed a familial quarrel that turned them into steadfast adversaries. It had developed in this manner. Many princes vied for the hand of Devaki, who would become the mother of Sri Krishna, when she was a young maiden. Somadatta and Sini engaged in a fierce struggle for her hand. After winning, Sini brought Devaki with him.

The two clans have been at odds since that tragedy. Satyaki was Sini's grandson, while Bhurisravas was Somadatta's son. It was only inevitable that when they found themselves on opposing sides in the battle of Kurukshetra, Bhurisravas would challenge Satyaki to a duel the moment he set eyes on the young warrior.

"Oh Satyaki, I know you strut around believing yourself a man of great prowess," shouted Bhurisravas. "I've looked for this meeting for a while. You'll pass away today and enter Yama's abode, just as Indrajit destroyed Dasaratha's son Lakshmana, cheering the hearts of countless grieving widows."

Satyaki chuckled. "Finish your boasting," he cut in. "Words are not deeds, and they do not terrify warriors who are in battle. Show your courage by deed and refrain from dry thunder like autumn clouds."

Following this verbal exchange, the fight started, and it resembled a duel between two ferocious lions.

Both of their chariots were destroyed, along with their horses and bows. They were now fighting while seated on the ground, using swords and shields until both of their weapons were destroyed. Then, without using any weapons, they were engulfed in a lethal embrace. They rolled together on the ground, leapt up and sprang on each other, fell back down, and the fight continued for a considerable amount of time.

Partha missed this fight between Satyaki and the son of Somadatta since his attention was at the moment on Jayadratha's actions. However, Satyaki's charioteer Krishna, who was aware of the family dispute, was very worried about Satyaki's fate.

"Satyaki is worn out," Krishna said to Dhananjaya. "Bhurisravas will immediately execute him."

Still, Arjuna was merely observing what Jayadratha was doing.

Krishna repeated, "Satyaki, who arrived after a tough struggle with the Kaurava soldiers, has been compelled to accept Bhurisravas' challenge. This conflict is incredibly unfair. The beloved Yuyudhana will be killed if we don't assist him."

"Yuyudhana is dead!" All the warriors in the Kaurava army around him cried out. Bhurisravas picked Satyaki up and sent him crashing to the ground as Krishna was speaking.

"Satyaki, the best member of the Vrishni clan, is lying almost dead on the field," pleaded Krishna once again. "Before your eyes, someone who came to aid you is being killed. You are just watching and being inactive."

Bhurisravas grabbed hold of him while he was on his knees. Satyaki was pulled on the ground like an elephant by a lion.

Arjuna was intensely anguished. "I have not challenged Bhurisravas to a fight, nor has he invited me to war. How can I attack Bhurisravas when he is talking to someone else? Even while it's true that a friend who came to rescue me is being killed right in front of my eyes, my mind shudders at the thought of such a thing."

As soon as Arjuna completed speaking to Krishna, Jayadratha's arrow cloud began to cover the sky. With a hail of arrows, Arjuna responded. But he kept turning in agony to Satyaki, who was being held captive by Bhurisravas.

Krishna urged Arjuna to take Satyaki's condition into account once more. "O Partha, Satyaki has no more weapons and is now powerless under Bhurisravas' control."

When Arjuna turned, he found Bhurisravas standing over Satyaki's lifeless body with his sword lifted in preparation to kill him. Before Bhurisravas could strike the deadly blow, Arjuna fired an arrow that flew like lightning. The elevated arm dropped to the ground with the sword still in it the very next second. All in awe, Bhurisravas turned to look at the perpetrator.

He screamed, "Son of Kunti, I had not anticipated this of you! This kind of behind-the-back shooting is not appropriate for a fighter. You attacked me without warning when I was fighting someone else. It is very true that no man is able to resist the negative effects of the company he keeps.

"What account would you give Dharmaputra of this brave act, Dhananjaya? Who, Arjuna, taught you this crude trick? Did your father Indra or your instructors Drona and Kripa teach you this? You have dishonourably tarnished your reputation by acting in a lowly man's manner. You weren't naturally inclined to do it. A person with noble blood in his veins would never consider such a heinous act. I am aware that disdainful Krishna inspired you to do it."

In the Kurukshetra battlefield, Bhurisravas angrily denounced Krishna and Arjuna with his right arm cut off.

Partha said, "Bhurisravas, you are old and it appears that ageing has clouded your judgement. You falsely accuse me and Hrishikesa. How could I stand by and do nothing as you killed my friend, who was like a right hand to me, right in front of my eyes? You were going to stab him as he was laying defenceless on the ground. If I hadn't stepped in, I would have earned my place in hell. You claim that by hanging out with Madhava, I am destroyed. Who in the world wouldn't want to be so destroyed?

"You challenged Satyaki to a duel, despite the fact that he was underprepared and worn out when he arrived here. You defeated him. He lay on the ground, defeated and helpless. What code of honour gave you the right to raise your sword, pierce the body of the dead warrior, and kill him? Do I not recall how you applauded the person who killed my son Abhimanyu as he stood dazed, worn out, without a weapon, and with his coat of armour ripped off?"

When Bhurisravas heard this, he did not respond. Instead, he used his left hand to spread his arrows out on the ground and create a seat for meditation. All of the Kaurava soldiers were profoundly touched by the sight of the old warrior practising yoga. They praised Bhurisravas while criticising Arjuna and Krishna.

"Brave soldiers, I swear to protect any friend within bowshot of me, and I cannot allow an adversary to kill him," said Arjuna. "It is my solemn promise. You blame me, but why? Tossing out criticisms without giving them much thought is improper."

He addressed Bhurisravas after addressing the field warriors who had reprimanded him, saying, "O great among courageous men, you have protected those who have sought your assistance. You are aware that your mistake is to blame for what transpired. The act of blaming me is unjust. If you'd like, let's all place the blame on the violence that permeates kshatriya society."

When Bhurisravas heard this, he bowed his head in respect.

Satyaki regained consciousness and stood up. Overcome with anger, he grabbed up a sword. Bhurisravas' body was still in the position of meditation. He knocked off the old warrior's head, even while everyone else was screaming in terror and before Krishna and Arjuna, who had hurried to the scene, could stop him.

From above the battleground, the gods and siddhas bestowed blessings to Bhurisravas. The entire field denounced Satyaki's behaviour.

"The adversary of my family attempted to kill me after I collapsed senselessly," Satyaki insisted, adding: "After I came down senselessly, this enemy of my family placed his foot on my prostrate figure. In whichever position he chooses, I may kill him." But nobody endorsed his actions.

Jayadratha Slain

"THE crucial moment has arrived, Karna," said Duryodhana. "If Jayadratha is not killed before this day's sunset, Arjuna will feel humiliated and commit suicide since he has not kept his word. With Arjuna's passing, the Pandavas will be destroyed and this country will be ours. We shouldn't let this chance pass us by.

"Everything is dependent upon you. Your exceptional combat prowess is being tested today. Show your worth today. You can see how the sun has descended in the west. I don't believe Partha will be able to go to Jayadratha in the short amount of time that remains before dusk. The next several hours before dusk, you, Aswatthama, Salya, Kripa, and I must watch over Jayadratha and do everything in our power to prevent him from falling into Arjuna's hands."

"My king," Karna responded, "I have been wounded all over by Bhimasena, and I am so exhausted that my limbs lack any strength. Nevertheless, I shall exert all of my strength. I'm only here to help you."

While Karna and Duryodhana were making these plans, Arjuna was launching a massive assault on the Kaurava army and exerting all of his strength in an effort to reach Jayadratha before dusk.

Krishna put his Panchajanya in his mouth and blew a loud note in the rishabha swara. This was a sign for his charioteer Daruka to immediately approach with his chariot. When it arrived, Satyaki took his place in it and fought Karna fully by attacking him forcefully and deftly.

Due to Satyaki's skill with the bow and Daruka's driving prowess, the gods were summoned down to observe the battle. The charioteer was removed, and Karna's four chariot horses were rendered inoperable. The chariot was then destroyed, and the flagstaff was chopped in half.

The enormous Karna was left without a chariot, and the Kaurava army was much stirred by the incident. Karna was forced to flee and board Duryodhana's chariot. "Here," Sanjaya informs Dhritarashtra, to whom he was recounting the episode, "Krishna, Partha, and Satyaki are the three finest archery masters. No fourth can compare to them!"

Arjuna overcame the Kaurava resistance and made it to Jayadratha. Arjuna battled in a rage brought on by the memory of Abhimanyu's murder and all the significant wrongs committed by the Kauravas. Being savyasachin, he fired shafts from the Gandiva with one hand and then the other, terrifying and confusing his opponents into believing that Death had descended upon the battlefield with gaping jaws.

The battle between Arjuna and Aswatthama and the other strong warriors who defended the king of Sindhu can only be fully described by the poet of the Mahabharata. Despite their fierce combat, they were all ultimately victorious and unable to stop Arjuna from getting to Jayadratha.

As soon as Jayadratha was attacked, a protracted fight ensued. Since the day was coming to an end, both sides were continually scanning the west. Since the Saindhava was no weak adversary, Arjuna's strength and skill had to be put to the test. The struggle continued as the sun reddened and fell below the horizon.

"The remaining time is quite limited. Jayadratha appears to have been saved, and Arjuna's challenge appears to have failed. The pledge is broken, and Arjuna will be humiliated," chuckled Duryodhana to himself.

After then, both armies cried out in the darkness, "It's dusk, and Jayadratha hasn't been killed." While the Kaurava army erupted in cheers, the Pandavas were dejected.

Since the sun was not yet visible, Jayadratha glanced to the western horizon and declared to himself, "I am rescued!" He believed the period of danger from Arjuna had passed.

Krishna, however, interrupted Arjuna at that very time and stated, "Dhananjaya, the Sindhu raja is looking at the horizon. I am to blame for this gloom. The sun has not set and is still in the sky. Get to work. The time is right since Jayadratha is unprepared."

Jayadratha's head was dragged away by a shaft that emerged from the Gandiva like a vulture swooping down on a chicken.

"Listen, Arjuna, and send your shafts in quick succession so that the head won't fall to the ground and land in Vriddhakshatra's lap."

And Arjuna fired his magnificent arrows, which lifted the head into the air, making for an odd sight.

When his son's head softly slid into his lap, Vriddhakshatra was deep in evening meditation and sitting in the open in his ashrama. He had his eyes closed. The head rolled down and hit the ground as the elderly king was about to stand up after finishing his meditation. Vriddhakshatra's head split into a hundred pieces as predicted. Together with his father, Jayadratha travelled to the home of the brave.

When Kesava, Dhananjaya, Bhima, Satyaki, Yudhamanyu, and Uttamaujas blew their conches, Dharmaraja heard the joyful sounds and understood that it signalled Arjuna's fulfilment of his word and the death of the Saindhava. Then Yudhishthira led his troops against Drona with ferocity.

Even though it was getting dark, the rule that the fighting must stop at dusk was disregarded on the fourteenth day of the conflict. The restrictions and limitations started to fall apart one by one as the passions increased day by day.

Drona Passes Away

EVERYONE who has heard the Mahabharata epic is familiar with Ghatotkacha, Bhimasena's illustrious son by his asura wife. Among the characters from the Mahabharata, there are two young men who exhibit all the virtues of heroism, fortitude, strength, courage, and amiability. They are Ghatotkacha and Abhimanyu, sons of Bhima and Arjuna respectively. At the battle of Kurukshetra, they both lost their lives.

When the sun went down on the fourteenth day, the conflict continued under the light of torches. Because asuras are most powerful at night, Ghatotkacha and his asura forces took advantage of the cover of darkness to assault Duryodhana's army. As Ghatotkacha and his demon army moved in the air and attacked, Duryodhana watched as thousands of his soldiers were killed.

"Kill this person immediately; if not, our entire army will soon perish." All of Karna's bewildered Kauravas pleaded as such.

After being struck by an asura's arrow, Karna found himself confused and furious. He did have the unfailingly effective spear that Indra had given him. But it had just one use and had been carefully guarded for use exclusively against Arjuna. However, Karna launched the rocket at the young giant out of nowhere amid the chaos and fury of that spooky melee.

Arjuna was saved in this way, but at a high price. Ghatotkacha, Bhima's adored son, died when he was shooting fatal arrows at the Kaurava army from above, leaving the Pandavas inconsolable.

The conflict continued. Drona's persistent strikes caused havoc and terror in the Pandava army.

Krishna said, "No one, O Arjuna, can overcome this Drona when they engage in combat while abiding by the stringent laws of battle. Without abandoning dharma, we cannot deal with him. We don't have any other options. There is only one thing that can convince him to stop fighting. Drona will become completely disinterested in life and lay down his weapons the moment he learns that Aswatthama has died. Therefore, someone needs to inform Drona that Aswatthama has been killed."

The idea made Arjuna cower in terror since he couldn't bring himself to tell a falsehood. The people around him rejected the notion as well since no one wanted to participate in deception.

Yudhishthira stood still for some time, thinking hard. He declared, "I shall carry the weight of this sin."

It was unusual. But did not Rudra step forward to ingest the dread poison that threatened to engulf the gods while the ocean was stirring at the beginning of the world? Rama was compelled to kill Vali against the principles of fair play in order to save the friend who had entirely depended on him. Yudhishthira likewise made the decision to accept the dishonour now because there was no other option.

Bhima raised his iron mace and struck the enormous Aswatthama elephant in the head, killing it instantly. Bhimasena approached the division led by Drona after slaying the elephant Aswatthama and screamed for everyone to hear. "I've murdered Aswatthama!"

Bhimasena had up until that point had never committed or even considered committing an ignoble deed. He was deeply humiliated as he spoke these words.

They pounded against his heart, but were they really true? Drona was about to discharge a brahmastra when he heard these remarks. "Is it true that my kid has been killed, Yudhishthira?" Dronacharya questioned, addressing Dharmaputra. The acharya believed that Yudhishthira would not speak falsely even for the kingship of the three realms.

Drona's question caused Krishna much agitation. "We are doomed if Yudhishthira fails us right now and hesitates to speak the truth. The Pandavas will be destroyed because of Drona's unquenchable power and his brahmastra, he declared".

As he stood quaking in fear of what he was about to do, Yudhishthira himself was equally driven by the will to triumph. He said to himself, "Let it be my sin," hardened his heart, and proclaimed out loud, "Yes, Aswatthama has been killed."

However, as he was saying it, he once more felt embarrassed and added, "Aswatthama, the elephant," in a low, trembling voice. These words, however, were lost in the clamour and were not heard by Drona.

Sanjaya described the battle's events to the blind Dhritarashtra, telling him, "O king, so was a tremendous sin committed."

When Yudhishthira spoke lies, his chariot's wheels immediately descended and touched the ground. Up until that point, they had always stood and travelled four inches off the ground. Yudhishthira, who had before distanced himself from the world's abundance of lies, all of a sudden merged with it. His chariot descended to the common road of men because he, too, craved victory and erred by going down the path of deceit.

Drona's bond to life broke when he learned that his adored kid had been killed, and desire faded as if it had never existed. When the military commander was in that frame of mind, Bhimasena spoke aloud, harshly indicting him. "You brahmanas, abandoning the proper duties of your varna and taking up the kshatriya profession of arms, have brought devastation to rulers. The princes would not have been guided to this devastation if you brahmanas had not strayed from the responsibilities that were naturally yours. You preach that non-killing is the highest kind of morality and that the brahmana is its protector and provider. However, you have disregarded the insight that is naturally yours. Your descent into this immoral existence was our misfortune."

Drona, who had already lost the desire to life, suffered severe suffering as a result of these taunts from Bhimasena. He laid down in a yoga position on the floor of his chariot, gave aside his weapons, and quickly fell into a trance. Dhrishtadyumna arrived at this time, sword drawn, and entered the chariot. He removed the senior warrior's head to fulfil his destiny as Drona's killer, heedless of the howls of horror and scorn from everyone else. And the son of Bharadwaja's soul erupted into a discernible blaze of light and ascended into heaven.

Section VIII

Karna Parva

The Death Of Karna

THE Kaurava army rulers appointed Karna as Generalissimo after Drona's passing. In his stunning war chariot, driven by Salya, Karna rose to his feet. The Kauravas were encouraged by his fearless assurance and his illustrious military career. Another war started.

The Pandavas chose the favourable hour for their bloody fight after consulting readers of the stars. With Bhimasena at his back, Arjuna spearheaded the assault on Karna.

Bhima was the target of Duhsasana's focused attack as he was hit by a hail of arrows. "I now have this wretch safely in my hands," Bhima smiled to himself. "I'll fulfil my promise to Draupadi today. My oath has been waiting for performance much too long."

As Bhima considered what Duhsasana had done to Draupadi, his rage flared up uncontrollably. He threw down all of his weapons, leaped from his chariot, and pounced on Duhsasana like a tiger on its prey, flinging him to the ground and breaking his limbs.

"Wicked beast, was that awful hand holding Draupadi's hair? I rip the body's root out right here. If there is somebody here who wants to assist you, please let him step forward and attempt!"

As Duryodhana bellowed this challenge, Bhimasena tore off Duhsasana's arm and tossed the bleeding limb onto the battlefield while glaring venomously at him. The horrible oath he had made thirteen years earlier was then carried out by him. He danced on the field, enraged with passion, sucking and drinking the blood from his enemy's body like a predator.

"I've accomplished it," he roared. "I have seen the redemption of the oath I took against this great offender. The only thing left to do is fulfil my promise to Duryodhana. The offering fire is prepared. Let the victim get ready, too."

Everyone shivered at the scene. Even the mighty Karna was alarmed when he saw Bhima in this rage-filled rapture.

Salya instructed Karna not to flinch. "You should not display any behaviour that could be interpreted as fear. It is wrong for you to lose hope when Duryodhana is standing trembling with despair. The army's only chance is you, now that great Duhsasana is dead. Seek out Arjuna in single combat like the brave warrior you are, and you will earn eternal glory on earth or in the heaven of the soldiers!"

Karna found his resolve at these words. He instructed Salya to lead the chariot toward Arjuna when his eyes were crimson with rage and unshed tears.

In a sincere tone, Aswatthama pleaded with Duryodhana, "Enough of the fighting. Let's put an end to this terrible hostility. Make peace with the Pandavas, dear friend. Stop the conflict."

"What? Did you not hear what the obstinate Bhima said as he danced over my brother's dismembered body and devoured human blood like a ravenous beast? What peace dialogue is possible at this time? Why do you use meaningless language?" cried Duryodhana.

Thus, he ordered a new arrangement of the forces and issued the order to attack.

Then a significant conflict ensued. The son of Surya launched a fiery arrow that made Arjuna look like a serpent with its flame-tipped tongue. The serpent-shaft then almost missed Partha's head but struck off his helmet. Krishna, Arjuna's charioteer, had just enough time to press the vehicle down five fingers deep in the muck!

In order to put an end to Karna, Arjuna fastened a dart to his bow while he was crimson with humiliation and rage. As predicted, the left wheel of Karna's chariot suddenly sank in the bloody muck as his fated hour had arrived. To remove the wheel from the mud, he jumped to the ground.

"Wait a moment!" he pleaded. "My chariot has buried itself. As a great warrior and as one who understands dharma, you would never intentionally use this mishap. I'll immediately fix my chariot and offer you all the resistance you need."

Arjuna paused. Due to the mishap, Karna was now a little upset. He reminded Arjuna of the curse that had been placed on him and made another appeal to his sense of honour.

Krishna stepped in. "It seems very important that you now remember that chivalry and fair play exist!" he said. "You recall them now that you are struggling, but how did you completely forget them when you humiliated Draupadi in the Hall of Assembly? You encouraged Dharmaputra, who enjoyed playing but lacked skill to gamble, and you defrauded him. Where had your fair play retreated to then? Was it right to withhold Yudhishthira's kingdom after the requirements of the were been met?

"You engaged in a plot with the evil people who wanted to poison and kill Bhima. When the Pandavas were asleep in the palace of wax into which they had been seduced, you consented to the plan to burn them alive.

"Over all that time, what had happened to dharma? What did Dharma say to you, as you watched in awe when violent hands were placed on Draupadi? When her husbands abandoned her, did you not insult her by telling her to find another husband? The tongue that did not feel embarrassed to say those things now speaks of valour. Indeed, chivalry! Was it gallantry when a group of you surrounded the young Abhimanyu and brutally killed him? Wicked man, stop talking about gallantry and fair play because you have never upheld them!"

Karna bowed his head in shame and said nothing. He discreetly ascended the chariot, leaving the wheel still mired in the muck. He then drew his bow and shot Arjuna with an arrow with such accurate aim and force that it temporarily paralysed him.

Karna took advantage of the break to raise the chariot wheel, but the curse was too strong for him, and the great warrior's luck had run out. Even with all of his considerable muscle, the wheel would not budge. Then, as Parasurama had said, he tried to remember the mantras of powerful astras he had learned from him, but he was unsuccessful.

"Arjuna, don't waste any more time," shouted Madhava. "Send your arrow and kill your evil foe."

Arjuna's thoughts were confused. His hand felt reluctant to take an unchivalrous action. However, the poet writes that once Krishna stated this, "Arjuna acknowledged this command of the Lord and dispatched an arrow that cut and removed the Radheya's skull."

The poet lacked the courage to blame Arjuna, who represented nobility, for this deed. Arjuna was provoked to kill Karna by the Lord Krishna as he futilely attempted to extricate his chariot from the mud in which it had become trapped. It was entirely wrong in accordance with the laws of war and code of honour in effect at the time. The only person who may be held accountable for violations of the dharma is the Lord Himself.

The message is that hoping to correct wrongdoing by physical harm and conflict is vain. By using physical force to fight for what is right, many wrongs are produced, which ultimately creates adharma.

Section IX

Salya Parva

Duryodhana

DURYODHANA'S sadness knew no boundaries when he saw Karna die. Duryodhana's anguish caused Kripacharya to say: "Moved by ambition and avarice we placed too big a load on friends. They have cheerfully endured it, sacrificed their lives on the battlefield, and reached the joyful regions above. You only have one option remaining, which is to make peace with the Pandavas. O King, stop carrying on this destructive battle."

Even in his extreme distress, Duryodhana did not appreciate this advice.

"Maybe there was a time for it, but that time has long since passed. With all this unfathomable blood between us—our loved ones' blood and theirs—how can there possibly be any discussion of peace between the Pandavas and us? How can I escape the scorn of the world if I give up to avoid dying? What joy can I possibly expect from a life so dishonourably saved? What happiness can I possibly hope to find in a peace that is secured by sovereignty after all of my brothers and relatives have been killed?"

The others roared in approval at Duryodhana's statements. They agreed with his position, decided on Salya, and gave him immediate ultimate authority. Salya was as courageous and strong of limb as any of the fallen warriors. The army was positioned under his command, and the conflict erupted vehemently.

Yudhishthira was now personally in charge of the onslaught against Salya on behalf of the Pandavas. Everyone was shocked to see the man, who up until that point had been the epitome of tenderness, fighting so vehemently.

Long before Yudhishthira threw his spear at Salya and struck him, the fight was evenly matched. Salya's body lay motionless and covered in blood on the field, similar to the large flagstaff at the conclusion of a joyous event.

The Kaurava army had no hope left after Salya, the last of the great generals, died. But the remaining sons of Dhritarashtra banded together and surrounded Bhima. He killed all of them. Since Draupadi was insulted in the Hall of Assembly thirteen years prior, the son of Vayu had been nourishing his raging resentment. He grimaced and thought to himself, "I have not lived in vain, but Duryodhana still lives."

The division attacking Sahadeva was spearheaded by Sakuni. After some time, Sahadeva released a sword-arrow with a jagged edge, calling out, "Fool, here is the reward for your enormous sin." The head, which was the source of all the Kauravas' evil acts, rolled to the ground as the arrow travelled straight and cut through Sakuni's neck like a blade.

Without a leader, the shattered army dispersed and fled in all directions before being chased down and wiped out by the victorious adversaries. Sanjaya described the disaster to the blind king, "Thus your army of eleven Akshauhinis was completely destroyed. Out of the thousands of kings, who championed your cause in their pride and power, only Duryodhana could be seen on that battlefield, fainting and badly wounded."

Duryodhana tried everything in his power to rally his defeated army, but in vain. Almost all by himself, he picked up his mace and headed for a body of water. The water drew him in because his entire body was burning like fire. As he stepped into the sea, he thought to himself, "The wise Vidura knew what would happen and he told us. What use is wisdom that is acquired too late? The actions taken must have an effect, and that result must be painful. That is the law."

In ferocious pursuit of their formidable foe, Yudhishthira and his brothers made their way there.

Yudhishthira screamed, "Duryodhana! After destroying family and tribe, would you spare yourself death by hiding in this pond? What happened to your pride? Do you not feel shame? Come on up and battle. Are you, a kshatriya by birth, afraid of conflict and death?"

After being shocked by these remarks, Duryodhana politely responded, "Dharmaputra, I have not come here as a runaway for my life. I didn't come here out of fear. I entered the water to put out the fire burning inside of me. I have neither a desire nor a fear of dying, so why should I fight? I no longer have anything left to fight for on earth! All those who supported me have died. I no longer seek the kingdom. I give you the entire planet without a fight. Enjoy it in absolute authority."

"Now, it is incredibly kind of you, especially considering that you previously indicated you wouldn't give us even a tiny bit of land. You rejected our request when we begged for peace and urged you to give us a share. Now you say we could take everything. We do not battle for a kingdom or a piece of land. Do I need to list all of your sins? You can only atone for the wrongs you did to us and the cruelty you showed to Draupadi by giving your life."

"When your son Duryodhana heard these harsh and brutal remarks made by Dharmaputra, he immediately rose from the water with a mace in his hand," Sanjaya, who told the events to the blind old king, stated.

The unlucky Duryodhana stepped out of the water and said, "Come, one by one, all of you, for I am single. You five won't conspire to attack me since I'm defenceless, without armour, exhausted, and damaged all over."

"Tell us, then, of how Abhimanyu was attacked and slain," Yudhishthira responded angrily. "Did you not approve of the throng uniting and attacking the boy who was by himself in your company? Yes, men do preach dharma and chivalry in the face of adversity. Don your coat of armour. Select any of us and engage in combat. Win and become king, or perish and go to swarga."

As a result, Bhima and Duryodhana started fighting. When their maces collided, flames flew. Due to the equal strength and skill of Duryodhana and Bhima, the conflict lingered in question as the combat continued for a long time.

Those who were standing by and watching were debating who would win. Krishna said to Arjuna that Bhima would fulfil the vow he made in the Hall of Assembly and break Duryodhana's thighs. When Bhima heard this, the recollection of the enormous indignation suddenly flashed vividly across his mind.

He jumped like a lion and landed with his mace on Duryodhana's thighs, breaking them, causing Duryodhana to fall heavily to the ground and eventually die from his injuries. Bhima leaped onto the enemy's prostrate body, stomped his huge foot on his head, and performed a dreadful dance.

"Bhima, stop!" yelled Dharmaraja. "You have settled the debt. Duryodhana is a prince and a cousin. It is not right to put your foot on his head."

Krishna said, "Soon the wicked man's soul will depart from the body. Sons of Pandu, Duryodhana and his friends have been slain. Why linger here? On to your chariots."

When Krishna said this, the face of the fallen Duryodhana glowed like a blazing fire with anger and hatred. Turning his eyes towards Krishna he said: "By base tricks you contrived the death of warriors, who fought bravely according to the laws of war. You could not have dreamt of victory in fair fight with Karna or Bhishma or Drona. Have you not a spark of shame left?"

Even dying, Duryodhana felt no regret for all that he had one.

"Duryodhana," said Krishna, "you accuse others in vain. Greed and pride of power led you to unnumbered wicked deeds and you are reaping as you sowed."

"Wretch!" replied Duryodhana. "I was a great prince, generous friend, and a terrible foe. All human joys, such joys as kings wish for in vain, and even gods do not despise, have been mine, in their fullness. A warrior's death is the fitting crown of such a life. Dying, I go triumphantly to swarga to join my friends. My brothers who have gone there already and are waiting to welcome me. You remain here below, your objects defeated and yourselves the object of contempt of all kshatriyas. I do not mind Bhima putting his foot on my head as I lie helpless on the ground with legs broken. What care I? In a few minutes more will not the feet of crows and vultures settle on my head?"

When Duryodhana said this, flowers were showered down from the heavens by the gods. Inordinate desire took Duryodhana into the wrong path, whence ensued anger and numerous breaches of dharma. But no one could question the unconquerable spirit of Dhritarashtra's son.

The Pandavas Reproached

BALARAMA arrived at Kurukshetra as the war was about to end after visiting all the sacred sites. He arrived just as Bhima and Duryodhana were about to engage in their final fatal struggle. When he saw Bhima aiming the fatal blow that broke Duryodhana's thighs, his rage at this major violation of the norms of single combat flared up.

"Woe be to you all! Any kshatriya willing to strike below the navel? This is Bhima's most egregious violation of the rules," he cried out, approaching his brother Krishna angrily and yelling, "I cannot bear to see such filthy fighting!"

After saying this, he moved with an elevated plough toward the offended Bhima. On the most important occasions, Balarama used the plough, just as Krishna used the discus.

When Krishna noticed his older brother moving passionately in the direction of Bhima, he became frightened. "The Pandavas are our closest friends and relatives," he shouted as he charged forward to intercept him.

"Before you judge Bhima, you should consider all the wrongs the Kauravas committed against the Pandavas. They have endured unconscionable wrongs at Duryodhana's hands. Bhima made a promise to kill Duryodhana and crush his two thighs with this mace in battle when Draupadi was insulted in the Assembly Hall. At the moment, he made public this solemn oath, which was known to all. Duryodhana was fully aware that Bhima had vowed to kill him and crush his thighs when he challenged the resentful Pandavas to a fight. A kshatriya has a responsibility to fulfil the commitment he has gravely made. How can you consider that what Bhima did was wrong?"

Balarama's perspective was unaffected by Krishna's teachings, but his rage subsided.

"Duryodhana will enter the joyful realms set aside for the courageous. Bhima's reputation will always be tainted. Men will talk about how Pandu's son attacked Duryodhana in violation of the rules of war. It will always be a serious stain on his reputation. I detest having to stay any longer." Balarama headed towards Dwaraka soon after expressing this indignantly.

Krishna questioned Yudhishthira, "What is the cause for this unusual silence?"

"Oh Madhava, I felt pain when I saw Bhima pounce on my cousin Duryodhana's lifeless body and crush his head. I can see our race's splendour coming to an end. I am aware of the depth of Vrikodara's sorrow and rage, and I don't want to unfairly point the finger at him. What good does it do now to discuss the morality of it or consider the propriety of a greatly injured man's retaliation after we have killed Duryodhana, who was suffering from incontinence and a lack of understanding?"

Yudhishthira was greatly anguished. With his keen intelligence, Arjuna remained mute. He didn't express support for Bhima's behaviour but did not rebuke it either. However, the remaining attendees were vocal in their criticism of Duryodhana and kept reminding one another of all of his transgressions and mistakes.

"Warriors, it is not fitting we go on declaiming against an enemy who has been defeated and is lying mortally wounded," Krishna said as he turned to face them. "We should not speak ill of a dying man. He was unwise and brought about his own end. He fell into the company of evil men and was ruined. Let us go."

Duryodhana, who was stretched on the ground in intense agony, when he heard Krishna say this, went into a paroxysm of rage. He half raised himself on his arms in spite of the excruciating pain, and exclaimed: "Wretch! Son of a slave! Was your father not Kamsa's slave? You have no business to sit or move with princes. You speak like a shameless wretch.

"Do you think I did not see you, making as though casually talking to Arjuna, pointing to your thigh, but really indicating to Bhima that he should strike me on the thighs? Did you not contrive the death of the grandsire Bhishma through stratagem by advising Sikhandin to be placed in front? You brought about the end of Dronacharya by making Dharmaputra utter a falsehood. Did you not look on without protest when that wretch Dhrishtadyumna attacked and killed the acharya who had stopped fighting? Was it not you who wickedly contrived to make Karna hurl the fatal spear at Ghatotkacha instead of reserving it for Arjuna as he had resolved to do?

"O great sinner, surely it was you who instigated Satyaki to butcher Bhurisravas when his right arm had been foully cut off and he stopped fighting and spread his arrows for a seat for holy meditation. It was you who brought about the death of Karna by inducing Arjuna to attack him in a cowardly manner. Oh worthless man, sole cause of our destruction, the whole world has condemned your act when, by sorcery you made it appear as if the sun had set, and made Jayadratha, the Sindhu king, believe that the day was over and he was past danger, and thus he was slain when he was off his guard."

Thus did Duryodhana pour his denunciation against Krishna and then, exhausted by the pain of his wounds and the violence of his rage, he fell prostrate again.

"Son of Gandhari," said Krishna, "Why do you let your anger add to the pain of your last moments? It is your own misdeeds that have brought about your end. Do not attribute it to me. Bhishma and Drona had to die on account of your sins. So also were you the cause of the death of Karna and others.

"Need I recount all the wrongs that you were guilty of against the sons of Pandu? What punishment can be too severe for the great outrage which you inflicted on Draupadi? The animosities and passions that resulted from your misdeeds cannot be made ground for condemning others. All the deceptions and lapses you charge us with were forced on us by reason of your wicked conduct. You have paid off on the battlefield the debt incurred by your greed. But you are dying the death of a brave man. You will go to the happy regions reserved for kshatriyas who lay down their lives on the field of battle."

"Krishna, I go to swarga with my friends and relatives. But you and your friends will live on earth to suffer," said the stubborn Duryodhana. "I studied the Vedas. I have given gifts ordained by law and I have reigned supreme over all. While I lived, I stood upon the humbled heads of foes. All human joys, such joys as even the Gods cannot despise and kings sigh for in vain, were mine.

"Dying now, such death as warriors deem the crown of kshatriya life, I go to meet in heaven my friends and brothers gone before, eager to welcome me. Who is more blest, I, or you who, doomed to linger here, mourning for slaughtered friends in desolate homes, find the long-sought triumph but ashes in your mouth?" said Duryodhana and the gods showered flowers down on the dying warrior and the gandharvas played music and the sky was illuminated. Vasudeva and the Pandavas felt small.

"There is truth," said Krishna, "in what Duryodhana said. You could not have defeated him by fair means. This wicked man was invincible in battle."

Section X

Sauptika Parva

Aswatthama

ASWATTHAMA'S mind had been troubled by the Pandavas' use of deceit to bring about his father's demise. He soon discovered how Duryodhana had been smitten down mortally against all standards of chivalry. Hurrying to the location where Duryodhana was laying, took an oath that he would that night consign the Pandavas to the realm of Yama.

Duryodhana, who was in the last physical agony of departing life, was overcome with ecstasy when he heard Aswatthama swear this pledge. He quickly instructed those who stood around to place Aswatthama as Supreme Commander of the Army. After the appropriate ceremony was completed, said to him, "All my hopes are in you."

It was sunset and the forest was in absolute darkness when Kripacharya, Kritavarma and Aswatthama halted for repose under a great banyan tree. They were so weary that Kripacharya and Kritavarma went fast asleep as soon as they laid down. Aswatthama, however, was unable to sleep because he was consumed by grief, outrage, and hatred.

On the branches of the banyan tree, under which the three warriors were resting, hundreds of crows roosted. Before a large owl arrived and started to kill the birds, everyone was still and asleep. Aswatthama had an idea when he saw this.

"These wicked Pandavas and the Panchala that killed my father and all their supporters can easily be killed by us, if we surprise them when they are sleeping in their tents at night. Thus can I avenge the deeds of foul play they have practised on us. There is no offence in adopting plans to suit one's altered circumstances. We can lawfully attack an enemy when his army is tired or when his forces are scattered. Why then should not we, who have lost our armies, attack our enemies when they are asleep? There can be nothing wrong in it. We have no other course open."

Aswatthama made up his mind and he immediately woke up Kripacharya and informed him of his plan. Kripacharya, who heard it, was astonished.

"This can never be," said he. "It is wholly wrong. To attack men who have retired to sleep has never been done before. It would be an unprecedented crime against the laws of kshatriya conduct. Aswatthama, for whom are we fighting? The man for whose sake we joined in this war has been fatally wounded and his end has arrived. There is no purpose now in our continuing the fight. Let us go to Dhritarashtra, the wise Vidura, and the faultless Gandhari and place ourselves at their disposal. They will tell us what lies before us to do."

When Kripacharya spoke thus, Aswatthama's grief and indignation increased and he spoke bitterly, "Everyone is certain that what he thinks is the only right and proper thing to do. One's understanding naturally limits one's vision. These Pandavas have been guilty of the foulest conduct. They killed my noble and trustful father through a lie. I have no doubt in my mind that what I propose to do is quite proper vengeance for all these foul deeds. I have decided on it and I do not propose to alter my plan. I am going tonight to the tents where they are sleeping having cast off their armour. There I will kill the Pandavas and Dhrishtadyumna while they are asleep."

Kripacharya was deeply grieved to hear Aswatthama speak thus. "You have attained a great name among men," he pleaded. "Your spotless character will by this be blemished."

"What dharma has been left for us to follow? These Pandavas butchered my father when he had thrown away all his weapons and sat down in prayer. If by killing the sleeping Panchalas, who butchered my great father, I may be doomed to rebirth in the body of a foul bird or of a wriggling worm, I do not care. I seek such a birth!"

Saying this and, without waiting for an answer, Aswatthama proceeded to harness his horses and get his chariot ready to start. When he was about to leave, Kripacharya and Kritavarma cried, "Stop. What are you resolved upon doing, Aswatthama? We cannot approve of it, but neither can we desert you in your desperate enterprise. The path you are bent on treading, we shall also follow. Let us share in the sin you are resolved upon." So, they went along with him.

They reached the Pandava camp. Dhrishtadyumna had removed his armour and was plunged in deep slumber in his tent. Aswatthama leapt on the sleeping warrior and, before he could put himself into a posture of defence, cruelly kicked him to death.

The same process was relentlessly repeated until all the Panchalas and all the sons of Draupadi were killed one by one when they were plunged in sleep in their tents. After having done this deed, the like of which had never before been considered possible among kshatriyas, Kripacharya, Kritavarma and Aswatthama came out of the tents and set fire to the camp.

When the fire spread, the sleeping soldiers were awakened and fled hither and thither in confusion, even like the crows on the banian tree under which they had rested in the forest, and they were mercilessly slaughtered by Aswatthama.

"We have done our duty," said Dronacharya's son. "Let us go and give the glad news to Duryodhana, if we can reach him before he expires. Let him die pleased."

The three of them accordingly hurried to Duryodhana.

AVENGED

"O Duryodhana, hear the news and be glad! The Panchalas have all been killed. The Pandavas' sons have likewise all been put to death. Their entire army has been wiped out. We attacked them at night while they were resting. On the Pandava side, there are now only seven survivors. I, Kritavarma, and Kripacharya are still alive on our side."

Aswatthama thus addressed Duryodhana, who was on the verge of passing away. Duryodhana slowly opened his eyes upon hearing this and gasped, "Aswatthama, you have done for me what neither the mighty Bhishma nor the brave Karna could manage! You have made my heart smile, and I will die joyful." Duryodhana passed away after saying this.

Yudhishthira lost in to despair and sobbed as he realised his army had been completely destroyed at the very moment of victory due to the unexpected attack while he was sleeping. "In fact, the defeated have won. Our carelessness has caused the offspring of Draupadi, who survived the assault of the powerful Karna, to be trampled and exterminated like vermin. As a merchant ship that has successfully navigated the high seas returns home but capsizes in a ditch and is lost, we have allowed ourselves to be destroyed."

Draupadi was overcome with unquenchable sorrow. She approached Dharmaputra's side and sobbed. She wailed, "Is there no one to destroy this big sinner Aswatthama and avenge the slaughter of my children?"

The Pandavas quickly set out to find the killer after she said this. Finally, they located him on the Ganga bank, hiding behind Vyasa.

Aswatthama silently picked up a blade of grass, charged it with the mantra of destruction, and flung it forward, saying, "May this kill the race of the Pandavas," as the Pandavas and Janardana approached.

It immediately entered Uttara's womb, where she gave birth to Abhimanyu's baby. If not for Sri Krishna's intervention, who preserved the kid in the mother's womb, the race of the Pandavas would have been wiped out. When the Pandavas retired to the wilderness, Yudhishthira later crowned Parikshit, who was this child.

Aswatthama conceded defeat by prying the dazzling jewel from his head and giving it to Bhima before retreating to the wilderness.

When Bhima reached Draupadi, he exclaimed, "Angel of pristine purity, this is for you. The person who murdered your cherished sons has been defeated. It has been destroyed, Duryodhana. I've consumed Duhsasana's blood. I have paid off my debts and exacted revenge for the terrible outrage."

"Yudhishthira deserves to wear this jewel in his crown," Draupadi said and accepted it.

Section XI

Stri Parva

Who Can Give Solace?

AFTER the fight, Hastinapura was a city in grief, with all the women and children sobbing and mourning their lost loved ones. Dhritarashtra entered the field of combat with tens of thousands of grieving ladies. The blind monarch wailed openly as he remembered everything that had happened in Kurukshetra, the scene of tremendous destruction.

"O King, comforting words cannot take away sorrow. For your sons, thousands of kings have devoted their lives in combat. It is now time for you to set up respectable funeral rites for the deceased," Sanjaya told Dhritarashtra.

"Crying for those who lose their lives in war is improper. Lives emerge from nowhere, and upon death, they go back into nothing. Why do we need to cry for them? Those who lose their lives in war after a valiant effort are hosted by Indra. You cannot obtain anything in the nature of dharma, pleasure, or money while grieving for the past." The wise and righteous Vidura made numerous further attempts to comfort the grieving king.

Also tenderly approaching Dhritarashtra, Vyasa greeted him and said, "Dear Son, there is nothing left for you to learn from me that you do not already know. You are well aware that all living things eventually pass away. According to Lord Vishnu Himself, the purpose of this tremendous fight was to lighten the burden on Earth. Because of this, the disaster could not be avoided. Yudhishthira is now considered to be your son. You should make an effort to love him and, in doing so, bear the weight of life while letting go of sorrow."

Yudhishthira made his way past the group of sobbing women and bowed before Dhritarashtra. There was no affection in Dhritarashtra's embrace of Yudhishthira.

The blind king was then informed of Bhimasena.

Dhritarashtra called out, "Come."

Vasudeva was intelligent. Since he was aware of Dhritarashtra's extreme rage, he gently shoved Bhima aside and set an iron figure in front of the blind monarch. Dhritarashtra tightened his hold of the metal statue to his chest, and suddenly he realised that this man had murdered all of his sons. The image was shattered in his grasp as his rage reached a fever pitch.

"Ha!" Dhritarashtra wept. "I have been tricked by my fury. Dear Bhima, I have slain you."

Krishna then addressed the blind king and said, "Lord, I averted the catastrophe. Bhimasena has not been killed by you. Only an iron picture was destroyed. I hope what you have done has calmed your rage."

The monarch eventually regained his composure and blessed Bhima and the other Pandavas before they left to travel to Gandhari.

Gandhari was with Vyasa. "Oh queen, don't get upset with the Pandavas," the rishi advised. "Did you not say to them before the fight even started, 'Where there is dharma, there will be victory?' That did happen. It is improper to let one's mind linger on the past and harbour anger. You must now appeal for help with your impressive resolve."

"Bhagavan, I do not envy the Pandavas' triumph. It's true that my understanding has been taken from me by my sadness over the loss of my sons. My sons are these Pandavas as well. I am aware that Duhsasana and Sakuni were responsible for the annihilation of our people. Bhima and Arjuna are innocent. I don't bemoan it, though. Bhima summoned Duryodhana to battle, and they engaged in combat as Vasudeva watched. However, Bhima knew that Duryodhana was stronger than him and could not be destroyed in a single combat. That is why he struck him below the navel and killed him. Vasudeva was observing. This was incorrect, and I am unable to forgive it for that reason."

Hearing this, Bhima approached and said, "Mother, I did this to save myself in war. Your son was unbeatable in battle, therefore I unquestionably made a mistake out of self-preservation. He tricked Yudhishthira by inviting him to a game. Your son had mistreated us in so many ways. You wouldn't have blamed us if we had shot your son dead on the spot for acting inappropriately in the Assembly Hall, I'm sure of it. We struggled to control ourselves because we were bound by Dharmaraja's pledge at the time. Since then, we have paid off the debt owed to honour and discovered joy in conflict. Mother, you ought to pardon me."

"Dear Son, I and my old husband would have found comfort in that surviving son for the rest of our lives if you had slain all but one of my hundred boys and satiated your rage. Where is Dharmaputra?"

As he approached Gandhari, whose eyes were wrapped in a handkerchief as a loyal lifetime penance for her husband's blindness, Yudhishthira shuddered as he said this. "Queen, the terrible Yudhishthira, who killed your sons, appears before you fit to be cursed," he said, bowing down in front of her. "Curse me, for I have done tremendous sin. I don't care about life or kingdom." As he was saying that, he collapsed to the ground and touched her feet.

Gandhari let out a long sigh before remaining silent. She turned her head away because she was aware that if she looked at the downcast Yudhishthira through the material that was binding her eyes, he would instantly burn to ashes. Even though she moved her face away, she could still see Yudhishthira's toe through a little opening in the napkin. The poet claims that the toe became burned black instantly.

Arjuna hid himself behind Vasudeva because he was aware of the severity of grieving Gandhari's fury.

The sage and upright Gandhari restrained her rage and despatched the Pandavas to Kunti with blessings.

Gandhari turned to face Draupadi, who was weeping after losing all of her sons. "Do not mourn, my girl," Gandhari said. "Who can comfort both you and I? This wonderful tribe was completely wiped off because of my error."

Yudhlshthlra's Anguish

THE Pandava family spent a month camped out on the banks of the Ganga performing til-and-water rituals for the comfort of the deceased warriors' souls.

Narada once came in front of Yudhishthira. "Son, you were victorious and are the sole ruler of the land because of Krishna's favour, Arjuna's bravery, and the strength of your dharma. Are you content?" he inquired.

"Bhagavan, it is true that I now own the country," Yudhishthira responded. "However, I see this victory as a significant defeat. O Narada, even Karna, who stood rooted like a rock in his honour and whose bravery the world admired, was slaughtered because we mistook him for an adversary. Our wicked devotion to our possessions led to this horrible deed of murdering our own brothers. He didn't murder us, though, because he maintained the promise he made to our mother.

"Oh! I'm an evil man who killed his own brother; I'm a sinner. At this notion, my mind is extremely troubled. Karna's feet resembled those of our mother in so many ways. When the terrible act was perpetrated in the huge hall and I became enraged, I let my anger fade when I noticed that his feet resembled Kunti's feet so much. Now that I am reminded of it, my sorrow has increased." Yudhishthira sighed deeply when he said this.

Karna and the many curses that had been pronounced on him were fully described to him by Narada. Karna once asked Drona to teach him how to use the Brahmastra after realising that Arjuna was better at archery than he was, but Drona declined.

Karna then travelled to the Mahendra hills, pretended to be a brahmana, and tricked Parasurama into becoming his student. He taught him how to utilise numerous astras and how to shoot an arrow.

One day, while practising with his bow near Parasurama's asrama, Karna unintentionally shot and killed a brahmana's cow. Karna was cursed by the brahmana, who was furious, saying: "In battle, your chariot-wheels will stick in the mud and you will be done to death, even like this innocent cow which you have slaughtered."

Parasurama was incredibly fond of Karna. He taught him everything he knew about archery and gave him thorough instructions on how to use and remove the Brahmastra. However, Karna was cursed by Parasurama in his rage when he learned that he was a kshatriya because of his well-known hatred of them.

Karna was uninhibited in his gift-giving. The father of Arjuna, Indra, once came to Karna and pleaded with him for a gift of the celestial jewellery and armour he had been born with. Indra was dressed as a brahmana. Karna removed them and distributed them when necessary. From that point forward, Karna's power decreased.

"Karna's promise to his mother Kunti that he wouldn't kill more than one of the five of you, Parasurama's curse, the wrath of the brahmana whose cow Karna slaughtered, the way his charioteer Salya depressed him by downplaying his bravery, and Vasudeva's cunning plans—together, these deeds brought about Karna's demise. Do not mourn while feeling responsible for his death on your own."

Narada said as such, yet his words did not comfort Yudhishthira.

"Don't hold yourself responsible for Karna's demise," replied Kunti. "The sun lord himself, his father, begged him. He pleaded with him to abandon the evil Duryodhana and come with you. I also made a lot of effort. But he was unreceptive to our arguments. He caused his own demise."

Yudhishthira exclaimed, "You tricked us, mother, by not telling us the truth about his birth. As a result, you contributed to this terrible sin. May ladies never again be able to maintain a secret."

This is the poet's account of how Yudhishthira, distraught about having killed his own older brother, cursed all women.

Yudhishthira Comforted

WHEN Yudhishthira thought of all his slain kin, he was overcome with a deep sense of regret. To atone for his transgression, he made the decision to leave the world, travel to the forest, and perform penance.

He told his brothers, "I see no joy or good in accepting the post of king or in earthly enjoyment. Do govern the land yourself so I can go to the forest free."

Arjuna discussed the beauty of family life and all the good one may accomplish without sanyasa. Bhimasena spoke angrily. "You speak unwisely, like a man who has memorised the texts of the sastras without comprehending their meaning. The dharma of the kshatriyas is not sanyasa. A kshatriya's job is to lead an active life and carry out his assigned duties, not to retreat to the wilderness and give up work."

In addition, Nakula questioned the legitimacy of Dharmaputra's proposition and argued that the path of work was the proper one to choose because the path of sanyasa was fraught with obstacles. The same argument was made by Sahadeva, who pleaded: "You are my father, my mother, my teacher, and my brother. Keep with us; do not depart from us."

Draupadi spoke. "The execution of just punishment is one of a king's obligations. It is an unavoidable need of the role of the monarch and cannot be neglected. There is absolutely no reason for regret. It is now your solemn obligation to shoulder the responsibility of running the country in accordance with dharma. Stop weeping."

After giving Yudhishthira a thorough explanation of his obligations and providing examples, Vyasa urged him to travel to the city and assume the responsibility of governing the region.

At Hastinapura, Yudhishthira was rightfully crowned. Yudhishthira went to where Bhishma was waiting to die on his bed of arrows. He asked for his blessing and dharma guidance before assuming the responsibilities of the State.

The well-known Santiparva of the Mahabharata is this advice given by Bhishmacharya to King Yudhishthira. After the speech was finished, Bhishma's soul died. In accordance with an old tradition, the king went to the Ganga and offered libations for the comfort of the deceased.

Following the ritual, Yudhishthira climbed the bank. He stood there for a long until the awful events all flooded back into his mind, and after being overpowered by immense anguish, he collapsed to the ground like an elephant that has been shot by a hunter.

Bhima approached his older brother, giving him a loving touch and comforting words. Additionally, Dhritarashtra stood up and addressed Yudhishthira, saying, "Doing what corresponds to the office of king is your current duty. Leave the grieving to Gandhari and I. In accordance with the dharma of warriors, you prevailed in combat. The tasks related to that victory are now awaiting your attention. Being the fool I was, I disregarded Vidura's advice and made a serious mistake. But now I have you as my son. Do not be sad."

UTANGA

AFTER the battle, Krishna said goodbye to the Pandavas and departed for Dwaraka. He ran upon Utanga, an old brahmana acquaintance, while travelling. When Krishna came to a stop, he saluted the brahmana while getting out of his chariot. Utanga acknowledged the greeting and then went on to ask the customary questions about the wellbeing of family members.

Madhava asked, "As brothers ought to, do your cousins the Pandavas and the Kauravas love one another? Are they happy and thriving?" he inquired.

The epic struggle that had been fought was unknown to the naive recluse. The question from his brahmana acquaintance shocked Krishna. He hesitated for a moment, then revealed what had occurred.

"Sir, the Pandavas and the Kauravas had engaged in a horrible war. I used all available tools to break up the argument and bring them together in harmony. But they remained unresponsive. On the battlefield, almost all of them had died. Who is able to stop fate's hand?" Then he explained everything that had occurred.

Utanga was incredibly angry when he heard the story. He addressed Madhava while his eyes were bloodshot with rage, asking, "Vasudeva, were you there watching this happen and did you permit it? You have, in fact, done your task poorly. Without a doubt, you have misled them and practised deception. Get ready to get my curse right away!"

"Peace, peace," Vasudeva remarked with a smile. "Do not let your anger consume the rewards of your severe penances. After you have listened to what I have to say, you are free to curse."

The viswarupa, Krishna's all-encompassing form, appeared to the enraged brahmana and calmed him down.

"I occasionally inhabit different bodies in order to preserve the world and uphold the good, and whatsoever body I am born in, I must act in accordance with that body's nature. I pleaded fervently with the foolish Kauravas. They ignored my advice because they were conceited and drunk on power. I attempted to intimidate them and failed. I was furious and displayed even my Viswarupa to them. They persisted in their sin and died as a result. You have no justification for being furious with me, O greatest among brahmanas."

After hearing this account of Krishna, Utanga regained his composure. Krishna was happy.

"I want to grant you a blessing. What do you want?" questioned Krishna.

"Achchyuta," Utanga said. "Is it insufficient that I have seen Thee and Thy Universal Form? I don't have any more desires."

But when Krishna persisted, the poor, travelling brahmana replied, "Well, my Lord, if you must grant me some blessing, let me always be able to find water to drink. Give that to me, please."

Indra grinned. "Is that it? Have that then," he ordered before continuing on his journey.

When Utanga was desperate for water one day and couldn't find any in the desert, he remembered back to the blessing he had received. As soon as he accomplished this, a filthy-rag-clad nishada materialised in front of him. He wore a water-skin slung to his shoulder and was holding five hunting hounds on a leash. "You seem thirsty," the nishada said with a smile to Utanga. He gave the brahmana a bamboo spout from his water-skin to drink from, saying, "Here is water for you."

Utanga expressed contempt as he said, "Friend, I do not need that, thank you," while staring at the man, his dogs, and his water-skin. He was repeatedly pressured by the pariah nishada to relieve his thirst, but this only made him angrier and he refused to drink. The hunter vanished along with his hounds.

Utanga wondered, "Who was this? He was not a legitimate nishada. It was undoubtedly a test, and I failed badly."

A little while later, Madhava himself showed in carrying a conch and a discus. "Purushottama, please!" Utanga cried, "You put me through a trying ordeal. Was it proper of you to subject me to such a test by giving me, a brahmana, dirty water to drink?"

"Oh Utanga, I asked Indra to bring amrita to you and deliver it to you as water when you used my boon for your benefit. He claimed that while he was willing to do anything, he could not grant an immortal the gift that would grant him immortality. I accepted the challenge assuming you had acquired jnana and transcended externals, but I persuaded him. He consented, providing I let him do it as a chandala and tested your understanding and found you willing to take water from a chandala. But you forced me to experience Indra's loss as a result of what you did."

Utanga regretted his error and felt humiliated.

Yudhishthira Rules

AFTER defeating the Kauravas, the Pandavas established themselves as the undisputed kings of the land. They began their responsibilities and completed them in accordance with dharma. However, they did not experience the euphoria they had anticipated from winning.

Vaisampayana, who read Vyasa's Mahabharata to the king, narrates the story. King Janamejaya inquired, "How did the Pandavas treat Dhritarashtra when they won and got the kingdom?"

The Pandavas showed the highest respect to Dhritarashtra, who was drowning in a sea of sadness. They treated their elderly relative in a routine manner. They made an effort to cheer him up but did nothing to make him feel ashamed. No directives were given by Yudhishthira without his consent. With sisterly love and devotion, Kuntidevi took care of Gandhari, whose one hundred sons had vanished like dream wealth, while Draupadi diligently served them both with respect.

Yudhishthira equipped Dhritarashtra's home with opulent furniture, beds, decorations, and anything else that was required. He sent the most delectable and exquisite meals that the royal cook had made for him. Dhritarashtra's companion, Kripacharya, shared a residence with him. He was consoled by Vyasa with enlightening tales from bygone eras intended to ease his anguish.

Dhritarashtra was consulted by Yudhishthira in the management of the State's affairs. Yudhishthira behaved in a way that gave him the impression that the kingdom was run on his behalf and that he was still in charge as the family's eldest member. Yudhishthira was extremely cautious when speaking, never allowing himself to utter anything that would hurt the grieving old man. The princes from all over the world who flocked to Hastinapura accorded Dhritarashtra the same honours they had in the past, as if he were still the emperor.

Gandhari had little opportunity to experience her declining estate thanks to the female servants. Since their uncle had lost all of his sons, Yudhishthira had given very strong instructions to his brothers that nothing should be done to even remotely hurt him. The brothers scrupulously adhered to this directive, probably with the exception of Bhima.

Dhritarashtra also treated the Pandavas with kindness. He didn't have any animosity toward them, and they didn't treat him unfairly either.

But after a while, Bhima started to occasionally cause offence. He occasionally disregarded the old man's directions out of irritation. He would utter phrases like "Those perverse cousins of ours have themselves to thank for their demise," in front of Dhritarashtra. Bhima was unable to forget or pardon Duryodhana, Karna, or Duhsasana.

When Gandhari observed that Bhima had spoken in a way that hurt Dhritarashtra, she was deeply grieved. Nevertheless, she had a noble and wise soul,. She would turn to Kunti if she was troubled by whatever Bhima said and find comfort. For Kunti was a true example of dharma and a source of patience. In this way, fifteen years elapsed.

Section XII

Ashramavasika Parva

Dhritarashtra

KING Yudhishthira ruled for fifty years before elderly Dhritarashtra was unable to handle the weight of sorrow. He had no desire to accept the courtesies and luxuries that were offered per King Yudhishthira's orders because he was hurt by Bhima's sporadic reprimands. He kept a secret fast and performed difficult penances without the Pandavas' knowledge. Gandhari also kept numerous fasts and subjected herself to hardship.

Dhritarashtra once sent for Dharmaputra and addressed him as follows: "Son, blessings on you. I've lived with you happily for fifteen years. You have taken the best care of me. Over the years, grieving Gandhari has attended to my bodily needs while putting aside her own sorrow. Now is the moment for me to work with Gandhari to accomplish what has to be done for our upcoming state. These robes must be swapped out with worn-out, ragged clothing appropriate for a Vanaprastha's lifestyle. I want to move into the woods and stay there while I pray for you. I need your permission to do this. Let me continue our fathers' tradition. You will benefit from my atonement as king."

When Yudhishthira heard Dhritarashtra say this and saw him, he was startled. "I was deceived into thinking you were taken care of and content. You have experienced grief, father, and there is no consolation for that. I don't think kingdoms or pleasures are beneficial. I was deceived into doing this by desire and ambition. Let Yuyutsu, your son, or anyone else you want rule. Or, if you like, you might assume the king's responsibilities and take care of the populace yourself.

"I'm going to the woods. Let me close this error-filled chapter. I beg you to spare me from scorching embarrassment and additional insults. I'm not the ruler. You are in charge. How can I grant you permission or deny it? My resentment towards Duryodhana has vanished completely. Even like Duryodhana and his brothers, we are your children. I consider both Gandhari and Kunti to be my mothers, and as such, I must treat them with the same respect and filial piety.

"I must accompany you if you go to the jungle so that I can help you there. What delight would I have as king if you withdraw to the woods and leave me here? I bow down in front of you and beg your pardon for the mistakes we have made. Serving you will bring me great happiness and serenity. Give me that chance and that privilege. Don't leave me behind."

Dhritarashtra was brought to tears. However, he remarked: "Kunti's dear son, my thoughts are firmly bent on going to the forest and performing penance. I have no peace within me right now. I've been living under your roof for a long time. You and the rest of your people have devotedly served me. You must now give me permission to leave and fulfil my wish."

After addressing Yudhishthira, who was shaking and standing with his hands clenched, Dhritarashtra turned to Vidura and Kripacharya. "I implore you to console the king and convince him to answer my petition. The forest is all I can think about. I'm out of words at this point. My throat feels dry right now. Age may be the cause. I've spoken far too much. I am worn out." As he said this, he swooned and leaned helplessly on Gandhari.

The big old man, who had the muscles of an elephant and the strength to break the metal statue of Bhima into powder, was in such misery that Yudhishthira was unable to bear it. He was so thin and malnourished by this point that his bones could be seen through his skin, pitifully leaning helplessly on Gandhari like a homeless person.

He asked himself, "Have I caused all this? I am a miserable and unworthy person who lacks wisdom and knowledge of the dharma. A curse on my education!"

He moistened Dhritarashtra's face with water and tenderly caressed him with his hands. Upon regaining consciousness, the elderly man gently hugged the Pandava to his chest. Hesighed, "My little boy, how beautiful is your touch! I am content."

Vyasa then walked in. When he learned what had happened, he instructed Yudhishthira to carry out Dhritarashtra's wishes as the Kuru eldest. "Allow him to enter the woods. He is older. His sons all passed away before him. He won't be able to hear his sorrow for very long. Gandhari, whom God has endowed with wisdom, has bravely endured her suffering. Dhritarashtra must not wither away here. Let him go and leave the worries of the world behind, living among the honey-filled blossoms of the forest and inhaling their aroma. He must now make amends, and soon. Allow him to leave with your wholehearted approval and without harbouring any malice.'

"So be it," Dharmaraja commanded.

Vyasa then went back to his hermitage.

The Passing Away Of The Three

YUDHISHTHIRA had finally given his approval for Dhritarashtra to retire to the jungle. So Dhritarashtra and Gandhari returned to their home and broke their fast. While eating, Kunti sat next to Gandhari. Yudhishthira was requested to sit by Dhritarashtra as he bestowed his final blessings.

The elderly man then left the palace while keeping his hand on Gandhari's shoulder as he made his way toward the woodland. Gandhari put her hand on Kunti's shoulder and walked slowly. She had given up using her eyes and had always covered her face with a napkin because her husband was blind.

Kunti had made up her mind to visit the forest with Gandhari. She was addressing Yudhishthira as she continued to walk, "Son, never let your speech be furious when you speak to Sahadeva. Remember Karna, who died a hero's death on the battlefield, with affection. He was my son, but I broke the law by keeping it a secret from you. Draupadi should get unfailing careful care. Never cause Bhima, Arjuna, Nakula, or Sahadeva any distress. Remember this at all times, son. All of the family's responsibility now falls on you."

Up until that point, Kunti had been assumed by Dharmaputra to be accompanying Gandhari only briefly in order to bid her farewell. He was shocked and rendered speechless for a few moments when he heard her say this. After his horror subsided, he exclaimed, "Mother, do not go like this! You blessed us and gave us the order to fight. You shouldn't have left us and gone to the forest just now."

However, Yudhishthira's pleadings proved ineffective. Kunti stuck to her plan. "Wherever my lord and husband is at the moment, I must join him. I will live in the discipline of the forest with Gandhari and shortly join your father. Come back calmly. Come back to the city. May the dharma always remain stable in your mind." After giving her legendary son a blessing, Kunti left.

Yudhishthira remained silent. He and her other sons saw Kunti's infrequent glances as she continued on her journey. The poet speaks of the three tribal elders making their way to the forest while holding hands and leaning on each other's shoulders. He captures this image so clearly that it makes the reader experience serious anguish as if the separation had just occurred in his own family.

For three years, Dhritarashtra, Gandhari, and Kunti lived in the forest. They had Sanjaya with them. The forest was on fire when Dhritarashtra returned to their hermitage after finishing his rituals one day. The flames spread throughout the area as the wind blew. The herds of deer and wild boars dashed wildly in all directions toward the waters.

Sanjaya was informed by Dhritarashtra. "This fire would engulf us all. You should protect yourself." Gandhari and Kunti then sat down on the ground in a yoga position facing east and surrendered peacefully to the fire.

Sanjaya had been the blind king's sole source of illumination for the entirety of his existence and had appeared to him as clear as life itself. He spent the remainder of his days as a sanyasin in the Himalayas.

Section XIII

Mausala Parva

Krishna Passes Away

IN the thirty-six years that followed the conclusion of the battle of Kurukshetra, Krishna ruled Dwaraka. The Yadavas who made up Krishna's tribe, the Vrishnis, the Bhopas, and other branches, lived in opulent splendour and unbridled self-indulgence.

A few rishis once visited Dwaraka. With a practical joke, the haughty and disrespectful Yadavas mocked these rishis. They turned one of their young men into a woman and asked the esteemed visitors, "O ye wise men, tell us whether this lady will have a boy or a girl," before presenting him to them.

"This individual will give birth to a mace, not a boy or a girl, and that mace will prove to be Yama to your tribe and destroy you all," the rishis shouted in anger after realising the joke's irreverence.

The gullible Yadavas were upset by this unfortunate conclusion to what they had believed was a funny joke. They were shocked to learn the following day that Samba, the man who had been dressed as a woman, had experienced labour pains and had given birth to a mace! As a result of the rishis' curse, they felt as though their demise was drawing closer.

After much thinking, they eventually pounded the mace into a fine powder and sprinkled it in the sea, believing they had neutralised the threat.

There was a long period of silence. Seasons went by. When it rained, a thicket of rushes appeared close to where they had scattered the terrible club's fine dust on the shore. The Yadavas were curious and amused when they witnessed this, because they had completely forgotten about the guests' curse.

The Yadavas went to the beach for a picnic one day, a long time later, and spent the entire day dancing, drinking, and having fun. The alcohol started to work. They started off joking around, but as they got more agitated, they started bringing up old grudges and fighting over nothing.

Kritavarma and Satyaki, two Yadavas, had fought on opposite sides, the Kauravas and the Pandavas.

"Would a kshatriya strike and murder soldiers who were asleep, O Kritavarma?" Satyaki taunted Kritavarma, "You have inflicted a big and enduring dishonour on our tribe." Several inebriated Yadavas cheered the assault.

The insult was too much for Kritavarma to handle. He yelled, "Like a butcher, you butchered the great Bhurisravas when sat in yoga after his right hand was chopped off and you, coward, dare to ridicule me," and some of the partygoers joined him in mocking Satyaki for his heinous act.

Soon, all of the Yadavas were involved in the argument on one side or the other, and soon after, they exchanged punches after exchanging words, which quickly turned into a free brawl. "This is the end of the coward who slaughtered sleeping warriors," cried Satyaki as he lunged at Kritavarma with his sword drawn.

Others instantly rushed Satyaki with their pots, drinking bowls, and whatever else they could get their hands on.

Krishna's son Pradyumna rescued Satyaki. After this, there was a frantic melee in which both Satyaki and Pradyumna perished.

Krishna cut the tall rushes that surrounded him on the seashore because he knew the time had arrived. As a result, all of the Yadavas followed suit, and there was widespread indiscriminate killing. The rishis' curse had started to take effect.

The fated men's insane rage caused them to pluck each of the rushes that had grown out of the mace, turning it into a mace. They all soon perished in this drunken struggle after using them deadly effectively on one another.

Balarama, who was witnessing all of this, collapsed on the ground out of shame and disgust. He committed suicide while in a yoga trance and drowned into the water in a stream of light that emanated from his forehead like a silver snake. Thus came to a close Narayana's Balarama avatar.

Krishna believed that everyone in his tribe would eventually destroy themselves. He wandered the wilderness in intense concentration after witnessing Balarama's death and thought about the fulfilment of his avatar. He thought to himself, "The time has arrived for me to depart," and he dozed off while lying on the ground.

Vasudev was lying on the ground at that forested seashore when a hunter came by and initially thought he was a wild animal lazing around. He cocked his bow, aimed at the man on the ground, and fired an arrow that pierced his foot in the instep and completely through his torso. The mighty Vasudeva left the realm of men in this manner.

Section XIV

Svargarohana Parva

Yudhishthira's Final Trial

HASTINAPURA learned of Vasudeva's death and the Yadavas' destruction. When the Pandavas heard the news, they abandoned earth. The five brothers and Draupadi left the city with Parikshit, son of Abhimanyu.

They went on a pilgrimage and reached the Himalayas. Seven pilgrims climbed the mountain on their last pilgrimage, accompanied by a dog. One by one, they died while climbing the mountain.

The youngest fell first. Draupadi, Sahadeva, and Nakula were each freed from flesh. Arjuna and Bhima followed. Yudhishthira witnessed all their deaths. The light of Truth burned bright before him, so he knew what was shadow and what was substance. Yudhishthira's dog remained loyal to him and followed him up the mountain.

As he climbed, Indra appeared in his chariot. "Your brothers and Draupadi are here. You've fallen behind and are weighed down. Join my chariot. I shall take you

Yudhishthira climbed into Indra's chariot, and the dog followed. Indra replied, "There are no dogs in swarga," he said, pushing the dog away.

But Yudhishthira refused to board the heavenly chariot if he had to leave his friend behind. Dharma was pleased with Yudhishthira's test of loyalty, and the dog disappeared.

Yudhishthira visited swarga. The Kuru prince Duryodhana was there, sitting on a beautiful throne and glowing like the sun. The goddess of heroism and other angels attended him.

Yudhishthira was dumbfounded. "Where are my brothers? I see only this greedy, narrow-minded man. He killed friends and family out of envy and spite. We were tied by dharma to inaction as innocent Panchali, our sacred bride, was dragged to the Assembly Hall and insulted. This man disgusts me. Where are my brothers? I want to be there." Yudhishthira then turned away from Duryodhana's throne.

The heavenly rishi Narada smiled disapprovingly at Yudhishthira and said, "Prince, stop! No ill will exists in swarga. Don't insult Duryodhana. Duryodharra's current status is due to kshatriya dharma. You have a human body, so you have inappropriate feelings. It is wrong to let fleshly things breed ill-will."

Yudhishthira answered, "Duryodhana, a sinner who fed enmity and anger and killed countless good men, has attained this swarga of warriors. Where is my brave and good brothers and Draupadi's land of greater glory? My mother Kunti wanted me to offer libations to Karna after the battle. Even now, I'm saddened by it. I killed Karna without knowing he was my brother. I can't wait to see Bhima, who is dearer to me than life, Arjuna, who was like Indra, Nakula, Sahadeva, and dharma-obeying Panchali. I miss them all. Why should I be in heaven, away from my brothers? That's swarga to me, not this place!"

Angels replied, "O Yudhishthira, if you want to be with them, go immediately." They ordered a servant to take Yudhishthira.

Yudhishthira followed the messenger. As they went, it became dark and strange, revolting things could be seen in the gloom. Blood and offal slime covered him. Carrion, bones, and dead men's hair littered the path. Worms were everywhere, and the air stank. Bruised bodies were everywhere.

Yudhishthira was dumbfounded. His mind raced as he walked. "How far must we travel?"

The messenger replied quietly, "We can turn back."

Yudhishthira considered leaving because of the stench. As if divining his intentions, familiar voices began lamenting loudly. "Don't turn back, Dharmaputra! Stay a while. Your presence eased our torture. You brought a sweet, pure breeze that eased our suffering. Son of Kunti, seeing you eases our suffering. Stay only briefly. Never return. While you're here, we can relax."

Yudhishthira was bewildered by the loud lamentations around him. Overwhelmed by pity for faintly remembered voices, he exclaimed,

"Poor souls! Who mourns so? Why?"

"I'm Karna," someone said. Another said, "Bhima." A third voice: "I'm Arjuna."

Another voice cried, "Draupadi." "Nakula," "I am Sahadeva," "We are Draupadi's sons," and so on, came doleful voices from everywhere, until Yudhishthira couldn't bear the pain.

He asked, "What sin have they committed? What good deeds did Duryodhana do to sit in heaven with Mahendra while these are in hell? What's going on? Am I insane?"

Yudhishthira cursed the gods and denounced dharma. He told the angel-attendant, "Return to your masters. I'll stay where my brothers are tortured in hell for their devotion to me. Come with me."

Yudhishthira's message was relayed to Indra.

So passed thirteen hours. Indra and Yama appeared before Yudhishthira as he wept. When they arrived, the darkness and horrifying sights vanished. Yama, the dharma god, smiled at Yudhishthira as a fragrant breeze blew.

"Wise man, I've tested you three times. For your brothers, you chose hell. Kings and rulers must suffer, if only temporarily. So you were doomed to hell's pains for thirty minutes. Savyasachi and Bhima aren't in hell. Nor Karna, nor anyone else you thought doomed to suffering. It was a test illusion. Swarga, not hell. Do you not see Narada's three-world travels? Stop mourning."

Yama then transfigured Dharmaputra. He became a god without a mortal body. With the body, anger and hatred vanished. Yudhishthira saw Karna, all his brothers, and the sons of Dhritarashtra, serene and without anger, having attained godhood. Yudhishthira thus found peace and happiness in this reunion.

GLOSSARY

Abhimanyu	Son of Arjuna and Subhadra who was married to Uttara, daughter of King Virata.
Acharya	Teacher or Guru.
Adhiratha	Karna's foster-father
Alambasa	A raksasa friend of Duryodhana who had joined his forces but Satyaki compelled him to flee from the battlefield.
Astra	A missile charged with power by a holy incantation.
Aswathama	Son of Dronacharya and last supreme commander of the Kaurava forces.
Kalinga, Magadha, Matsya, Panchala, Salva	States the kings of which were friendly to the Pandavas.
Balarama	Elder brother of Sri Krishna (also called Baladev)
Bakasura	A voracious, cruel and terribly strong rakshasa or demon who lived in a cave near the city of Ekachakrapura whom Bhima killed to the great relief of the citizens.
Bhagadatta	King of Pragjyotisha, a Kaurava ally.
Bhagawan	Form of address to Gods and great rishis: e.g. Bhagawan Sri Krishna, Narada, Vyasa.
Bharata	Son of Kaikeyi and King Dasaratha, step-brother of Rama, who was exceptionally devoted to and loved Rama.
Bharadwaja	A rishi, father of Yavakrida.
Brahma	Creator of the universe.
Brahmastra	A divine weapon, irresistible, one given by Lord Brahma himself.
Brahmacharin	A religious student, unmarried, who lives with his spiritual guide, devoted to study and service.
Brihannala	Name assumed by Arjuna while living at Virata's court in incognito.
Brihatbala	A daring warrior who charged at Abhimanyu caught in the Kaurava army's net.
Bhima	The second Pandava brother, excelled in physical prowess as he was born of the wind-god.

Bhishma	The old grandsire to whose care were committed the five Pandavas by the rishis when the eldest Yudhishthira attained the age of 16 for their proper upbringing including mastery of the Vedas, Vedanta and various arts especially those pertaining to the Kshatriyas. Later he intervened but without success to bring about peace and understanding between the Kauravas and the Pandavas who ruled separately from Hastinapura and Indraprastha respectively. He was the eighth child of King Santanu and Ganga. Appointed supreme commander of the Kaurava armies.
Bhurisravas	One of the powerful kings on the side of the Kauravas.
Chala	A Kaurava warrior.
Chandala	A person of a degraded caste, whose conduct was much below standard and whose contact was supposed to cause pollution.
Chekitana	Head of one division of the Pandava army.
Chitrangada	Elder son of Santanu born of Matsya-gandhi (Satyavati) who succeeded his father on the throne of Hastinapura.
Chitrasena	A Kaurava warrior.
Dasaratha	King of Ayodhya and Rama's father.
Devaki	Mother of Sri Krishna
Devavrata	The eighth child of Santanu and Ganga who in time mastered the art of wielding arms and learned the Vedas and Vedanta as also the sciences known to Sukra was crowned Yuvaraja heir-apparent, but later vowed to celibacy and was known as Bhishma.
Devayani	The beautiful daughter of Sukracharaya preceptor of the demons, who fell in love with Kacha, son of Brihaspati, preceptor of the Devas.
Dharma	Righteous course of conduct.
Dharmagranthi	Assumed named of Nakula at Virata's court.
Dharmananda	The delighter of Dharma-a name of Yudhishthira, the son of Dharma or Yama.
Dhananjaya	One of the names of Arjuna.
Dhristadhyumna	Supreme commander of the Pandava forces, eldest brother of Draupadi.

Dhritarashtra	Elder son of Vichitravirya and Ambika, born blind, father of Duryodhana.
Dharmaputra	The son of Yama-epithet of Yudhishthira.
Dhartarashtras	Sons of Dhritarashtra.
Draupadi	Daughter of King Drupada, King of Panchala who married all the five Pandavas though Arjuna had won her in the Swayamvara, because of the vow that they would share everything in common.
Drona	Son of a Brahmana named Bharadwaj; married a sister of Kripa and a son Aswathama was born to them; learnt military art from Parasurama, the master; later he became the instructor of the Kaurava and Pandava princes in the use of arms.
Drupada	King of Panchala, father of Draupadi who became the wife of the Pandavas.
Duhsasana	Duryodhana's brother who dragged Draupadi to the hall of assembly pulling her by her hair.
Durdhara	A son of Dhritarashtra killed by Bhima in the war.
Durjaya	A brother of Duryodhana who was sent to attack Bhima, to save Karna's life, but lost his own.
Durmarsha	A son of Dhritarashtra killed by Bhima.
Durmata	A son of Dhritarashtra who got killed by Bhima.
Durmukha	A chariot-borne warrior on the Kaurava side.
Durvasa	A sage known for his anger who visited the Kauravas.
Ganapati	Amanuensis of Vyasa who agreed to write down without pause or hesitation the story of the Mahabharata dictated by Vyasa.
Gandhari	Dhritarashtra's wife and queen-mother of the Kauravas.
Gandharvas	A class of celestial beings regarded as specialists in music.
Gandiva	Arjuna's most potent bow.
Gangadwara	A place where sage Agastya and his wife performed penance.
Ghatotkacha	Son of Bhima from Hidimba
Govinda	One of the epithets of Sri Krishna and Vishnu; it means cow- keeper and refers to Krishna's occupation in Gokula, the colony of cowherds.
Guru	Revered preceptor, teacher.

Hanuman	Wise and learned monkey devotee of Sri Rama, who possessed extraordinary powers of discrimination and wisdom and who searched and found Sita in her confinement in Lanka.
Hastinapura	Capital city of the Kauravas.
Indra	King of the Gods.
Indrasena	A kinsman of the Pandavas.
Iravan	Arjuna's son by a Naga wife who fell in the battle on the eighth day.
Janamejaya	A king who conducted a great sacrifice for the well-being of the human race.
Janardana	A name of Krishna.
Jarasandha	Mighty king of Magadha of whose prowess all kshatriyas were afraid. Killed by Bhima in a thirteen-day non-stop physical combat, with Sri Krishna and Arjuna as witnesses.
Jatasura	A demon killed by Bhima.
Jaya	A son of King Dhritarashtra who was killed by Bhima in the war.
Jayadratha	A warrior on the side of Kauravas who closed the breach effected by Abhimanyu in the Chakravyuha military formation by Dronacharya and trapped him inside.
Jnana	Knowledge of the eternal and real.
Kacha	Grandson of sage Angiras and son of Brihaspati, who went to seek knowledge under Sukracharya as a brahmacharin
Kamsa	Maternal Uncle of Sri Krishna and son of Ugrasena, also son-in-law of Jarasandha, whom Sri Krishna killed.
Kanka	Assumed name of Yudhishthira at Virata's court.
Karna	A matchless warrior, son of the Sun-god and Kunti. Disciple of Parasurama. Also son of Radha, his foster-mother, and was known as Radheya.
Kekaya	A brave warrior on the Pandava side into whose chariot Bhima got during the fighting on the sixth day.
Kesava	One of the names of Sri Krishna.
Khandavaprastha	The ancient capital from where the ancestors of Pandavas, Nahusha. and Yayati ruled. The Pandavas rebuilt the ruined city and erected palaces and forts and renamed it Indraprastha.

Kesava	One of the names of Sri Krishna.
Khandavaprastha	The ancient capital from where the ancestors of Pandavas, Nahusha. and Yayati ruled. The Pandavas rebuilt the ruined city and erected palaces and forts and renamed it Indraprastha.
Kichaka	Sudeshna's brother, commander-in-chief of Virata's army, who made advances to Sairandhri (Draupadi), was invited to meet her at night at the ladies' dancing hall and was met instead by Valala (Bhima) dressed up as a female who killed him (Kichaka).
Kripacharya	Aswathama's uncle who advocated a combined assault on Arjuna in battle as against Karna's boast that he could take him on single-handed.
Krishna-Dwaipayana	Sage Vyasa.
Kritavarma	A notable Yadava warrior fighting on the side of Kaurava forces.
Kundinapura	Capital of Vidarba.
Kunti	She was the daughter of Sura and was known as Pritha. She was given in adoption to the king's childless cousin Kuntibhoja and was named Kunti after her adoptive father. She was given a mantra by Sage Durvasa. She gave birth to a son by invoking the Sun god; ashamed, she placed the child in a sealed box and set it afloat. The box was picked up by a childless charioteer and became known as Karna. Later, Kunti chose Pandu as her husband at a Swayamvara.
Kunti-Madri	Queens of King Pandu who gave birth to three and two sons known as the Pandavas in the forest where he spent many years for having committed some sin. The sons were known as Yudhishthira, Bhima. Arjuna, and Nakula, Sahadeva.
Lakshmana	Younger step-brother of Rama and son of Sumitra and King Dasaratha. Duryodhana's gallant young son also bore this name.
Lord Narayana	Refuge of men; Mahavishnu.
Madhava	One of the names of Krishna. It means the Lord of Lakshmi.
Madhusudana	Another name of Krishna, the slayer of the asura Madhu.
Mahendra	A King who had attained heaven.

Maitreya	A sage who visited the court of Dhritarashtra, expressed sorrow at the Pandava's plight, advised Duryodhana not to injure the Pandavas for his own good.
Mantra	An incantation with words of power.
Mandavya	A sage wrongly punished by the king by being impaled
Nakula	Fourth brother of the Pandavas.
Nara	Arjuna or Dhananjaya.
Narada	The sage who suddenly appeared before Dhritarashtra and Vidura as the latter was describing the departure of the Pandavas to the forest and uttered a prophecy that after fourteen years the Kauravas would be extinct as a result of Duryodhana's crimes and vanished as suddenly.
Narayana	Sri Krishna or Krishna; Vishnu.
Narayanas	Krishna's kinsmen
Panchali	Another name of Draupadi, Queen of the Pandavas and daughter of King Drupada
Pandu	Second son of Vichitravirya and Ambalika who succeeded to the throne of Hastinapura on his father's death, as his elder brother Dhritarashtra was born blind, father of the Pandavas.
Parikshit	Son of Abhimanyu and grandson of the Pandavas who was crowned king after the holocaust claimed the Kauravas and the Pandavas.
Partha	Arjuna
Phalguna	Arjuna
Pradyumna	Sri Krishna's son.
Pritha	Mother of Karna, Kunti before her marriage.
Purochana	An architect who built a beautiful wax palace named "Sivam" in Varanavata.
Purumitra	A Kaurava warrior.
Purushottamma	An epithet of Sri Krishna. It is one of the names of Vishnu and means the Supreme Being.
Radheya	Son of Radha a name of Karna, who as a foundling was brought up as a son by Radha, the wife of the Charioteer Adhiratha.
Rajasuya	A sacrifice performed by a king to be entitled to assume the title of "Emperor".

Rishabha	The second note of the Indian gamut (Shadja, rishabha, gandhara, madhyama, panchama, daivata, nishada—sa, ri, ga, ma, pa, dha, ni.)
Rudra	One of the names of Siva.
Rudra dance	Siva's cosmic dance of destruction.
Rukma	Heir-apparent to the throne of Vidarbha. When defeated by Balarama and Krishna he established a new city Bhojakata, ashamed to return to Kundinapura, the capital of Vidarbha, and ruled over it.
Sahadeva	Youngest of the Pandava princes who offered the first honours to Krishna at the Rajasuya sacrifice.
Sairandhri	A maid servant or female attendant employed in royal female apartments.
Sakuni	He played dice on behalf of the Kauravas and succeeded in defeating the Pandavas by a stratagem. As a result the latter had to go and live in the forest for 13 years. According to the conditions of the game, the thirteenth and last year of exile was to be spent incognito. If discovered by anyone they were again to repair to the forests for a like term. He was considered to be the evil genius, who beguiled Duryodhana to take to evil ways.
Salva	Friend of Sisupala, who besieged Dwaraka to avenge his death.
Salya	Ruler of Madradesa and brother of Madri and uncle of the Pandavas who because of having received hospitality from Duryodhana went over to his side.
Sanga	Son of Virata. When king Virata was wounded, he had to get into Sanga's chariot, having lost his chariot, horses and charioteer.
Sanjaya	The narrator who tells blind Dhritarashtra the war's progress everyday. He told the king that a victim of adverse fate would first become perverted and lose his sense of right and wrong. Time would destroy his reason and drive him to his own destruction.
Santanu	King of Hastinapura, father of Bhishma.
Sanyasin	One who has renounced the world and its concerns.
Sarmishtha	Princes and daughter of king Vrishaparva who got angry with Devayani and slapped and pushed her into a dry well.
Satanika	Virata's son whose head was severed by Drona.

Satyajit	A Panchala prince, a hero who stood by Yudhishthira to prevent his being taken prisoner by Drona, while Arjuna was away answering a challenge by the Samsaptakas (the Trigartas).
Satyaki	A Yadava warrior, friend of Krishna and the Pandavas who advocated collecting their forces and defeating the unrighteous Duryodhana.
Satyavati	A fisherman's daughter who possessed uncommon beauty and emanated a divinely sweet fragrance and king Santanu became enamoured of her married her and made her his queen.
Satyavrata	Warrior on the Kaurava side.
Saugandhika	A plant that produced a very beautiful and fragrant flower that Bhima went to get for Draupadi.
Sikhandin	A girl turned man, warrior on the Pandava side who restored order among scattered, subdued soldiers. Drupada's son.
Saindhava	Jayadratha.
Sini	One of the suitors to Devaki's hand. A kinsman of the Kauravas.
Sisupala	King of Chedi. Died at the hands of Krishna at the time of Dharmaputra's Rajasuya sacrifice.
Subhadra	Wife of Arjuna, sister of Sri Krishna and mother of Abhimanyu.
Sudeshna	Queen of King Virata whom Sairandhri (Draupadi) served.
Supratika	Name of King Bhagadatta's elephant.
Susarma	King of Trigarta, a supporter of the Kauravas who backed the Proposal to invade Matsya, Virata's country.
Sri Rama	Also known as Rama, Ramachandra or Sri Rama. Hanuman tells Bhima how he was deeply thrilled when he happened to touch Rama's body, This king of Ayodhya was banished to the forest for 14 years, killed Ravana the king of Lanka who abducted his wife, Sita.
Srinjayas	Pandava supporters.
Srutayu, Astutayu	Two brothers fighting on the Kaurava side attacked Arjuna but were killed.

Srutayudha	A Kaurava warrior whose mace hurled at Krishna rebounded fiercely. killing Srutayudha himself. His mother Parnasa had obtained that gift from Varuna who had specified that the mace should not be used against one who does not fight, else it would kill the person who hurls it.
Swarga	The heaven of Indra where mortals after death enjoy the results of their good deeds on earth.
Sveta	A son of King Virata who fell in battle to Bhishma's arrow.
Tantripala	Assumed name of Sahadeva at Virata's court.
Upaplavya	A place in Matsya Kingdom, where the Pandavas settled after their exile of 13 years.
Vaisampayana	Chief disciple of sage Vyasa who revealed the epic for the benefit of humanity.
Vaishnava mantra	An invocation which endows a missile with some of the irresistible power of Vishnu.
Valala	Assumed name of Bhima when he worked as a cook at Virata's court.
Vanaprastha	The third stage of the dvija's life, when he is required to relinquish worldly responsibilities to his heirs and retires to the woods with his wife for an anchorite's life.
Vandi	Court poet of Mithila who on being defeated by Sage Ashtavakra in debate drowned himself in the ocean and went to the abode of Varuna.
Varanavata	A forest in which the Pandavas were asked to stay in a wax-house which was to be set on fire at midnight in order to kill the Pandavas while they were asleep.
Vasishtha	A sage who had cursed the eight Vasus to be born in the world of men as sons of Ganga and Santanu. Ganga threw her seven children into the river with a smiling face.
Vasudeva	An epithet of Krishna. It means both son of Vasudeva and the supreme spirit that pervades the universe.
Vikarna	A son of Dhritarashtra who declared the Kauravas had not won Draupadi legally
Virata	King of Matsya, the country which was suggested by Bhima to live in incognito during the 13th year of their exile.
Viswarupa	All—pervading, all—including form. See the description in the Bhagavad Gita Ch. IX.

Vriddhakshatra	King of the Sindhus, father of Jayedratha into whose lap his son Jayadratha's head was caused to fall by Arjuna after cutting off Jayadratha's head.
Vrishnis, Kekayas	Tribals who were devoted to the Pandavas who with Sri Krishna visited the Pandavas in their exile.
Vrishasena	A warrior on the Kaurava side.
Vrikodara	Wolf-bellied-an epithet of Bhima, denoting his slimness of waist and insatiable hunger.
Vyasa	Compiler of the Vedas, son of sage Parasara.
Vyuha	Battle array.
Yama	God of death, god of dharma, whose son was Yudhishthira. It is he whose questions Yudhishthira answered correctly whereupon his dead brothers were brought back to life on the banks of the enchanted pool.
Yajna	A sacrifice.
Yaksha	A class of demi-gods, subjects of Kubera, the god of wealth.
Yavakrida	Son of Sage Bharadwaja who was bent upon mastering the Vedas.
Yayati	Emperor of the Bharata race who rescued Devayani from the well into which she had been thrown by Sarmishtha. He later married both Devayani and Sarmishtha. One of the ancestors of the Pandavas who became prematurely old due to Sukracharya's curse.
Yudhamanyu	A prince supporting the Pandavas.
Yuyudhana	Another name of Satyaki.
Yuyutsu	A noble son of Dhritarashtra who bent his head in shame and sorrow when Yudhishthira lost Draupadi. He also disapproved of the unfair way in which Abhimanyu was killed.